PIONEER PRINTER

Samuel Bangs in Mexico and Texas

PIONEER PRINTER

Samuel Bangs in Mexico and Texas

By Lota M. Spell

UNIVERSITY OF TEXAS PRESS • AUSTIN

Library of Congress Catalog Card No. 63–11190
Copyright © 1963 by Lota M. Spell
All rights reserved.

Manufactured in the United States of America
Printed by the University of Texas Printing Division
Bound by Universal Bookbindery, Inc., San Antonio

PREFACE

In this work I have tried to give some insight into the life of Samuel Bangs, the man who printed or helped to print the first document known to have issued in that form in Texas, and thereby to trace some aspects of the introduction and progress of the press in early Texas and in three other Mexican states.

For the preparation of such a study the Library of the University of Texas offered superb facilities. In the manuscripts and printed documents of the Bexar Archives, which were entrusted by Bexar County to this institution more than a half century ago, is the history of Texas as a Spanish province and as a part of the Republic of Mexico. When to these were added in 1921 the Genaro García Collection of Mexicana, and later the Hernández y Dávalos and the Prieto Papers, there was at hand detailed material dealing with the Eastern Interior Provinces of Mexico, which until 1824 included Texas. As a result, the larger part of the 359 "Extant Specimens of Bangs' Printing" listed in the Bibliography of this work are, in some form—original, photocopy, or microfilm—at the University of Texas or in my possession.

Originally I proposed to include the exact location—by collection, folder, or box—of each document cited, but the rapid expansion of library holdings in most important archival centers and repeated changes in directors and personnel, each with new ideas of classification—conditions to be expected in fast-growing institutions—finally taught me that no location is immune to change. For this reason I have generally indicated only the holding institution, leaving to archivists or library personnel the determination of exact location. The list of "Abbreviations Used for Location of Manuscripts and Periodicals," which precedes both the main text and the Bibliography, is suggestive of the wide geographical range of the archives and libraries which have contributed to this work.

v

Preface

There are many to whom I have been indebted through the years. Some of them, although deceased, should be mentioned. Among those are: Mr. E. W. Winkler, librarian and bibliographer at the University of Texas for more than a decade, who aroused my curiosity about Bangs by showing me Wagner's MS "Notes on early printing in the Provincias Internas"; Dr. James A. Robertson, who urged the preparation of my first article on Bangs, published in 1931; Dr. C. E. Castañeda, who secured for me photocopies of the Bangs-Uro y Lozano correspondence; and Señor Vito Alessio Robles, who, following my lead, located the record of Bangs' baptism in the Cathedral of Monterrey. I am also indebted to Miss Alice Cherry and her sister, life-long Galvestonians, for an interview in which they shared with me their knowledge of Bangs, his daughter-in-law, and his grandson; to Señor Israel Cavazos Garza, director of the Archivo General del Estado de Nuevo León at Monterrey, for locating and photocopying various *legajos* concerning early printing in that area; to Dr. Malcolm McLean and Mrs. McLean for references they found to Bangs; and especially to Miss Nettie Lee Benson, Librarian of the Latin American Collection at the University of Texas, for her tireless search for material that might throw light on Bangs and for her reading of the rough manuscript. Most patient and long-suffering has been my husband, Dr. J. R. Spell, who has served as copyist, critic, translator, and chauffeur during our extensive rambles in search of Bangs materials. For the excellent typing of the manuscript I am indebted to Mrs. Ona Kay Stephenson. To all of them and to the directors and personnel of the National Archives in Washington, D.C., Havana, Mexico City, and Madrid and of the many other libraries cited in my notes, I hereby extend my sincere thanks for the many courtesies shown me.

LOTA M. SPELL

Austin, Texas

CONTENTS

ILLUSTRATIONS

MAPS

Abbreviations for Locations of Manuscripts and Specimens of Bangs' Printing and for Titles of Periodicals

AAW American Antiquarian Society Library, Worcester, Massachusetts.

ACC Archivo del Congreso del Estado de Coahuila, Saltillo, Mexico.

AG Archivo del Gobierno, Victoria, Tamaulipas.

AGE Archivo General del Estado de Nuevo León, Monterrey, Mexico.

AGI Archivo General de Indias, Seville, Spain.

AGN Archivo General de la Nación, Mexico City, Mexico.

AGT Archivo del Gobierno del Estado de Tamaulipas, Victoria, Mexico.

AHE Archivo General de Historia del Estado de Coahuila, Saltillo, Mexico.

AHN Archivo Histórico Nacional, Madrid, Spain.

AS Archivo del Ayuntamiento, Saltillo, Mexico.

AM Archivo del Ayuntamiento, Monterrey, Mexico.

ASRE Archivo General de la Secretaría de Relaciones Exteriores, Mexico City.

BA Bexar Archives, University of Texas Library, Austin, Texas.

CBC Bancroft Library, University of California, Berkeley, California.

H-D Hernández y Dávalos Papers, University of Texas Library, Austin, Texas.

LC Library of Congress, Washington, D.C.

LMS Library of Lota M. Spell, Austin, Texas.

MA Matamoros Archives (originals burned). Photocopies, University of Texas Archives, Austin, Texas.

Mi Mier Papers, University of Texas Library, Austin, Texas.

NA National Archives of the United States, Washington, D.C.

NAG Nacogdoches Archives, Texas State Library, Austin, Texas.

P	Prieto Papers, University of Texas Library, Austin, Texas.
PRO	Great Britain, Public Record Office, London, England.
TGR	Texas Galveston Rosenberg Library, Galveston, Texas.
TLO	General Land Office of Texas, Austin, Texas.
TSA	Bexar Archives, County Clerk's Office, San Antonio, Texas.
Tx	Texas State Library, Austin, Texas.
TxU	University of Texas Library, Austin, Texas.
Yale	Yale University Library, New Haven, Connecticut.
SWHQ	*The Southwestern Historical Quarterly.*
HAHR	*The Hispanic American Historical Review.*

PIONEER PRINTER

Samuel Bangs in Mexico and Texas

Introduction

HE DATE and the personalities involved in the introduction of the press into the Southwest have been subjects for research and speculation for many years. As the region was once a part of Mexico, and earlier of Spain, the search for data which would throw light upon the problem has not been limited either to the United States or to English-speaking historians. José Eleuterio González, in writing of the neighboring state of Nuevo León,[1] expressed the belief that the Anglo-Americans who came into Texas in 1813 brought with them a press, which, he concluded, was captured at San Antonio by the Mexicans and taken to Monterrey, where an old press still existed; but neither in the official report of the battle near San Antonio nor in the list

[1] *Colección de noticias y documentos para la historia del Estado de Nuevo León* (Monterrey, 1867), pp. 356–357, quoting from unpublished notes of José Angel Benavides.

3

of captured goods is there any reference to a press or parts of a press.[2]

Other writers have referred to a press brought into Texas by the Long Expedition in 1819.[3] One of these, an eminent bibliographer of the Southwest, Henry W. Wagner, who knew of the existence of a printed proclamation issued at Monterrey, Mexico, on July 21, 1820,[4] came to the following conclusion: "There is no doubt that Long's second expedition had a press which was captured, and probably the printer himself, as Bangs was in the expedition and captured, and a short time afterwards he appeared as a printer."[5]

But who was Bangs, and how did he get either to Texas or to Monterrey? Was Wagner correct in his surmise that Bangs was with the Long Expedition? Both questions remained without an answer until the present writer in 1924 unearthed a letter, signed by Bangs himself, which revealed certain facts concerning his introduction to Texas and Mexico.[6] Soon afterward a chance perusal of the *Life* of Benjamin Lundy gave a clue to where the printer came from.[7] Later his name was noted as the publisher of the first newspaper of the Mexican War.[8] It became increasingly

[2] The report of José Joaquín de Arredondo, who commanded the Mexican troops in this battle, to Félix María Calleja, the viceroy of Mexico, is enclosed with his letter from San Antonio de Bexar, September 18, 1813, of which the original is in the Archivo General y Público de la Nación, Mexico City, Mexico (hereafter referred to as AGN), Historia 23, Operaciones de Guerra, Arredondo IV, 1813–1820, fols. 179–193. It is translated in the *Quarterly of the Texas State Historical Association*, XI (January, 1908), 220–236. This publication and its successor, *The Southwestern Historical Quarterly*, will hereafter be referred to as *SWHQ*.

[3] Mirabeau B. Lamar, "Life of General James Long," MS in the Texas State Library (hereafter Tx). Printed in *The Papers of Mirabeau Buonaparte Lamar* (C. A. Gulick et al., editors), II, 59. Hereafter referred to as Lamar Papers.

[4] Copies of this are in the Bexar Archives, Library of the University of Texas, which is hereafter referred to as TxU.

[5] MS, "Notes on Early Printing in the Provincias Internas." Photocopy, TxU.

[6] Samuel Bangs, Saltillo, Mexico, to Servando Teresa de Mier, July 13, 1822. In the Mier Papers, TxU. See Appendix I, Document 3.

[7] Benjamin Lundy, *The Life, Travels and Opinions of Benjamin Lundy, including his Journeys to Texas and Mexico. . . .*, p. 154.

[8] *Corpus Christi Gazette*, January 1, 1846. TxU.

evident that the details of even twenty years of Bangs' life would throw considerable light on the history of the early press in Texas and in northeastern Mexico. The search for them has extended over thirty years and has led from Massachusetts to Mexico City and from London to Madrid, with many stops en route. The facts discovered by 1930 and the conclusions then reached were made known by the writer in a bibliographical article, "Samuel Bangs: The First Printer in Texas," in 1931; it was reprinted in Texas in 1932; and, translated into Spanish, it was published in Mexico City that same year.[9] During the following decade it furnished the substance for several articles and books by others; it also gave impetus to attempts to solve some of the problems it had brought to light.[10]

Of these attempts the most important was the disproof of some seemingly well-established facts which threatened, for a time, to make Bangs' priority unsupportable and to rob him of the distinction of being the first to print in Texas. Among these facts were: (1) that José Alvarez de Toledo had brought a printing press into Texas in 1813; (2) that a newspaper which bore the title of *Gaceta de Texas* was reputed to have been published at Nacogdoches on May 25, 1813; and (3) that another, *El Mexicano*, was believed to have issued from the same press. Together these facts seemed to support the contention that at least two newspapers antedated Bangs' arrival, if, as Wagner surmised, he had come with the Long Expedition in 1819.

In spite of this seemingly incontrovertible evidence all claims that the *Gaceta de Texas* and *El Mexicano* were printed in Texas

[9] Lota M. Spell, "Samuel Bangs: The First Printer in Texas," *Hispanic American Historical Review*, XI (May, 1931), 248–258. Hereafter *HAHR*. See Bibliography for reprintings.

[10] Douglas C. McMurtrie, "Pioneer Printing in Texas," *Southwestern Historical Quarterly*, XXXV (January, 1932), 173–193; Ike Moore, "The Earliest Printing and First Newspaper in Texas," *ibid.*, XXXIX (October, 1935), 83–99; Vito Alessio Robles, *La primera imprenta en Coahuila* (México, 1932); Alessio Robles, *La primera imprenta en las Provincias Internas de Oriente* (México, 1939); and revisions of these in Alessio Robles' *Coahuila y Texas . . .* (México, 1945–1946), 2 vols.

Pioneer Printer

were invalidated by two sentences in a letter written at Natchitoches, Louisiana, on June 20, 1813, by William Shaler, a special agent of the State Department of the United States, to James Monroe, then the Secretary of State. These sentences read: "The enclosed gazette was prepared for publication in Nacogdoches but on account of our departure printed here at our return. *The Mexican* in Spanish and English will appear in a few days." Enclosed with the letter was a copy of the *Gaceta de Texas*, dated Nacogdoches, May 25, 1813; and, in the letter, the circumstances of the hasty exit from Nacogdoches of José Alvarez de Toledo and his associates, among them Shaler, are described in detail.[11] With them, by muleback, went the type already set for the *Gaceta*. But neither that paper nor *El Mexicano* was printed in Texas.

With this fact definitely established there remained the press of the Long Expedition to be accounted for. Its owner and operator, Eli Harris, who was a native of North Carolina, took his whole printing "office" into Nacogdoches in 1819 after he entered "Texian" service with the rank of captain under the command of General James Long. There, shortly after the General arrived (July 29, 1819), he established a newspaper. After the Royalists broke up the Expedition, Harris returned to Louisiana, but was recalled to the coast, where commissioners from Mexico offered each officer his regular pay, and to him *double pay* "on account of the loss of my printing office which the Royalists had destroyed."[12] Horatio Bigelow, a member of the Supreme Council of the Provincial Government of Texas, was the editor of the newspaper.[13]

[11] MS in the National Archives of the United States (hereafter NA), State Department, [Communications from] Special Agents, "William Shaler," II (1810–1815), Document 82, p. 103. The discovery of this document was announced by Julia K. Garrett, in "The First Newspaper of Texas—Gaceta de Texas," *SWHQ*, XL (January, 1937), 200–215; and also in *Green Flag over Texas*.

[12] Eli Harris, Providence, Louisiana, to Mirabeau B. Lamar, January 18, 1841, MS in Tx; printed in *Lamar Papers*, III, 483.

[13] Mirabeau B. Lamar, "Life of General James Long," MS in Tx; printed in

6

Introduction

At least three issues of the weekly *Texas Republican,* dated August 14, 21, and 28, were published by Eli Harris at Nacogdoches before the press was destroyed. The Natchez, Mississippi, *Republican* of August 31, 1819, reported the receipt of the first number of the *Texas Republican;* the Fort Gibson *Correspondent* of September 25 reprinted an article from the *Texas Republican* of August 21, and in its issue of September 18 mentioned that of August 28; while the September 25 *St. Louis Enquirer* announced the first number of the *Texas Republican* as dated at Nacogdoches on August 14, 1819. The *Gazette de la Louisiane* of September 4, in announcing the arrival of the first number of the *Republican,* added that it was printed by Eli Harris.[14] The arrival in Philadelphia in October of one of these issues was duly reported to the Spanish government by its consul general as "a newspaper in English published by the Republic of Texas which first saw the light last August at Nachitoches."[15] Geographically, the consul was slightly confused.

But the name of Bangs appears nowhere in connection with the *Republican* or with the Long Expedition, and for good reason. He was elsewhere.

Lamar Papers, II, 59 (Lamar's statement); III, 483 (Eli Harris' statement).

[14] E. W. Winkler, *"The Texas Republican"* in *SWHQ,* VI (October, 1902), 162–165; VII (January, 1904), 242–243; XVI (January, 1913), 329–331; and also C. S. Brigham, "Bibliography of American Newspapers, 1690–1820" in *Proceedings of the American Antiquarian Society,* New Series, XXXV (1925), 98.

[15] Mateo de la Serna to Manuel González Salmón, Philadelphia, October 21, 1819, MS in Archivo Histórico Nacional, Madrid, Sección de Estado, Legación en los Estados Unidos, Legajo 5645. This archive will hereafter be referred to as AHN.

ONE

With the Mina Expedition

ᏒᏒᏒᏒᏒᏒᏒᏒᏒᏒᏒᏒᏒᏒᏒᏒᏒᏒᏒᏒᏒᏒᏒᏒᏒᏒᏒᏒᏒᏒᏒᏒᏒᏒᏒᏒᏒ

O N A HOT MIDSUMMER DAY in 1816 a small British vessel, the *Caledonia*, came quietly to anchor at Norfolk on Chesapeake Bay, after a hectic voyage of forty-six days from Liverpool.[1] On board were members of a projected military expedition—a motley lot—under the command of an impetuous young Spanish general, Francisco Xavier de Mina.[2] In the group were a few Spaniards and Italians, some of whom had served with the British army in Spain; several Englishmen, among them James A. Brush[3] and Daniel Stewart (the Stewart

[1] William D. Robinson, *Memoirs of the Mexican Revolution including a Narrative of the Expedition of General Xavier Mina*, p. 54. See n. 8 for discussion of this source.

[2] Robinson included (pp. 43–51) a biographical sketch of Mina.

[3] Brush was reported a member of the Expedition by Luis de Onís (Spanish minister to the United States) in correspondence with Juan Ruiz de Apodaca (viceroy of Mexico), Philadelphia, July 23, 1816; Historia, Operaciones de Guerra, Notas Diplomáticas, I, fols. 237–238 v., AGN. His official correspondence with the captain general of Cuba and the secretary of state of Spain also

With the Mina Expedition

family had contributed substantially toward equipping the expedition);[4] and an intelligent and courageous Mexican ecclesiastic, Servando de Mier,[5] who, like Mina, was fired with enthusiasm over the undertaking. The object of the expedition was to help Mexico attain her independence. For six years her people had been trying to rid themselves of Spanish rule, but they lacked military leadership and supplies. These necessities this expedition proposed to provide. Already in the hold of the *Caledonia* were arms, munitions, equipment, and a small portable press—all contributed by friends of Mexico and of Mina.

Mier and the young general—he was only twenty-six—landed at Norfolk and went at once to Baltimore[6] with the hope of securing information there concerning conditions in Mexico. As soon as their arrival became known they were joined by representatives of other Spanish-American countries which were also struggling to throw off the Spanish yoke. Among these were General Mariano Montilla, Juan G. de Roscio, and Manuel Torres from Venezuela; José Rafael Revenga, who had been the secretary of Simón Bolívar, the fiery revolutionary leader in South

---

furnish details concerning the personnel. While with the Expedition Brush kept a diary which is cited by Robinson (Introduction, p. iii) as his principal source. A MS "Journal of the Expedition and Military Operations of General Don Fr. X Mina in Mexico, 1816–1817" in the Huntington Library is assumed to be this diary, although the entries are not daily jottings and discrepancies between it and Robinson are numerous.

[4] Domingo Luacey, in a letter to Agustín de Iturbide, from Veracruz, March 24, 1822 (H-D), recommends Daniel "Stuart" as one who has influential friends in the British Cabinet and whose family had furnished large funds for the Expedition. For ready reference to H-D see the *Calendar of the Juan E. Hernández y Dávalos Manuscript Collection,* compiled by C. E. Castañeda and J. A. Dabbs.

[5] Both the letters of José Servando Teresa de Mier Noriega y Guerra and his testimony while a prisoner of the Inquisition (included by José E. Hernández y Dávalos in his *Colección de documentos para la historia de la Guerra de Independencia de México,* Volume VI, and hereafter referred to as *Documentos*) throw much light on the Expedition and its members, although his testimony, for reasons which will become clear later, is not entirely trustworthy. See his "Declaración," October 6, 1817, p. 806.

[6] Mier to "Frasquito," from Norfolk-Baltimore, July 1–13, 1816, says they reached Norfolk on June 30 (*Documentos,* VI, 806); Harris G. Warren (*The Sword Was Their Passport,* p. 151) says June 20.

9

America; Miguel Santa María, a deputy from Mexico to the Spanish Cortes who had lately escaped from a Spanish prison; Joaquín Infante, a Cuban who had worked persistently since 1810 for independence; and Pedro Gual, the official representative of Venezuela and Colombia in the United States. After Mina laid his plans before them, all agreed to assist him and some volunteered to join the Expedition. Gual then announced through the local press the arrival of Mina and Mier, and included a sketch of the career of Mina in Spain, where he had proved himself a daring and fearless leader.[7]

The fame, and especially the personality, of Mina,[8] the elo-

[7] *The American*, Baltimore, Maryland, July 17, 1816.

[8] The first published work covering the Mina Expedition is that of William Davis Robinson entitled *Memoirs of the Mexican Revolution including a Narrative of the Expedition of General Xavier Mina . . .*, published in Philadelphia in 1820. He cites as his principal source concerning the expedition (Introduction, p. iii) a "Diary of James Brush."

Robinson's work, which includes (pp. 43–51) a biographical sketch of Mina, was reprinted in London in 1821, and a Spanish translation, made by J. J. Mora, was published in London in 1824. Before this reached Mexico, Carlos María Bustamante, an active participant in the Mexican struggle for independence, had begun telling the story of the conflict, with the addition of many firsthand documents, in his *Cuadro histórico de la Revolución Mexicana*. In his first volume he included a letter of José Servando Teresa de Mier Noriega y Guerra, a member of the Mina Expedition, which covers events from April to June 25, 1816; and in his fourth volume (1826) he wrote the story of Mina, following Robinson to some extent but adding original documents. Other original documents, especially letters and the testimony of Mier when a prisoner of the Inquisition, which throw much light on the details of the Expedition and its members, were published later (1877–1882) by José E. Hernández y Dávalos in his *Documentos*.

Other sources are the official correspondence of the minister of Spain to the United States with the U.S. secretary of state, the captain-general of Cuba, the viceroy of Mexico, and the secretary of state of Spain (1816–1821); and the Diplomatic Dispatches from the U.S. minister in Spain to the U.S. secretary of state (1818–1821). In the unpublished Hernández y Dávalos Papers (hereafter H-D) at the University of Texas are numerous pertinent documents. In Mexico City in the Archivo General de la Nación (hereafter AGN) is the correspondence of the viceroy (Juan Ruiz de Apodaca, Conde del Venadito) and General Arredondo, the commandant of the Eastern Interior Provinces, which then included Coahuila, Nuevo León, Nuevo Santander (later Tamaulipas), and Texas. In the Archivo de Indias at Seville (hereafter AGI) is an "Account of Mina's Expedition" by Isaac W. Webb, which, like the testimony of Mier, must be taken with

quence of Mier, and the prospect of Mexico as a new market for goods aroused such enthusiasm in business circles in Baltimore that over a hundred thousand dollars was advanced toward financing the expedition.[9] It was not Mina's intention to recruit troops, as he expected the Mexican revolutionary government to furnish these; he proposed, instead, to provide the much needed munitions and leadership in the form of experienced and fully equipped officers and technicians.

But how to get in touch with the insurgent leaders in order to cooperate with them was Mina's first problem. He found no representative of their government in either Baltimore or Washington and was assured there was none on the eastern seaboard. All he could learn was that there was such a representative in New Orleans, José Manuel Herrera, and that he had appointed as governor of Texas a Frenchman, Louis Aury,[10] who was cruising in the Gulf of Mexico and preying mercilessly on Spanish shipping. Mina then went to Philadelphia and Mier to New York in order to leave no stone unturned. In Philadelphia Gual published a manifesto of Mina[11] and, through articles in the *Weekly Aurora*, made known the purpose of the expedition.[12] But after both Mina and Mier were unsuccessful in their quest, Mina decided to dispatch Mier by the quickest route to New Orleans in order to establish contact with either Herrera or Aury while he prepared to follow.

His main problems otherwise—ships, men, and supplies—were

---

a grain of salt, as it was written while Webb, who had been a member of the Expedition, was a prisoner of the Mexican government, and the document was forwarded to Spain as an enclosure with a letter of the viceroy to the Spanish government.

In this chapter I have followed Robinson in the main, but have also utilized these other firsthand sources. Hereafter his work will be cited as *Memoirs*.

[9] Mier, "Declaración," November 13, 1817; Hernández, *Documentos*, VI, 817.

[10] The decree of Herrera naming Aury governor of Texas was published in the New Orleans *Commercial Advertiser*, October 18, 1816 (Brush, "Journal," p. 33).

[11] Mier,"Declaración" (October 9, 1817), Hernández, *Documentos*, VI, 807.

[12] *The Weekly Aurora*, Philadelphia, July 30 and August 6, 1816. Quoted by Warren, p. 153.

rapidly solved. With the funds provided in Baltimore, he purchased three boats, including a sailing brig pierced for guns, as well as additional military stores.[13] There was no difficulty in securing men; soon more than two hundred of various nationalities had volunteered as officers—among them many who had served in either the British or United States army. As all were eager to be off and an intimation reached Mina that the United States government might prevent their sailing on such a mission, he hastily fitted out the *Caledonia* as a transport for some two hundred men and dispatched it in August to Port-au-Prince with a Spanish schooner hired to carry a company of artillery, the cannon, and other heavy arms.

For himself and his staff Mina retained the brig. In this group was an experienced United States Army officer, Colonel Guilford Young, of Connecticut, who brought with him a number of trained officers and technicians—largely outstanding young men from New England.[14] Among them was a young fellow named Samuel Bangs, who had been attracted to the Expedition by the offer of the rank and pay of an artillery officer[15] and by the opportunity it would afford him to see something of the world. He had heard tales of southern seas and of Spanish America, where vessels from New England ventured at their peril, but was himself neither a sailor nor a soldier—merely a simple printer who was recruited to operate the portable press Mina had brought from England. While only a slip of a boy, the young printer had a pleasant smile and a hearty laugh and was soon popular among his older companions, although his ignorance of military terms and usage furnished them, for a time, much amusement, to which he responded good-humoredly.

Like the rest of the group, he was eager to be off. Although Mina was conscious of this general feeling, he repeatedly de-

[13] Robinson, *Memoirs*, p. 56.
[14] Luis de Onís to [José Cienfuegos], captain general of Cuba, from Philadelphia, August 28, 1816; AGN, Historia (Operaciones de Guerra, Notas diplomáticas), I, fols. 249–249 v.
[15] *American Flag*, Brownsville, Texas, May 17, 1848.

layed his departure, hoping to get authoritative information about conditions in Mexico and the best place to land. Reports were in circulation that only a few insurgent leaders remained in the field and that these not only lacked almost all the essentials of warfare but were jealous of each other. Besides, the viceroy of "New Spain," as Mexico was officially known, had lately made an offer of amnesty which many, feeling that the situation was hopeless, had accepted. In spite of these uncertainties, Mina finally set sail for Port-au-Prince on September 26.[16]

With perfect weather, the brig moved forward so smoothly and so rapidly that the spirits of all on board ran high. Cloudless skies and cool sea breezes inspired the conviction that quick success awaited them. The young printer became more certain each day that he had done well in joining the group. He was not idle, either, during the journey southward. Like many of the staff officers, the boy knew no Spanish, nor did the other printer, John McLaran. To remedy that situation, Mina assigned an officer to give Spanish lessons daily, and all possible means were employed to introduce all, and especially the printers, to the language they would soon have to use.

But—unknown even to Mina—troubles were already brewing. In the slow voyage across the Atlantic in May and June some of the Spaniards he had befriended in London and given free passage to America became disgruntled. While he and Mier were away they left the ship and reported what they knew of Mina's plans to the Spanish consul in Baltimore.[17] This information was promptly forwarded to the Spanish minister in Philadelphia and by him relayed to Cuba, Mexico, and Spain. While it had occurred to Mina that the deserters might cause some trouble, he left the United States completely unprepared for the dangers to which their treachery could lead.

[16] Bangs says "26" in his Application for Land, Saltillo, January 27, 1830 (Texas, General Land Office, Spanish Grants, XXX, 200).

[17] José Fernando Martínez de Pasamontes, sworn statement, [Baltimore], September 9, 1816. Remitted by Luis de Onís to Pedro Cevallos, secretary of state of Spain, Philadelphia, September 11, 1816; AHN, Department of State, Legation in the United States, Legajo 5641, No. 139.

The enthusiasm of the group on landing at Port-au-Prince the middle of October was considerably dampened by the discovery that a tropical storm a few weeks earlier had left the *Caledonia* dismasted, the schooner upset and grounded, and several of the men dead.[18] Mina had to have the *Caledonia* repaired and to replace the grounded schooner; besides, a number of his officers lost heart over the outlook and abandoned the group. The enforced delay irked all but the New Englanders, who, like Bangs, were basking for the first time in tropical warmth and luxuriating in the wealth of fruits and flowers. When the boats were finally ready, the little group of ships set sail—this time for the island of St. Louis (San Luis) on the Mexican coast.[19]

Barely were they again at sea when a calm set in, which further exasperated all, and led many to lament that they had not returned home from Port-au-Prince, as they might have done. Worse was soon to come. Yellow fever broke out on the *Caledonia* and soon spread to the other vessels. On the transport eight died, and within a few days no one on board the schooner was free of fever. That vessel was then taken in tow by the brig, which had lost only one man. For Bangs that was fortunate, for this fact, coupled with his youth, good health, and inexperience, kept him from suffering the fear of death that gripped many; but his confidence in his wisdom in joining the group was considerably shaken. However, before they reached Grand Cayman Island, northerly winds inspired renewed courage in all and restored some to health; fresh food from the Island did wonders for others. The schooner with its sick was left there. Almost a month after leaving Port-au-Prince—during which time more than thirty members of the Expedition had died—they reached St. Louis Island, just off the coast of the Spanish province of Texas.

Mina told his men that he was stopping there to confer with

[18] *Boletin I de la División Ausiliar de la República Mexicana* (Bulletin I of the Auxiliary Division of the Mexican Republic). Soto la Marina, 1817. See Appendix I, Document 2. Yale; photocopy, TxU and LMS.
[19] The Brush "Journal" begins at this point.

Commodore Aury, a French corsair whose headquarters were known to be on an island near the mouth of the Trinity River. The boats anchored off the island while Mina located the titular governor and then discussed his plans with him. Aury declined to recognize the Spaniard as a general, for Mina had as yet no status with the insurgents of Mexico, but, impressed by his sincerity and determination, agreed to cooperate with him. The Commodore nevertheless warned that the northers then prevalent might make a winter landing on the Mexican coast dangerous. At his invitation Mina then decided to wait there until that danger had passed; in the meantime he hoped to meet Herrera and be officially recognized.

When Bangs heard the order for both men and cargo to be landed, he began, for the first time, to lose heart. From the brig he surveyed in disgust the low, flat, almost treeless island covered with long prairie grass and intersected by countless bayous. The only settlement, called "Galvez Town," consisted of a few straggling huts and an unfinished fort at the eastern end. The disadvantages of the island were soon painfully apparent. The channel to the harbor proved dangerous and the water on the bar too shallow for the vessels to enter; as a result the entire cargo had to be unloaded on the beach and carried to the only feasible storage place found—the hulk of an abandoned ship on one of the shallow spots in the bay. Then, as it was not safe for the ships to remain at anchor on the open coast, they were ordered to New Orleans.

The transfer of the cargo proved both slow and difficult; here was real work for all, although some small craft assisted and Aury ordered his Negro troops to help. In spite of the winter season, the sun at midday seemed terribly hot, especially to the New Englanders, and the glare from the water was hard on their eyes. The heat and exercise increased their craving for water; that in the sand proved brackish, but some distance away they later found good water at a spot where ships had apparently been accustomed to fill their casks.

Mina selected a spot west of the settlement on which to pitch his camp. There, under a torrid sun, tents were set up, field pieces placed, and arms and clothing distributed. From his store of booty Aury supplied all with rations of excellent bread, salt beef, pork, oil, fish, and brandy; with these and the game and supplies the coasters soon offered, the division fared exceedingly well. And the nights, with the sea breeze, were wonderful for sleeping!

The technicians were put to work immediately.[20] The printing press was brought up and the boxes of supplies were unpacked and stacked near at hand. Shortly Bangs began to print the Daily Orders of the Camp and, as captured vessels were frequently brought in, the decisions of the Prize Court.[21] At once he and McLaran faced the difficulties inherent in printing in an unfamiliar language—for Spanish lessons had ceased in the face of yellow fever; but their errors were generously overlooked. During several weeks in December working in the tent that housed the press was fairly comfortable; then, after a day as balmy as in spring, a biting norther swept the Island. The winds howled continuously; the waves dashed high on the shore; and for days there was no relief from the cold, which seemed to penetrate even their bones. When the winds died down—which they did as unexpectedly as they had risen—the sun warmed all as before. But printing in the tent was repeatedly brought almost to a standstill by such cold snaps.

Mina did not permit his men to be idle while he waited for the season of northers to pass; he organized them and began daily drilling. The officers from the United States who did not understand Spanish were formed, in the interest of self-defense, into a company called the "Guard of Honor," commanded by Colonel Young; Mina expected these to be scattered after they learned the language. The First Regiment of the Line was placed in command of Major José Sardá, a Catalonian; Colonel Myers com-

---

[20] Robinson, *Memoirs,* pp. 60–77, and Brush "Journal," pp. 30–35, cover the Galveston stay.

[21] Undated manuscript in the Dyer Collection, p. 9. Texas Galveston Rosenberg Library, Galveston, Texas. Hereafter TGR.

manded the artillery, and the Count de Ruuth, the cavalry. The engineering, commissary, and medical departments, as well as the technicians—printers, carpenters, blacksmiths, and tailors— were also organized, and daily reports were required from each body.[22] While many were inclined to grumble over the enforced delay, good order generally prevailed.

When Mier arrived from New Orleans early in December, Bangs thought him one of the most peculiar figures he had ever seen. Some fifty years of age, he was less than average in height and stocky in build. His skin and hair were fair; his eyes, vivacious and penetrating, were gray; both beard and eyebrows were "slightly black."[23] He carried regularly a wide green umbrella, and on feast days he wore purple bands on his black clerical robe. On one arm shone a gold bracelet set with a large topaz, and on his breast hung a golden cross from a heavy chain.

To Mina he brought the bad news that Herrera had left for Washington before Mier reached New Orleans, and that he had been unable to establish any contact with the revolutionists. He had also hired a schooner and dispatched it to every point on the Mexican coast that had been reported in insurgent hands; at each place Spanish forces were found in possession. Undismayed by this discouraging report, Mina sailed for New Orleans to make a personal effort to locate some representative of the insurgent government.

Mier meanwhile turned his attention to the camp personnel and soon showed a marked interest in the young printer; in both of them there was a strong underlying streak of humor. As the boy came to know the prelate, who constituted himself both Spanish teacher and supervisor of the press, he found him a man of decision and profound knowledge; Mier entertained Bangs by the hour with tales of his thrilling experiences. As a young Dominican friar a quarter of a century earlier, he had fallen into

[22] Report of the secretary, Regiment of the Union, [Expedition of F. X. Mina], Galveston, February 24, [1817], accounts for 91 men (H-D, Calendar No. 952, p. 180).

[23] Hernández, *Documentos*, VI, 663–664.

17

the clutches of the Inquisition, as a result of his independent thinking and speaking in the Mexican capital, and he was then sent as a prisoner to Spain. There he escaped repeatedly, and finally went to Rome, where he was secularized, he said, by the Pope. When the troops of Napoleon entered Spain in 1808, he returned there and, as a chaplain, preached resistance against the invaders; but, like Mina, he finally had to take refuge in England. In London he published the first history of the Mexican Revolution and pamphlets in behalf of freedom of the press and of the independence of Spanish America; in Baltimore he furnished similar articles to the press; and while in New Orleans he had issued, under the name of Domingo Noriega, biographies of the two Minas—Francisco Xavier and his uncle Francisco Espoz y Mina. The unbounded enthusiasm of this man, in spite of all he had suffered, and his unshakeable conviction of the ultimate success of the expedition made Samuel realize more fully the importance of the mission on which they were bound and the necessity of a command of the Spanish language. Besides, he now had someone with whom he could talk over his problems, no matter what they were. For Mier came to take the place of a father for him, and also for many of the younger men.

All rejoiced when Mina returned flying the Mexican colors on the brig whose name he had changed to *Mexican Congress*.[24] Preparations for departure were well under way when the General was hastily recalled to New Orleans, leaving the division under the command of General Montilla. His absence at the moment was particularly unfortunate, for the whole camp was much shaken by the discovery that a member of the Expedition, Segundo Correa, whom Mina had gotten rid of after he found the fellow trying to excite a mutiny among Aury's troops, was a spy of the Spanish government and that his purpose in joining the group, at the instigation of the Spanish minister in the United States, had been to kill the leader. Not until after Mina had let him slip through his hands did the full extent of his in-

[24] Robinson, *Memoirs*, p. 69.

tended treachery become known. Then the captured letters, which revealed the whole scheme and which had been published in the United States, were reprinted by Bangs in an order of the day.[25]

For the printers the first two months of 1817 passed quickly, as they were kept busy printing not only the Orders of the Day and the Prize Court decisions but a *Proclamation* of Mina. He had originally written it in London and had had it printed there prior to his departure, under the date of May 2, 1816.[26] In this he reviewed his early career, his struggle to free Spain from the oppressive rule of Ferdinand VII, and the motives which impelled him to help Mexico secure independence. In justification of his attitude toward Spain, he cited William Pitt, who had gloried in the resistance of the American colonists to British rule. In Baltimore this *Proclamation* had been rewritten by Gual, but Mina did not like that version and ordered his secretary Revenga to make certain changes in it. To these Revenga added some touches of his own; among them, at Mier's suggestion, the epithets "impious" and "sacrilegious" were applied to the Inquisition. In this form and with the original title it was reprinted at Galveston and dated February 22, 1817. The printers' names appear on the verso of the broadside as Juan J. M'Laran and S. Bancs [*sic*].[27]

About a week later, with Mina still away, Aury discovered that a hundred Americans who had enlisted with Colonel Perry to serve in an invasion of Texas had decided instead to join the

[25] Robinson, *Memoirs*, pp. 69–71. *Boletin I* (Appendix I, Doc. 2).

[26] Exposición de D. Xavier Mina a los Españoles y Americanos. Londres, 2 de mayo de 1816. Hernández, *Documentos*, VI, 850. A copy bearing this date was among Mier's books and papers captured at Soto la Marina.

[27] No original of this printing has been located. It was reprinted by Carlos María Bustamante in his *Cuadro histórico de la Revolución Mexicana* (México, 1823–1832, 6 volumes), IV (1826), Parte segundo de la tercera época, Carta 16, pp. 7–12. In Carta 18, p. 1, fn. 2, he says: "Ignoro si será el mismo que se ha insertado; pero este se data en Galveston a 22 de febrero, y en el reverso se dice que está impreso por Juan J. M'Laran y S. Bancs." As the Spanish translation of Robinson's *Memoirs* had reached Mexico, Bustamante offered many corrections and included many firsthand documents as evidence.

Mina Expedition. Thoroughly enraged—and the Frenchman had an ungovernable temper—Aury imprisoned Perry and some of his officers in their quarters. When he realized that the men intended to defend Perry, the Commodore drew up his other troops, mostly Negroes and cutthroats. At once Mina's men were aroused; and Montilla, while trying to prevent any encounter between the two groups, took the precaution of supplying his own with ammunition and placing all on call to arms. Aury then wisely released those under arrest and permitted any who wished to join Mina's force.

While Mina was in New Orleans he bought an old ship, the *Neptune*, and another transport, the *Cleopatra*, to replace the *Caledonia*, which he released, according to his original agreement. He came back on March 16 with a few new recruits and found the whole division ready for departure. He then informed some of the members of his staff that he had decided to land at Soto la Marina, a small settlement on the Santander River, where the Royalists would not be expecting them, and that Aury would accompany them there. He also expressed displeasure over some of the terms used in the *Proclamation*. At once several officers resigned, among them Montilla, Revenga, and Roscio, as they questioned the wisdom of such a landing.

While the men on board, ignorant of their destination, were impatiently awaiting a favorable wind, two captured brigs were brought in for condemnation, but as the wind sprang up just at that moment they were ordered to take Perry and his men aboard and proceed with the expedition. Mina's division, consisting of some three hundred men, was then redistributed, and on March 27 all sailed. On an armed schooner went Aury with a company of artillery and the cavalry of De Ruuth; on the *Cleopatra* went Captain Hooper, General Mina and his staff, the Guard of Honor, the First Regiment of the Line, and the printers; and on the *Neptune* went Captain Wisset with the commissariat and stores. A schooner, the *Ellen Tooker*, arriving just as the fleet was leaving, decided to accompany it, as did also a small sloop. All were ordered to assemble at the mouth of the Rio

Bravo del Norte (the Rio Grande). The remains of the encampment at Galvez Town were set afire.[28]

Shortly after sailing it was discovered that provisions on the *Cleopatra* were inadequate, and by the time the Rio Bravo del Norte was reached, her water supply was so exhausted that it had to be replenished. As the fleet, then anchored at the mouth of the river, was temporarily flying Spanish colors and as Major Sardá, who went on shore with several men, was a Spaniard, the Royalists permitted them to take water from the river and even drove up some wild cattle for their use. But the shallowness of the water on the bar made it so difficult to get fresh water that a Spanish officer who had left England with Mina was drowned in the attempt. Worse still, four men deserted.

During the days spent at the mouth of the river Bangs was not idle, for here he began to print a proclamation which Mina issued on April 12 to his "Companions in arms." In this he tried to rectify some of the expressions used in the Galvez Town *Proclamation* by reminding his men of their common purpose—not to conquer but to aid the country in freeing itself from oppression.[29]

No sooner was a new start made than up came a gale which scattered the vessels. With the *Neptune*, which was carrying the stores, out of sight, the *Cleopatra* was again without sufficient supplies. Food had to be rationed; for almost a week each man's daily allotment was only half a biscuit, a few almonds, and a pint of water. In spite of this hardship the *Cleopatra* arrived first at their destination. They were met by a couple of friendly peasants who offered to serve as guides, but quickly disappeared.

[28] Robinson, *Memoirs*, pp. 75–77. At this point Mier takes up the story in a letter to Bustamante dated September 9, 1823 (*Cuadro histórico*, I (1823), Epoca 1, Carta 22, p. 10, to Carta 24, p. 4). The substance and much of the text is the same as in his "Memorias" and "Manifiesto Apologético" (MSS, Mi). On departing from Galveston he also wrote a poem on the settlement (Carta 22, p. 10), one stanza of which reads:

Acabó como vivía	It ended as it had lived
Entre guerras y motín	In the midst of war and riot.
Regal fué su Rostachin.	Regal [one of the engineers] was
	its Rostachin.

[29] Reprinted in *Boletin I* (Appendix I, Doc. 2).

The other boats came in the next few days; and by the twenty-first of April disembarkation of all had been accomplished without interference of any kind.[30] The General had been persuaded to land at this spot by a Mexican boy, a native of the place, who assured him, in New Orleans, that the town of Soto la Marina was only a short distance from the mouth of the Santander River; but a reconnaissance revealed that it had been moved many miles upstream.[31] The mouth of the river proved to be very narrow and the bar so obstructive as to prevent all the vessels from crossing. Inside the bar the stream widened for many miles but then again narrowed, so that had the vessels been able to pass the bar they could have almost reached the new town. The country near the beach was intersected by large bayous and shallow ponds which extended some distance northward, but the town itself was on a high spot on the north bank.

The press and its equipment were promptly unloaded and set up, and Bangs was put to work on the beach, a hot, sultry spot most of the day. And now that it was almost May the sun was considerably hotter than it had been during the winter. The first publication he issued from the small English press after establishing it on the mainland of Mexico was a *Patriotic Song* composed by Joaquín Infante, the auditor of the Expedition, in honor of their successful debarkation. On this piece of work, of which Bangs was quite proud, he placed his name as printer of the Division.[32] As soon as that was finished he began work on an abbreviated version of the Galveston *Proclamation* which Mina wanted to have ready to distribute in the towns he expected to enter. With it he hoped to attract to his own forces members of the Spanish army in Mexico.[33]

[30] Robinson covers this part of the trip (pp. 78–79), and calls the river the "Santander"; Brush calls it the "Saint Anders." Today it is the Soto la Marina.

[31] At this point the Brush "Journal" becomes much more detailed. Pp. 36–53 cover the Soto la Marina period to the departure of Mina for the interior.

[32] Made from an original now at Yale. It was reprinted by Bustamante (*Cuadro histórico*, IV, Letter 17, pp. 5–6).

[33] Included in *Boletín I* (Appendix I, Doc. 2). Reprinted in Hernández, *Docu-*

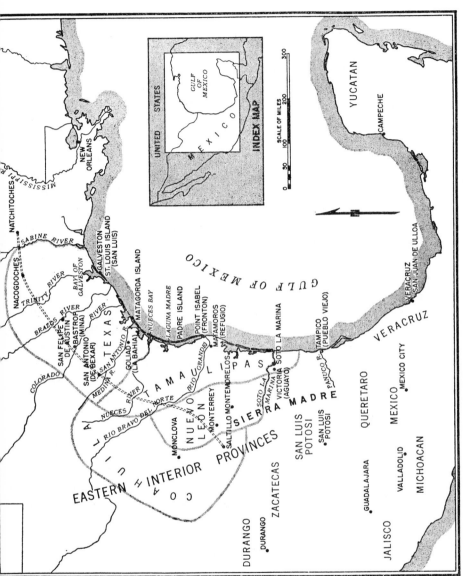

Mexico and the Eastern Interior Provinces, 1823.

While the printer and a helper worked on the beach, boats with a fieldpiece, some stores, and a detachment of artillery went up the river, and troops set out on foot and by horse for the new town. The progress of those on land was very slow, as the men suffered intensely from the heat and from lack of water after the road turned away from the river, for they had no canteens. This experience taught them that people in such climates traveled only in early morning and late afternoons; during the midday they rested.[34] Bangs, too, found that a siesta at midday helped in getting his work done.

Before many days passed news came down the river that the advance guard, which was made up of volunteers from the Guard of Honor and the cavalry under Sardá, had entered Soto la Marina without meeting any opposition. The General and Mier were welcomed with open arms by the curate of the village, and the citizens, surprised and overjoyed at being well treated, were very friendly.[35] The place was a straggling village of some eight hundred souls; the houses were built of adobe bricks and the roofs thatched with tall grass or reeds. Most of them were huddled close together along narrow dusty streets or lanes. Around the town mesquite brush and straggling grass provided food for small herds of horses and cattle. The clothing of the women was nondescript but modest; small children were entirely naked. The men wore leather coverings over their clothes, especially over their legs to protect them from the thorns of the mesquite or other prickly shrubs, and used iron spurs fastened over long gaiters. Food consisted largely of thin corncakes with jerked mutton or beef flavored by a sauce made from red peppers they called *chile*. Water was carried in *ollas* from the river, and cooking was done either in the open or on *braseros*—clay receptacles in which charcoal was coaxed to burn. Primitive as was their life, the people seemed kind and good-hearted.

---

mentos, VI, 862–865, from a copy whose imprint reads: "Reimpreso por Don Teodosio López de Lara. Impresor del Gobierno Mexicano."

[34] Robinson, *Memoirs*, p. 82.
[35] Brush, "Journal," pp. 42–43.

Encouraged by the cooperative spirit they encountered, Colonel Novoa ordered a more ambitious publication prepared for distribution. In this three-page *Bulletin I of the Auxiliary Division of the Mexican Republic* the story of Mina's exertions in the cause of liberty in Spain is told, his motives in coming to the aid of the suffering colonists are explained, and some of the difficulties he had experienced in reaching Mexico are recounted. In it, too, the *Proclamation* Mina had issued to his men on April 12 at the mouth of the Rio Bravo del Norte and the April twenty-fifth version of the Galvez Town *Proclamation* were reprinted.[36] Copies were promptly sent up the river and widely distributed to the native population. Some fell into the hands of troops in the vicinity, and soon over a hundred sturdy fellows joined Mina's ranks. Later others came, among them two Royalist officers, the Rubio brothers, who supplied the badly needed horses. In spite of these encouraging reinforcements, De Ruuth, the commander of Mina's cavalry, resigned and returned to Aury's vessel; Colonel John Maylefer, a valiant Swiss officer, succeeded him. The troops were then reorganized, armed, and issued colorful uniforms, ready for action. But the uniforms, suited to neither the season nor the climate, soon had to be discarded.

Mina sent out small scouting parties freely in all directions; one even advanced as far as Aguayo, the capital of the province on another branch of the river. But the Royalists never attacked, and it seemed the settlers had been instructed to retire whenever one of Mina's parties presented itself. Colonel Perry came to close quarters with some troops, but held his own with small losses, although he had to abandon some supplies he had captured.

During several weeks, while Mina waited expecting to be attacked, he occupied his men in bringing up stores from the beach, including the press and all its equipment, and in throwing up a small breastwork for the protection of the supplies and

[36] An original issue of the *Boletin* is in the Yale University Library and photocopies of it are at TxU and in possession of the writer. It is reproduced in Appendix I as Document 2.

25

themselves in case of a siege. He himself proposed to head for the interior and join the patriot army; he then expected to return with enough native troops to utilize the extensive supplies he had brought. Before he left he started the construction of a fort on an advantageous spot near the river. The whole division worked hard, the General and the technicians among them, and the peasants helped. Although the fort was built only of adobe bricks, all hoped it would be strong enough to offer some defiance to the enemy. As the river at this point was very narrow they planned to throw up defenses on the opposite bank to protect the rear of the fort and ensure safe access to water.[37]

While the men at Soto la Marina were working hard on the fort, Commodore Aury departed, taking with him those who had resigned and the prize brigs. Only two boats, the *Cleopatra* and the *Ellen Tooker,* remained at the mouth of the river, as the *Neptune* had been run on shore as soon as her cargo was discharged. Some of the cargo, including Mier's library, in which were many of his own and other works advocating the independence of Spanish America, was taken up the river. But still many stores remained at the landing place, and tents were pitched there as shelter for those guarding them.

All was serene, both in the town and on the beach, until the middle of May, when Captain Hooker, the crew of the *Cleopatra,* and those left to guard the stores unexpectedly appeared at Soto la Marina. They reported that when some Spanish ships came in sight the *Ellen Tooker* escaped; the *Cleopatra* was captured and burned. The Spanish crews had started to land, but the sight of the tents so alarmed them that they hastily returned to their boats. This part of the report raised the spirits of Mina's men considerably; that their enemy could be so easily frightened off amused them. Yet all realized that they were now cut off completely from any return by sea.

Undeterred, Bangs unpacked the press and set it up near the fort. There he completed the *Proclamation* of Mina, addressed

<hr />

[37] Robinson, *Memoirs,* pp. 84–87.

this time to the soldiers of Ferdinand VII, both Spaniards and Mexicans, urging them to join him. The single page bore the heading: *Don Xavier Mina, General and Chief of the Auxiliary Division of the Mexican Republic.* In substance it repeated his earlier plea for cooperation.[38]

When the fort was almost finished and guns from the fleet mounted, Mina made the final arrangements for his march to the interior. He ordered brought up two mortars, much ammunition, and more of the *Neptune's* cargo; cattle were killed and the meat jerked; corn was brought in; and the place was prepared as far as possible for defense. He then selected the troops to accompany him and encamped them some distance away across the river. Among those whom Bangs especially hated to see leave was Colonel Young, who had induced him to join the group and had proved himself an able officer and a gentleman.

While these preparations were under way, Colonel Perry, who had openly shown dissatisfaction with the situation, called his men together and told them he had decided to return to the United States; he explained the dangers that faced them and urged all to leave as soon as possible. Fifty-two officers and men went down the river, stocked themselves from the beach stores, and set off for Matagorda. Although dumfounded for the moment at the desertion of so many men at such a critical moment, Mina never wavered in carrying out his original plan.

For the defense of the fort he left detachments of the Guard of Honor, artillery and infantry; groups of the medical and commissary departments; and the printers, the mechanics, the sailors of the destroyed vessels, and some recruits. All were placed under the command of Major Sardá, who was instructed to hold out to the last. Mina assured him that he would return in time to force the Royalists to raise any siege attempted during his absence. On May 24, with over two hundred men, he departed.[39]

---

[38] Photocopy, TxU and LMS.

[39] Robinson, *Memoirs,* pp. 88–93. As Brush departed with Mina for the interior of Mexico and did not know until much later what happened at the fort, his "Journal" from page 54 could not have furnished Robinson a firsthand ac-

With Sardá in command, drilling of the recruits and the transfer of additional stores from the beach continued without disturbance for almost two weeks. Then news came that the Royalists were on the march, and two days later three members of a foraging party reported that the rest of their group had been either killed or captured. Among the latter was Captain Andreis, an Italian who had served in the British army and had come with Mina from London.

All were then ordered to help prepare the fort for defense. The peasant women killed and jerked more beef; the seamen worked hard in salvaging more stores from the beach. Bangs and his helper boxed the press and equipment, hid them among the general stores, and then joined in work on the entrenchments. In spite of the hard work under a scorching sun, not a murmur was heard.

On June 11 over two thousand troops under General Joaquín Arredondo were reported only three miles away. At the fort were ninety-three men; twenty, among them the printers, were assigned to protecting the stores. On the fort were nine guns, but the rear was entirely unprotected, as no defenses had been built across the river. During the next three days there was firing from the opposite bank, without material damage. Far worse, two days later, was the defection of Captains Martenich and Sala, an action which aroused both indignation and uneasiness. Sala,

---

count of the happenings at Soto la Marina. The information concerning the fate of the fort from May 24 to June 25 was obtained, Robinson says (p. 169), from an authentic source. It seems to have been secured from participants whose names at that time it was not wise to reveal.

Robinson himself had been captured by Spanish forces and was shipped to Spain via Havana on the *Ligero*. On the same boat went as prisoners José Torrens, François Dagahan, and Christian Tanke, all members of the Mina Expedition who had been captured at Soto la Marina. See George W. Erving to J. Q. Adams (U.S. Secretary of State), Madrid, March 4 and April 9, 1819, Nos. 98 and 99. Enclosed in the last of these is a statement signed by Torrens, Dagahan, and Tanke regarding the fate of other members of the Expedition. See Primary Sources, Manuscripts. United States, Department of State Diplomatic Dispatches. Spain. Vol. 16 (1818–1819). NA.

who, with his family, had been saved from starvation in London by Mina and brought to the United States at Mina's expense, had seemed loyal. As the senior engineer in possession of all details of the fort, he could easily assist in its fall. In spite of their danger, the officers in the fort held a council of war, crossed their swords, and swore to defend it to the bitter end. All felt added confidence in themselves and contempt for their enemy when some Royalist cavalry, who had come edging up to drive away some nearby cattle, were put to flight by a few infantrymen. The whole garrison and the technicians worked day and night on the fortifications, but met the enemy, whenever they appeared, with a steady fire, part of the men loading the guns while others fired. Bangs and his helper were rapidly learning the art of self-defense.

On the fifteenth a battery across the river exposed the fort to a crossfire which worked destruction at every shot. Then infantry cut the little garrison off from water. By noon the fort was almost disabled. Bugles, trumpets, and drums soon sounded the advance of the enemy, but they were greeted with a heavy discharge of cannon, musket, and shouts of "Long live liberty and Mina!" Three times the enemy fled, Arredondo, the commander, narrowly escaping a cannon ball. But incessant effort and intolerable thirst soon exhausted the defenders. The artillery was useless and most of the gunners were dead; the infantrymen could scarcely hold up a gun. Some of the recruits had fled. After the third onslaught, firing slackened, for the Royalists themselves had suffered such heavy losses as to leave no doubt concerning the courage and determination of those holding the fort.

At half-past one a messenger bearing a flag of truce demanded its surrender. It was refused, as all agreed they would rather die than submit to dishonorable terms. Another messenger arrived offering to spare the lives of the garrison; this was refused. After a third message was received, Arredondo's staff adjutant came up with an offer of honorable and liberal terms.

It was then agreed that all in the garrison or at the mouth of the river would surrender as prisoners of war, each to be treated according to his rank, and the officers paroled. Private property was to be respected and the foreigners were to be sent back to the United States at the first opportunity. The natives were to be sent to their homes, with their conduct condoned. The garrison would march out with the honors of war and stack arms. The commanding officer declared that he was authorized to agree to any terms he thought proper, and pledged his word of honor on behalf of his commanding officer that the conditions would be scrupulously observed. As Sardá knew that the honor of a Royalist officer thus solemnly pledged, if he was honorable, was better security than any written documents which could easily be destroyed, he did not insist on a formal capitulation with the signature of Arredondo.

Hostilties ceased; thirty-seven officers and men marched out with all the honors of war and stacked their arms before some fifteen hundred of the enemy. When Arredondo saw the little band, he asked in astonishment, "Are these the whole garrison?" and was answered in the affirmative.[40]

For the next two days all of them were at liberty, expecting soon to be on the way home. The following day they were placed under guard, and some of them forced to bury the dead and to destroy the defenses. Shortly afterward the men of the foraging party who had been captured, but so far well treated, were led, with the exception of Andreis, to the front of the camp and there, before the eyes of their horrified comrades, shot. Mier, who was

[40] Mier's account of the fall of the fort and also that of Colonel Antonio Elozua, an officer with Arredondo, are in *Cuadro histórico*, I (1823), Letters 22–23, which was published before the Spanish translation of Robinson. But see also Robinson's version, (*Memoirs*, pp. 170–178).

In the Report on the capture of the fort at Soto la Marina which Arredondo sent to Viceroy Apodaca, June 30, 1817, is inserted that of Colonel Juan José Echeandía to Arredondo, listing the goods and men captured, among them Torrens, Dagasan (*sic*), and Tanke (AGN, Historia, [Operaciones de Guerra, Arredondo, IV], fols. 257–261). For Arredondo's Report see fols. 253–256, 262–264.

the first put under guard and shortly afterward in chains, and repeatedly subjected to jeers and coarse insults, was sent off on a mule with a military escort. Most of the garrison were kept in close arrest for some weeks and then led off as prisoners.

Bangs was not among them, nor did his name appear on the list of those captured at the fall of the fort.

TWO

In the Hands of State and Church

ARLY ONE MORNING several months later Bangs was routed out of the hut in which he had been imprisoned and by the sign language ordered to take the road, with soldiers as guards. He obeyed, but wondered whether he was to be shot or to meet a worse fate. After the surrender of the fort he had seen Father Mier taken off in chains, although his meekness and serenity would have softened even savages. Weeks later he saw most of the other prisoners started in the direction of the coast under heavy guard. Now he was on the move, but alone. His limited knowledge of Spanish did not enable him to gather the import of the conversation of his guards, either with him or each other, but he realized before they had gone very far that the general direction they were taking was northwest. This meant he was headed inland. On the western horizon the outlines of mountains were clearly visible. He could think of no reason to be going that way and his scanty knowledge of Mexican geography did not assist him in identifying any of the sandy, straggling villages through which, at long intervals, they passed. The streambeds they crossed were largely dry and the country was bare, parched, and desolate, supporting only stunted mesquite shrubs and cacti, plants he had seldom seen before. Yet the region was dotted with churches, many of them small but some surprisingly large. Clustered about the main structure were trees, flowers, and grass, which made each seem the center of an oasis. By noon each day the heat became intense, and before long burned every exposed portion of the lad's body. In spite of his hunger, which was increased by the enforced exercise, he could still hardly stomach the native food. A drink resembling coffee, made from roasted beans, was given him in the morning before starting; then nothing until long past midday, when they paused at some roadside hut. Here the offerings consisted mainly of fresh or jerked meat in a red *chile* sauce; frijoles (beans) seasoned with garlic; and tortillas, a form of thin but tough pancake made from corn. By midafternoon the sun was blistering and the heat almost unendurable. The nights, which he spent on the ground, brought some relief. Then, seeing the stars above him, he felt, for a moment, freer; and his weary, swollen feet could rest.

After the first few days of steady travel, during which he offered no resistance to his guards, they lessened their vigilance and became slightly more human. The landscape, too, gradually changed. They occasionally crossed little valleys; through them small clear streams meandered. In the deep shade of the bordering pecan trees his escort, from time to time, would halt to rest. Progress became continually more tiring, for the circuitous road was climbing toward the mountains. Some days they came upon a charming, well-watered valley; here were orange orchards and other fruit trees. There were gardens, too, of vegetables and flowers—many he had never seen before. Groups of thatched huts, some almost covered by luxuriant deep red or purple vines, became more frequent; and the trails they had followed gave way to roads traveled by more men and burros. From time to time they met an ox cart whose two cumbersome wooden wheels creaked loudly; these carts transported anything a mule or donkey could not carry. When the drivers, who went on foot as if to set a good example for the weary oxen, stopped to exchange greetings with the guards, they looked curiously at the boy's blistered face, and wondered that he did not understand their language.

As they finally approached the mountains the boy was amazed to find them very different from those in New England; these were almost treeless. Bleak and bare, their steep sides were marked only by beaten trails or by unending miles of rocks piled to serve as boundary markers. Higher and higher the mountains rose above the road they traveled; they also stretched endlessly to both north and south. At long last—he had almost lost track of time and it seemed months since they left Soto la Marina—one of his guards pointed excitedly toward a distant mountain and cried out, "La Silla! La Silla!" ["The Saddle! The Saddle!"].[1] To the weary, homesick boy this meant only that they must be arriving somewhere. A few nights later he could no longer see the stars. Behind the bars of a jail, he slept on a stone floor.

He was awakened before day by the ringing of bells. From his windowless cell he could see little about him, but he sensed, from the type of building in which he found himself, that it was a larger and older place than Soto la Marina. Some days later, when he was taken out of the jail, he felt suddenly transported to another world. Before him was a large open square; on it faced an imposing stone church; and on the opposite side were large two-storied buildings whose arcades served as sidewalks. Tall trees shaded much of the plaza, and on the street in front of the church a number of ragged men were working.

He soon found himself among them, sharing their task of recobbling the street. When first assigned to this crew, the boy felt momentarily relieved; it was better to be working, he thought, than to be shot or to have to spend endless hours in

---

[1] Saddle Mountain, so-called because its peak resembles a saddle, rises to the southeast of Monterrey.

jail. Later he was not so sure. The work consisted of digging out, with very crude tools, the rocks that had become so embedded that they no longer served effectively as paving; these were to be replaced by larger ones so set that only a rounded surface protruded. Sand or clay was then tamped in the crevices. Guards sat about to see that the prisoners worked.

In the weeks that followed, the young New Englander learned what a prisoner of the Spanish government had to endure. Worst of all to him was the filth in the jail and out of it; the lack of a bath and of clean clothes. He tried hard to accustom himself to the daily routine. During the morning hours there was usually a cool breeze and he did not mind the work, although it was physically tiring. As the sun rose higher he was frequently almost prostrated by the heat, which at first was only slightly less intense than during those first days on the road from Soto la Marina. But as autumn came the days were cooler and the work more tolerable. Long past midday each prisoner was given six centavos (cents) with which to purchase food from one of the numerous stands around the square. By dint of perseverance he learned that a helping of *chile* and beans could be placed upon a tortilla held in his outstretched hand, and that by rolling the tortilla the whole could be eaten by bites without the aid of either plate or spoon. After the respite following this meal—which permitted a brief siesta—the prisoners worked on until almost dark; they were then returned to the jail, where each ate anything he had been able to salvage from his midday repast.

Through the early months he spent at this exhausting labor he was tormented by the question of where he was, and why. There was long no answer; in the meantime Bangs learned something of the place, the people, and their language and customs. He found them on the whole very kind-hearted; almost all passers-by gave him sympathetic glances as they approached, and even the children on the street tried to be friendly, sometimes giving him fruit or bits of food. Most of the other prisoners showed sympathy for him and relieved him as much as they could; indeed almost all regarded "El Americano" with respect.

For his part, he found most of them more sinned against than sinning. From them he learned that it was customary for the government to lease its prisoners to the municipal authorities to be employed on public works; in return the city paid a small amount per day for such labor and gave each prisoner the few cents daily for "rations."[2]

Little by little as time passed and he could understand what his guards and fellow prisoners were saying, he found out where he was, and why. He was in Monterrey, the capital of the province of Nuevo León and the headquarters of the commandant —the highest representative of the Spanish government in the Eastern Interior Provinces of Mexico. These comprised Texas, of which St. Louis Isle was a part; Nuevo Santander, in which Soto la Marina was located; Nuevo León, where he now was, and the adjoining province on the west, Coahuila. But he was shocked beyond words when he discovered that the dapper officer in ornate uniform who emerged from time to time from the "Purple House," as his headquarters were called, was none other than General Joaquín de Arredondo, the man who had accepted the surrender of the fort at Soto la Marina and then ordered its defenders imprisoned or killed.

The boy was to learn much, bit by bit, about Arredondo. There was gossip, even among convicts. He was reputed to be a member of an aristocratic family in Spain, and his father to have been the governor of Cuba. He had come to Mexico quite a while before, but for four or five years he had been the commandant in charge of the four provinces, and was said to have even more authority than the viceroy.[3] One convict reported that he had heard Arredondo's secretary say that the viceroy had ordered all the prisoners taken at Soto la Marina shot, and that Arredondo had said at that time that he would not leave a scrap

[2] Scattered through the Monterrey records from 1818 to 1820, usually in Legajo 1 of each year, are records of amounts paid by the City Council to the provincial government of Nuevo León for the services of prisoners utilized in public works. Such prisoners are not listed by name but by number. AGE.

[3] Vito Alessio Robles, *Coahuila y Texas desde la consumación de la independencia hasta el tratado de Guadalupe Hidalgo*, I, 67 (note) and 74.

of them.[4] And yet, when the time came, he shipped Mier to the capital and most of the others off somewhere—either to Veracruz or to Spain. But why, Bangs wondered, day after day, was he separated from the others and brought to this far-off place. If Arredondo intended to shoot him, why did he keep him working with the chain gang? What fate was still in store for him?

As more months passed, new convicts were added to the gang and others were released; but still there was no change in Bangs' status. At last he was taken from the gang, given an opportunity to bathe in the river and to change to the few remaining clothes he had brought with him in a bundle. The next day he was taken to a spacious but poorly lighted room on the ground floor of one of the largest buildings that faced the main plaza. It had no windows and only one door that opened onto the central patio of the building. The room was completely empty except for a stack of wooden boxes. With nothing better to do, he walked around them; their shapes seemed vaguely familiar. Closer inspection revealed that they were the cases in which he and his helper had packed the press and its equipment before they hid them among the supplies stacked near the fort. After a while a man whom he recognized as the secretary of Arredondo came in, and in a pleasant manner indicated that he was to open the boxes. Next he was told to set up the press and show how it worked.

That night a new question presented itself to him. How did they know that he was a printer? No satisfactory answer was to be had at the moment, but bit by bit, with the aid of the friendly secretary, he was able to piece the story together. It happened that the Commandant, while looking over the list of goods captured at Soto la Marina, had been struck by two lines:

Press.
Boxes with all equipment for it.

Although he recalled at the moment that the viceroy had or-

---

[4] Juan Ruiz de Apodaca (viceroy of Mexico) to Joaquín de Arredondo, México, May 29, July 24, and August 2, 1817; Hernández, *Documentos*, VI, 892–895.

dered Mier's books and papers, and a press, forwarded at once to the capital, Mexico City, the ruler of the four northeastern provinces decided to send the press to Monterrey and keep it for his own use. Some time later it occurred to him that to make use of the press he would need a printer, as none was to be found in Monterrey. Orders were then given to locate the man who had printed Mina's proclamations. The list of prisoners specified no such mechanic, but a thorough search through the captured material brought to light the *Canción Patriótica*, on which Samuel Bangs had so proudly placed his name. After it was found that that name did not appear on any of the lists of prisoners who had been dispatched, he was ultimately located among a handful of foreigners who had not yet been disposed of, because they did not fall into any specific category.[5] Orders were then issued to send him on to Monterrey. Unfortunately for him, he arrived long before the mules on which the press and other boxes were being shipped. In the meantime he was assigned to cobbling as was any pickpocket or cutthroat.

Overjoyed at his release from that work and at the prospect of again becoming a printer, Bangs explained as best he could that he would need a helper. As there had never been a press in Monterrey, they asked who had helped him at Soto la Marina. That individual, probably Jacob Peters, was also found among the undisposed-of foreign prisoners, and in time Bangs had a compatriot as a helper. Even after he arrived, Bangs could not begin to print because the ink shipped in kegs had dried up. More had to be ordered from Mexico City, over six hundred miles away. As freight seldom moved more than three miles a day, the two

[5] Report No. 602 of Joaquín de Arredondo to Apodaca, from Soto la Marina, June 30, 1817, with 3 enclosures. Enclosure No. 2 is the report of Juan J. Echeandía to Arredondo, from Soto la Marina, June 29, 1817, containing an inventory of the goods captured; Enclosure No. 3 is a list of the individuals who surrendered. At the end is a statement that three officers and twenty-six men were executed; two officers and one soldier died from wounds; and seven remained to be disposed of. The viceroy's orders of July 24, 1817, concerning the disposition of the prisoners follow. These orders were later superseded. Historia 23, Operaciones de Guerra, Arredondo IV, 232–267. AGN.

boys had an opportunity to enjoy some leisure, even though they were prisoners with only six cents a day for food.

In the course of their daily contacts with a better class of people, and in connection with their work after the press was in operation, Sam and Jacob learned Spanish in a hard but practical way—through sound, speech, and sight. As both proved capable and diligent workers, they were soon left completely unguarded and permitted to spend their few leisure hours as they pleased. Their scanty allowance for rations was increased to ten centavos a day, with which they purchased food on the street, but neither received any wages. They finally remedied their plight to some extent by engaging at night in other work,[6] thus increasing the few pennies they had to spend in the market, where vegetables and fruits were abundant and cheap most of the year. After some months they were permitted to sleep in the building that housed the press, but with the additional duty of sweeping and sprinkling the street early in the morning, as was required by law of householders. Neither operation was strenuous; an old bucket with holes in the bottom served as sprinkler. Another privilege highly appreciated was access to the Santa Catarina River nearby; in it they could bathe and wash their clothes. How could printers turn out clean sheets and cards without being themselves somewhat clean?

After they settled down, their work consisted mainly of printing various types of cards and letterheads for official use, although Arredondo interpreted this term to cover what others might have considered personal. Then they began to print simple forms, leaving blanks to be filled in with names, dates, and numbers. Only slowly did the Commandant realize the wider use to which the press could be put.

Even while he was still a member of the chain gang, Bangs had learned that Mina had been defeated and executed, and that most of the men who had set out with their leader from Soto la Marina had either been killed in action, as was Colonel

[6] Samuel Bangs to José Servando de Mier, from Saltillo, July 13, 1822. Mi. See Appendix I, Doc. 3.

39

Young, or shot by order of the viceroy.[7] Only a handful escaped. Of Father Mier no one seemed to know anything, but a rumor reached Monterrey, where he had many relatives, that he was again in the hands of the Inquisition. Long afterward news trickled in that some of the Soto la Marina survivors were in the dungeons of the fortress at Veracruz and that others had been sent to Spain and Africa.[8] Such reports of the fate of his former companions and news of further Royalist military victories, which the government *Gazette* persistently reported, made hopes for the independence of Mexico an idle dream. Spain still seemed to have a firm hold on the governmental reins, and on these two boys, citizens of the United States.

Of family or friends at home Samuel knew nothing. Nor had he been able to let them know that he was alive. A prisoner of war was not granted such privileges by the Spanish government; besides he had no means of sending a letter to far-away New England. From time to time travelers from Texas brought news that other leaders were still trying to free Mexico, or at least Texas, from Spanish rule; but as far as Monterrey was concerned, life moved uneventfully on. News of a marriage of the king, the birth of a prince or princess, or the death of a queen stirred the city mildly, but word of a probable Indian raid did induce action until the threat had passed. The people of Monterrey were, as a whole, poor and almost wholly dependent upon uncertain crops. The importance of the place derived largely from the fact that it was a northern outpost.

In their early days as printers in Monterrey the boys had visited the church, and while the whole service was strange to a young fellow who had known only Congregationalism, Bangs found the hours he spent in this Catholic place of worship very pleasant. After they were left unguarded they continued to go,

---

[7] *Gaceta del Gobierno de México,* July 15 and 16, October 31, and December 16, 1817.

[8] George W. Erving to John Quincy Adams, Madrid, April 9, 1819, enclosing statement from three American prisoners at Cadiz (United States, Department of State, Diplomatic Dispatches, Spain, Vol. 16, No. 99 NA).

as they were told to do. But as the months of their stay in that city faded into years, the ecclesiastical authorities, to whom Bangs was still a heretic, ordered him baptized into the Catholic Church. In the sacristy of the Monterrey cathedral, on the 16th of February, 1819, the young North American printer, who gave his age as twenty-one, was made a member of that religious body under the name of José Manuel María Julián Bangs. His parents were recorded as "Samuel Bangs" and "Hana H Grice"; his grandparents as "Samuel Bangs" and "Luce Sparge" (Sprague)—all natives of Boston in the "province" of Massachusetts. His godfather was a lieutenant of militia, Manuel L. Sada, a member of a prominent Monterrey family. Through that ceremony Samuel Bangs lost his identity; he became officially "José Manuel Bangs."[9] By that time the Catholic Church no longer seemed strange to him. Father Mier had introduced him in Galvez Town to its faith, as the good man scattered benedictions on each and all, and he had also taught the boy to respect Catholic forms. Mina, too, had insisted that his men respect the religion of the people they were hoping to free. Now he accepted his religious status as he had all other features of his imprisonment, calmly and good-naturedly. Inwardly he still nursed hopes of home and freedom.

During the early months of 1820 he was still engaged in printing, for the most part, forms for various purposes—acknowledgments of receipt of correspondence, notices of civil and military appointments, certificates of disability, and passports.[10] In April he printed portions of the announcement of the third marriage, the preceding autumn, of Ferdinand VII, the King of Spain, to a Saxon princess, María Josefa Amalia,[11] and also a decree regarding the succession to the Spanish throne. Of local and more personal interest was the invitation extended by the bishop of

---

[9] Monterrey, Mexico, Catedral, Libro de bautismos, 1817–1822, p. 128 v.

[10] Many of these, including a completed passport of 1821, are in a package labeled "1820," AHE. In it is also a "cordillera" which is described in No. 32 of Appendix II.

[11] Appendix II, No. 13.

Monterrey, the Commandant Arredondo, and his son-in-law, Captain José de Castro, to the funeral of the Captain's small son, which was to take place at the Cathedral at half-past ten on the morning of May 30.[12]

Up to that time no news had reached the citizens of Monterrey concerning the revolution in Spain, which began with a military revolt on January 1, 1820, and subsided on March 9 when the king took an oath to support the Constitution of 1812, although he had refused to sanction it on his return from France in 1814. Notice of this drastic change in the government of Spain and all her colonies reached Arredondo the middle of May, but he did not make it public.[13] The arrival of the May 31st decree of the viceroy ordering all officials to take an oath publicly to support the Constitution made further silence useless. He had Bangs add three lines of heading and four of closing to this printed decree,[14] and on June 13 copies were posted at various public places in Monterrey; others were dispatched to the main settlements in all four provinces. After the bando was posted, the City Council of Monterrey adjourned to the "Purple House," the headquarters of Arredondo, and with him repaired to the Cathedral, where the Bishop, the Commandant and the members of the Council as a body took the required oath. After the signing and the singing of the *Te Deum* there was a great bell-ringing.[15]

With the publication of that decree, a busy life began for Bangs. His ingenuity as a printer was taxed to the utmost, as demands on the press increased rapidly and its resources were limited. From this time on he was called upon to print not only the orders issued by Arredondo—these had earlier been made

[12] In package labeled "1820." AHE. Appendix II, No. 12.
[13] Arredondo to the viceroy, from Monterrey, May 16, 1820 (Historia 21, Operaciones de Guerra, Arredondo II, 1811–1820, No. 1087). AGN.
[14] Appendix II, No. 15.
[15] Minutes of the City Council of Monterrey, June 13, 1820, Vol. 1817–1822. AM.

known by the town crier or in script—but to reprint, in whole or in part, royal and viceregal decrees and issues of the official *Gaceta* published in Mexico City. When decrees that were to be posted (as bandos) were too lengthy for a sheet the press could accommodate—roughly 8½ by 12¼ inches—he used two or even three sheets, printed only on one side, and then joined them as a whole. When type of one font was exhausted, he utilized italics or any other font available; when lower-case letters failed, he used capitals. Of the lower-case italics, he resorted most often to *d, p, l* and *q;* of the capitals, *A* and *E* were most used as substitutes. Although Bangs managed to follow Spanish copy remarkably well, slips of spelling or syllabic divisions betrayed from time to time the foreigner. Accents were for him, at this time, no problem, for the English type of the Mina press provided few aside from a small acute accent over the lower case *a.* That, once introduced, was steadily employed. Accents appear on some of the early Monterrey decrees, but for these the body of each text was printed in Mexico City or in Spain and Bangs merely completed the heading or, usually, the conclusion. Otherwise the almost complete absence of accents is one means of identifying the work done on the Mina press.

Arredondo made no effort to simplify Bangs' task. Most of his orders and many of the decrees which he ordered reprinted carried the following elaborate heading:

D. Joaquin de Arredondo Mioño Pelegrin Bravo de Hoyos y Venero, Caballero de la Orden de Calatrava, Brigadier de los Exercitos Nacionales, Gobernador, Comandante General y Gefe Superior Politico de las Quatro Provincias Internas de Oriente en este America Septentrional, General en Gefe de Operaciones en Ellas, Subinspector de sus Tropas, y Sub-delegado de correos en las Mismas . . .

[Don Joaquin de Arredondo Mioño Pelegrin Bravo de Hoyos y Venero, Knight of the Order of Calatrava, Brigadier of the National Armies, Governor, Commandant General and High Political Chief of the four Eastern Interior Provinces of North America, General-in-chief of operations in them, Sub-inspector of its troops and Supervisor of Mails in them . . .]

Reprints of the *Gacetas,* which were frequently demanded by the Commandant, carried only the heading of the original. Most of his orders and the reprints of decrees were followed by the printed name of Arredondo, to or below which he added his rubric; the signature, either printed or written, and rubric of the secretary followed. The date the document was ordered printed or issued in Monterrey usually preceded the signatures. No identification of press or printer was given; that was considered unnecessary as Bangs' was the only press in the four provinces.

On July 6 Arredondo issued the decree of the Spanish Cortes of May 23, 1812, governing elections of members of city councils, with the king's authorizations of March 9 and 17, 1820; to this the Commandant added orders that such elections be held in the four provinces under his command;[16] and in the early days of August, Bangs printed the royal order that the Constitution be published on the fifteenth of that month and be obeyed throughout Spain and all the Spanish dominions.[17] Of more personal interest to the printer was the indult of the king, forwarded by the viceroy, ordering all but a few types of prisoners freed;[18] this Bangs completed on August 1 with high hopes for a change in his own status, but neither he nor his helper was released. Other decrees which followed in rapid succession authorized elections for members of the provincial deputation and for deputies to the Cortes in Spain. On September 8 he reprinted in pamphlet form the royal order that parish priests and teachers read and explain the Constitution to parishioners and students.[19] Celebration of the king's oath of allegiance to that document,

[16] AGE. Appendix II, No. 16. Photocopy, LMS.
[17] AGE. Appendix II, No. 20. Photocopy, LMS.
[18] A general pardon ordering all Anglo-Americans released. Madrid, December 20, 1819; México, April 13; Monterrey, August 1, 1820. AGE. Appendix II, No. 19.
[19] The decree was reissued on January 9, 1821. BA. Appendix II, Nos. 22 and 37.

which he had taken in July before the assembled Cortes in Madrid, was set for October 12 to 14.[20]

Those were gala days for Monterrey. Salvos of artillery were fired at dawn, midday, and sunset, as well as after the *Te Deum* on the fourteenth. Each night the band played on the plaza and there was dancing under the arcades. The young printers could hear the ripples of laughter and the strains of the music from their printing quarters, but they had no part in the merriment. However, from that time on a deluge of decrees of amnesty and individual pardons kept alive in both boys hope that freedom was not too far in the distance.

While various headings were used in the many pieces of printing they turned out, that of Arredondo was most frequently employed. In the conclusions for a time greater variety in wording and in length occurred, but by October the form of conclusion for most of the work issued by Arredondo had been to a large extent standardized. The form of closing generally adopted read:

> Y para que llegue a noticia de todos, mando se publique por Bando en esta capital y demas Ciudades Villas y Lugares de las quatro Provincias de mi cargo; circulandose para los propios fines a los Gefes, Magistrados, y justicias a quienes toca su inteligencia y cumplimiento. Dado en Monterrey a   de   de . Signed "Arredondo" [in print] with rubric.[21]

At last, in 1821, Bangs and his helper were technically released from prison, but they were retained—he, as the government printer at a wage of eighteen pesos a month, and Jacob as a helper at nine pesos. With this they had to feed and clothe themselves, for "raciones," miserable as they were, ceased.[22] How badly Sam needed clothes is revealed by a note he wrote on March 3 to Don Alejandro Uro y Lozano, a member of the City Council and proprietor of a small store, who had befriended

[20] Circular issued by Arredondo, Monterrey, October 11, 1820. TxU. Appendix II, No. 27.
[21] Conclusion of No. 28 (Appendix II), October 17, 1820, is a good example.
[22] Samuel Bangs to Mier, from Saltillo, July 13, 1822. Mi.

45

him while a prisoner. In it Bangs asked the brief loan of a pair of trousers in which to attend a wedding, as his only "best" pair was in tatters. To Don Alejandro he continued to sign himself "Sam" Bangs. But such a diversion as attending a wedding was still a rare event, and Spanish orthography was still an unconquered art.[23]

The calm of the governmental authorities in Monterrey, especially of the dictator Arredondo, was greatly shaken—the very day Bangs wrote his modest request—by news that General Agustín de Iturbide, a commander of the Royalist army in Mexico, had gone over to the revolutionary party and declared the independence of the whole country. While reprinting the viceroy's announcement of this (to him) most deplorable fact,[24] Bangs' hopes for complete freedom flared again, but he did not dare to give any evidence of his joy over the news, for Arredondo had made examples of several sympathizers with independence by having them shot, and had even ordered the school children taken out to witness the execution.[25]

As soon as the "Comandante General" learned the terms of the Plan of Iguala drawn up by Iturbide on February 24, which provided for the complete independence of Mexico from Spain, he ordered Bangs to print a *Proclamation to the people of the four Eastern Interior Provinces*. In it he assured them of his confidence in their loyalty, and also announced that if the revolution should reach their border (which he considered unlikely in view of the precautions he had taken) he would place himself at the head of the troops and protect them all from the fury of the enemy.[26] He then took stern restrictive measures to stem the

---

[23] Samuel Bangs to Alejandro Uro y Lozano, Monterrey, March 3, 1821. In Bangs-Uro y Lozano Correspondence, fol. 1. CBC. Photocopies, LMS.

[24] *Gaceta del Gobierno de México*, March 6, 1821; reprinted by Bangs in Monterrey, n.d. TxU.

[25] David Alberto Cossío, *Historia de Nuevo León*, IV, 273.

[26] This begins, "Habitantes de las quatro provincias." In it Arredondo announces defection of Iturbide and pleads for allegiance to Spain. Monterrey, March 13, 1821. BA. Appendix II, No. 45.

tide. He prohibited travel without passport in the four provinces and assessed severe penalties for violations; he restricted printing, although the Constitution granted freedom of the press and the Mina press was the only one within hundreds of miles; and prohibited the circulation of letters or proclamations giving any information concerning the uprising.[27]

Arredondo was not the only high official worried over the situation. In this respect, if no other, he and Apodaca, no longer termed the "viceroy" but the "high political chief and captain general of New Spain," were in complete agreement. A month later Bangs was reprinting an appeal from Apodaca for united support of the government against rebels and traitors; this closed with a strong assurance of the ultimate success of the Royalists. It was signed: "El Conde del Venadito," a title that had been bestowed on Apodaca. For the first time Bangs was authorized to designate the Monterrey press as the "Ymprenta del Gobierno."[28]

During the next three months the political picture in Mexico changed so completely that Bangs began to see a return home as a possibility. He even celebrated the Fourth of July with a little *baile* or dance, although he had to borrow a few small glasses from his friend Don Alejandro. He also asked the favor of a very small loan. This, he said in his note, he hoped would reach him before Judgment Day—a good-natured reflection on the Mexican lack of haste.[29] By that time insurgent troops had reached the adjoining province of Coahuila, and Arredondo had come to the conclusion that it might be wiser to take flight than to attempt to defend the people he had ruled so despotically since 1813. His last communication to them was a reprint of a circular of Iturbide reducing certain taxes, which was issued on

[27] The order begins: "Como la tranquilidad que felizmente ha reinado . . ." Monterrey, April 28, 1821. TxU. Appendix II, No. 50.

[28] *A los habitantes de esta Nueva España*, México, 5 de Abril 1821. Issued as a broadside in Monterrey, n.d. TxU. Appendix II, No. 48.

[29] Bangs to Alejandro Uro y Lozano, Monterrey, July 4, 1821. In Bangs-Uro y Lozano Correspondence, fol. 2. CBC. Photocopies, LMS.

July 27, 1821.[30] Within a week the once mighty man was headed by a devious route for Cuba and safety.

He was promptly succeeded as temporary commandant by a right-hand man of Iturbide, Lieutenant Colonel Gaspar Antonio López, who decided to set up his headquarters at Saltillo. Bangs had no idea that this decision would affect him personally until a month later when he learned that the provincial archivist had asked the City Council to provide transportation to Saltillo for a part of the provincial archives and the press. The Council refused, and referred the matter to its representative in Mexico City, the seat of the national government.[31] In an effort to conciliate Bangs and to reconcile him to the move to Saltillo, for López considered the press indispensable, he promised to raise his salary to thirty pesos a month, subject to the approval of the new captain general, his superior. Perhaps he was moved to that step by the decree of the Regency Council—then the governing body of the nation—to the effect that all who had taken part in the Revolution were to be pardoned, which might have meant that Bangs could leave.[32]

The celebration of the independence of Mexico ordered by the Regency Council began in Monterrey on November 13, when the Plan of Iguala and the Treaty of Córdoba were publicly read, and two individuals, chosen as representatives from each civic body, took the required oath of allegiance—this time to the new government of Mexico. On the following day there were elaborate services in the gaudily decorated Cathedral. In keeping with the order that the celebration be as magnificent as subscribed funds permitted, stalls which offered a great variety of nick-nacks, toys, and refreshments were set up on the main plaza; there men, women, and children milled around. During midafternoon all who could attended the bullfight; some

[30] Circular of June 20, 1821; reprinted at Monterrey, July 27, 1821. TxU. Appendix II, No. 51.

[31] Minutes of the City Council of Monterrey, August 27 and December 28, 1821; Libro 1817–1822. AM.

[32] López issues a decree of the Soberana Junta Provisional of October 23, 1821, in Monterrey, November 15, 1821. Appendix II, No. 52.

dropped into a tent where playlets were given through the late afternoon and evening. After dark the City Council provided a great show of fireworks.[33] While the band played the younger men and women promenaded on the other square in opposite directions under the watchful eyes of their elders, who occupied seats along the outer edge of the square. In this way both girls and men had the opportunity to survey leisurely the complete array of the opposite sex which the town had to offer. This practice was followed each Sunday and Thursday night when the band played.

Bangs celebrated as far as his slender means permitted. His eighteen pesos barely provided a subsistence; he still worked in the evenings to help to meet his barest needs. Without the permission of the government he could not leave the country, and he had no influential friends in Mexico City to help him secure it. Besides, he knew he would never be able to save up enough to pay his passage to the United States, even if he could get to either of the nearest ports, Refugio (later Matamoros) or Pueblo Viejo (later Tampico).

Yet he could not fail to realize that changes were taking place in Mexico. In the spring of 1822, when General James Long, who had been trying to make Texas an independent province, was brought through Monterrey as a prisoner on the way to the capital, well dressed and respectfully treated, he was anticipating an early return home. He promised to get news of Bangs to his family and to secure the help of the United States government in providing him transportation to Boston.

Cheered momentarily by this promise, Bangs kept doggedly at his printing in Monterrey until April 21, when he reprinted Iturbide's report to the Mexican people on the final military victories of his generals.[34] Then López, without further consultation, ordered the press and its equipment moved to Saltillo. As a

---

[33] Minutes of the City Council of Monterrey, October 19, November 5, 1821. Libro 1817–1822. AM.

[34] El Generalíssimo Almirante a los Mexicanos, México, April 4 and 6. [In script] Monterrey, April 21, 1822. BA. Appendix II, No. 94.

final concession to the printers he ordered horses and saddles to be furnished them,[35] and the transfer of the press was carried out expeditiously, although the journey to Saltillo involved a climb of some three thousand feet in less than sixty miles.

Saltillo was an older town than Monterrey and more pleasantly located—higher in the mountains. As a result the climate was considerably cooler. The fertile and well-watered valley in which it lay produced an abundance of grains, vegetables, and especially fruits. To Bangs' surprise and satisfaction food was more plentiful and cheaper. Here were pears, peaches, quinces, guayabas, apples, figs, and grapes in season; and also some varieties of vegetables entirely unfamiliar to him. The press was installed in the main government building, and he was given living quarters adjoining. And now, a free man, more familiar with the language and customs of the country, it was easier for him to cultivate a wider circle of friends. Few knew of his days in the chain gang; even to him it sometimes seemed like only a bad dream.

In May Bangs and his assistant were kept busy printing decrees and proclamations connected with the establishment of the Mexican empire and the elevation of Iturbide to the imperial throne. On May 26 they reprinted a decree dated May 13 at Mexico City that conspiracy against independence would be punished as *lèse majesté* had been before 1810;[36] the next day they reprinted Iturbide's proclamation of May 18 to the Mexican people; this bore at its head, by López' order, "Viva Nuestro Emperador Don Agustín de Iturbide."[37] In it the former Royalist general appealed to the people to extend to him the greatest proof of their love and confidence—in other words, the imperial crown, which was voted him, under pressure, the following morning. López announced this fact in a proclamation addressed

[35] A complaint of the owners of the horses and saddles which were hired for "los Americanos" and had not been returned is dated September 5, 1822—almost six months after the horses were engaged. AGE.

[36] TxU. Appendix II, No. 98.

[37] Appendix II, No. 99. This begins: "Mexicanos. Me dirijo a vosotros . . ." Saltillo, May 27, 1822. TxU.

to "The Inhabitants of the Four Provinces"; Bangs printed it three days later,[38] and on June 1 he issued Iturbide's address on accepting the crown.[39] Several weeks later he took pleasure in printing the June 8 decree of Congress that all those who had been dispossessed of their positions for having supported the independence movement should be returned at once to their posts.[40]

With access to the issues of the national *Gacetas* he was able to keep in touch with events in the country and to some extent with the outside world. For details of national affairs he needed only to acquaint himself with the import of material he was given to print. This had increased greatly in amount and variety since the proclamation of independence. One of the early pamphlets he printed in Saltillo, *The Disarmament and Embarkation at Tampico of the defeated Saragossans*, recounted in its ten pages the details of the surrender of one of the last contingents of Spanish troops to leave Mexico.[41] General Felipe de la Garza, the governor of Tamaulipas, a name that had replaced Nuevo Santander, had accepted their surrender and supervised their embarkation for Cuba.

Fresh hope of an early return home was aroused some three months later by news that Father Mier was not only alive but in the Mexican capital exercising the functions of a deputy to Congress from his native province, Nuevo León.

At once Bangs tried to get in touch with this survivor of the Mina Expedition, whose life since 1817 had been as eventful as his own had been dull. Mier had been held by the Inquisition as a prisoner until 1820, when that institution was abolished by the reestablished Spanish constitution. The viceroy then ordered

---

[38] Appendix II, No. 100. D. Gaspar Antonio López, Proclamation to the "Habitantes de las Quatro Provincias." Saltillo, May 27, 1822.

[39] "S. M. el Emperador." Appendix II, No. 102. See Iturbide.

[40] Saltillo, June 22, 1822. Appendix II, No. 108.

[41] *Los Capitulados de Zaragosa desarmados por el coronel don Felipe de la Garza gobernador del Nuevo Santander y obligados a embarcar por Tampico.* The surrender took place on May 5, 1822, at Tampico, but the last document included is dated June 10, 1822. Appendix II, No. 109.

him transported to Spain, but he escaped at Havana and made his way to Philadelphia, where he spent several months. While there he learned of Iturbide's plan to become emperor and immediately launched a press campaign against him. He then set out for Mexico to take an active part in the opposition; but, almost at his journey's end, he was captured by the Spanish troops who still held the fortress in the harbor of Veracruz. There he was imprisoned until the new government could secure his release. Indeed that was granted only because the commanding officer of the fortress realized that Mier, a strong supporter of constitutional government, would be a perpetual thorn in Iturbide's side, as indeed he proved to be.[42]

In Bangs' letter welcoming Mier home the young printer reaffirmed the respect and veneration he had long felt for the prelate, sketched lightly the course of his own life since being captured at Soto la Marina, and suggested that if Mier planned to establish a press in Mexico, he would like to become his printer. He added that he could also provide the press if he could get to the United States where he had means at his command. Nor did he fail to inquire whether he was eligible for the bounty being paid those who had engaged in the struggle for independence, even though it had been achieved in a manner different from that they had planned. He signed the letter "Samuel," but in a postscript he explained that his baptismal name was "José Manuel," to whom the reply should be directed.[43] Although he thought he had completely lost his own name, he was recorded in a list of subscribers to a fund to assist the government as "the printer, Samuel Bangs," who promised to donate two pesos monthly from his salary.[44] This he felt he could then afford as living in Saltillo was cheap and the promised increase in his salary had been approved.[45]

[42] For a calendar of Mier's papers, see Lota M. Spell, "The Mier Archive," *HAHR*, XII (August, 1932), 359–375.

[43] Bangs to Mier, from Saltillo, July 13, 1822. Mi.

[44] *Gaceta del Gobierno Supremo de México*, February 20, 1823. TxU.

[45] Anastacio de Bustamante to acting Commandant of Eastern Interior Provinces Gaspar Antonio López, from Puebla, November 14, 1822. AGE.

Mier's reply was long in coming, as he was swamped with congratulations and appeals for help from relatives, friends, and strangers. In the meantime Bangs worked out certain standard headings and forms of imprints by which the many decrees and circulars he printed during the imperial era are identifiable. For the briefer decrees and practically all the circulars he used the following heading:

> D. Gaspar Antonio Lopez, Coronel de Caballeria del Ejercito Imperial Mexicano de las Tres Garantias, Comandante General, Jefe Politico Interino de las Cuatro Provincias Internas Orientales, Comandante en Gefe de Operaciones en ellas, & &

At the end he printed "Lopez," to which the Commandant added, in his own hand, his rubric. The form of imprint Bangs employed most frequently was:

> Imprenta de la Comandancia General [de Oriente]. Saltillo, Año de 1822. Segundo de la Independencia [del Ymperio].

To this was usually added: "Jose Manuel Bangs, Impresor." To the reprinted issues or excerpts from the *Gaceta* he added only: "Reimpreso en [el] Saltillo. Imprenta del Gobierno."[46]

When the news reached Saltillo that Iturbide had dissolved Congress and that some of the deputies, including Father Mier, were under arrest, feeling ran high. Nor was it calmed when reports came of the defection of General Antonio López de Santa Anna. By the time Bangs had finished reprinting the letters and proclamations of General José María Lobato, he sensed the impending fate of the empire.[47] In that publication Lobato was promising his support to Iturbide against the machinations of the "infamous Santana," who was promising reforms and wealth to all who joined him in overthrowing the empire. It was, however, not the plan of Santa Anna, but that of José Antonio Echá-

---

[46] See the *Gaceta Extraordinaria* of October 27 and November 1, 1822 ("Extras"). TxU. Appendix II, Nos. 130 and 132.

[47] José María Lobato, [*Documentos y proclamas de.*] Reimpreso en el Saltillo el 21 de diciembre de 1822 . . . Imprenta de la Comandancia General de Oriente. Jose Manuel Bangs, Impresor. Appendix II, No. 144.

varri, which proposed creation of a republic, the calling of a constituent congress and the adoption of a constitution, that led to Iturbide's abdication on March 19, 1823, and his sentence to perpetual banishment.[48] But before reaching the decision to accept defeat, the Emperor issued on February 11 a proclamation calling upon the soldiers of the Trigarant Army for support; this Bangs reprinted on February 22.[49] The hoped-for response was not forthcoming.

With the fall of Iturbide, supporters of a federal republic, including the pioneer champion of Mexican independence, Father Mier, came into power. Commandant López was shortly succeeded by General Felipe de la Garza, the governor of Tamaulipas, who Mier believed would "take orders" from him and not succumb to the wiles of the leaders in Coahuila, especially of a relative, Miguel Ramos Arizpe. Among other orders, Mier told De la Garza to take the press, which he said was his, back to Monterrey.[50]

Such a move had already been anticipated. On April 12 an inventory of the press and all its appurtenances was made by a commission composed of Juan Fuentes, Joaquín Palou (the secretary of the Commandant), Pedro García de Hoyos, and Bangs. Each single piece of the mechanism was identified and accounted for, and the whole list signed by each member of the commission, including "Samuel Bangs."[51] But the press was not at once dismantled, for the next national proclamation, a *Manifiesto* dated April 4, was printed in Saltillo. It was signed by Pedro Celestino Negrete, Miguel Domínguez, and José Mariano

---

[48] Nettie Lee Benson, *La Diputación provincial y el federalismo mexicano,* pp. 90 ff.

[49] *Proclama de S. M. el Emperador al Ejercito Trigarante,* México, febrero 11; Saltillo, febrero 22, 1823. BA. Appendix II, No. 159.

[50] José Servando de Mier to Bernadino Cantú, from Mexico City, April 30, 1823, in Cossío, *Historia de Nuevo León,* V, 33–34.

[51] Inventario de la Imprenta de la Comandª Gral de Oriente que se halla en esta Villa, sus enseres, letras, erramientos y demás muebles de qᵉ se compone y se encontraron en el Reconocimiento qᵉ se hizo con asistencia de su Impresor Samuel Bangs. [At end] Saltillo, 12 de Abril de 1823. [Signed] Juan Fuentes. Joaquín Palou. Samuel Bangs. Pedro García de Hoyos. AGE.

Michelena, the three members who constituted the Regency Council, to which executive power had been delegated. The Saltillo reprint bore the following imprint: "Reimpreso en el Saltillo a 20 de Abril de 1823, Tercero de nuestra Independencia y Segundo de la Libertad. José Manuel Bangs, Impresor."[52]

Back to Monterrey went the press and back to Monterrey went Bangs; but both returned much more slowly than they had come. As soon as the press was set up in its former quarters Bangs began printing under orders of the new Commandant. One of the documents printed was De la Garza's communication to General Santa Anna that the citizens of the four provinces under his command had declared themselves on June 5 in favor of a federal republic; another was a bando making public new regulations for more effectively curbing robbery and assassinations.[53] Early in July, when plans for the election of deputies to the new Constituent Congress were under consideration, he printed, in the form of a four-page folder, the report of a committee which had been appointed to assist the president of the provincial deputation, Juan Antonio Rodríguez. This report, which was signed by Julián de Arrese and Agustín Viesca on July 5, suggested the subdivisions, for election purposes, of the provinces of Nuevo León, Coahuila, and Texas, and gave other instructions for the holding of the election. It was distributed by Bangs with a letter of Rodríguez of July 10 authorizing the circularization.[54]

When the federal decree of July 19 reached Monterrey, Bangs saw, for the first time, a chance to return home. This decree, honoring those who had lent their services to the cause of independence, ordered their employment by the government or other benefits by which the state could recompense such citizens. Pensions were to be granted even to those without a military record. Each applicant for any of the benefits was required to present

[52] *El Supremo Poder Ejecutivo de la Nación a sus compatriotas.* BA. Appendix II, No. 162.

[53] See Bibliography, México, Provincias Internas de Oriente, Comandante General (De la Garza). Appendix II, Nos. 163 and 164.

[54] See Bibliography, México, Provincias Internas de Oriente, Diputación provincial. Appendix II, No. 167.

certificates from well-known officials attesting the services performed.[55] In the case of Bangs this seemed simple; his work as a prisoner and as a printer was well known locally. The necessary papers were to be drawn up in Monterrey and forwarded to Mier, who with his own recommendation was to transmit them to the proper federal authority. But the year 1823 was a hectic one in Monterrey governmental circles. The appointment of De la Garza as commandant was followed by his resignation, which was not accepted by the National Executive Committee; there were also rapid changes in the office of *jefe político*; and the powers of the provincial deputation were rapidly broadened. De la Garza, who had been the governor of Tamaulipas, spent little time in Monterrey; Echeandía, the pro-tem *jefe político*, knew little of Bangs' work; and both Arredondo and López were gone. In spite of such difficulties the papers were eventually forwarded to Mier, upon whom an avalanche of similar documents had already descended. Indeed it seemed to Bangs that the official wheels now turned with no more speed than those of the oxcarts he remembered seeing while footing his weary way as a prisoner from Soto la Marina to Monterrey. Now he could only wait without even hearing the creaks.

De la Garza found it equally slow and difficult to get printing done in Monterrey. Two circulars embodying the congressional decree of June 27 and its implementation—these imposed upon every citizen an annual tax amounting to three days' earnings— reached him at San Carlos, Tamaulipas, early in August. On the eleventh he wrote the *jefe político* at Monterrey that he had written a member of the provincial deputation to have a hundred copies of these two circulars (Nos. 9 and 10 of the Treasury Department, which he enclosed) printed on the government press and the usual number circulated in the provinces; the re-

---

[55] Declaración en honor de los primeros héroes libertadores de la nación y los que los siguieron," in *Colección de órdenes y decretos de la Soberana Junta Provisional Gubernativa y Soberanos Congresos Generales de la Nación Mexicana,* II (2nd ed., 1829), 149–151.

mainder were to be sent to him for distribution in Tamaulipas.[56] None came. He wrote again on September 27 that Tamaulipas still had no circulars.[57] Not until October 6 did Echeandía, then the *jefe político*, reply that the circulars had been printed and circulated and that forty copies of each were then en route to Tamaulipas.[58]

It was fortunate that they were, for by that time Bangs had dismantled the press, made a new inventory of its parts, and packed the whole in boxes. Before so doing he checked each piece with Juan del Moral, an employee in the office of the Commandancy General, to whom he turned over the press, as instructed by the *jefe político*.[59] He had earlier asked for transportation to the United States,[60] and had been granted a *licencia* to leave the country. In return for his services and suffering in the cause of independence, he was at last rewarded with a modest bounty which permitted him to procure new clothes and to set out on the long-dreamed-of passage home.

[56] Felipe de la Garza to the jefe político at Monterrey, from San Carlos, Tamaulipas, August 11, 1823. Appendix II, Nos. 165 and 166. AGE.

[57] Felipe de la Garza to jefe político at Monterrey, from San Carlos, September 27, 1823. AGE.

[58] Juan J. Echeandía to Felipe de la Garza, from Monterrey, October 6, 1823. AGE.

[59] Lista de las existencias de Imprenta que tenía a mi cargo, y he entregado a Dⁿ Juan del Moral de orden del Sr. Gefe Político de esta Provᵃ coronel Dⁿ Juan de Echeandía. Monterey [*sic*] Octubre 7 de 1823. José Manuel Bangs [with rubric]. Recivi, Juan del Morál [with rubric]. AGE.

[60] Instancia del Impresor Samuel Bangs que pidió su transporte a los Estados Unidos su pais. AGE.

THREE

The Bangs and Boston

FAR MORE VERSED in the ways of the world than the Samuel Bangs of eighteen who sailed from Baltimore in 1816 was the José Manuel Bangs who left Mexico late in 1823 for his New England home, from which he had not heard a word during his absence of seven years. On the slow return trip he had ample time to speculate on the state in which he would find his family and his property, as well as to contrast life in Boston with that in the northeastern provinces of Mexico.

During the years preceding his departure from Baltimore he had seen little of his immediate family. Food and lodging, in addition to the twenty dollars a year he received after the first six months, were furnished him during the five-year term he served as printer's apprentice in the shop of a distant relative, Thomas G. Bangs, a printer,[1] but he was expected to be about the print

---

[1] *Boston Directory, 1816*, p. 58.

shop except on rare occasions. Before that he had lived with his widowed mother; he remembered her telling about her wedding in the New North Church with the Reverend Mr. Stillman officiating,[2] and how strange it seemed to write her name the first time as Hannah T. Bangs instead of Hannah Grice. Until he was about nine years old his sister Harriet was both his nurse and playmate; he had cried bitterly when she married a shipbuilder named John Marshall[3] in 1807. After his mother remarried the next year, his step-father, David Rice, headed the family.[4] He had never known his own father, Samuel Bangs the sixth, a glazier who had died the year his son was born, nor could he remember his grandfather, Samuel Bangs the fifth, who died two years later.[5] But he grew up knowing that his grandfather had provided for him and for Harriet in his will, and that the income from their property was paid to their mother for their support as long as they lived at home. Then it was left to accumulate, for they were not to receive the property until each reached legal age.[6]

Of his Bangs ancestors he had heard a great deal from the numerous relatives and from outsiders. The family had made its appearance upon the New England scene early in the history of the Massachusetts Colony in the person of Edward Bangs, who sailed into Plymouth Harbor on the good ship *Anna* in 1623.[7] As a boy he thought that American history began in New England,

[2] Dean Dudley, *The History and Genealogy of the Bangs Family* (hereafter cited as *The Bangs Family*), p. 81, gives the date as November 2, 1789; *A Volume of Records relating to the History of Boston containing Boston Marriages from 1752 to 1809, Boston Town Records*, XXX, 113, gives the year as 1788 (hereafter referred to as *BTR*).

[3] *Ibid.*, p. 225. *Births from 1700 to 1800*, p. 337 (*BTR*, XXIV) and Dudley, *The Bangs Family*, p. 82, say she was born in 1789.

[4] *BTR*, XXX, 269.

[5] His father, Samuel (the sixth), was born December 7, 1769, and died between 1798 and October, 1800; his grandfather, Samuel (the fifth), was born in 1733 and died in 1800. See Dudley, *The Bangs Family*, pp. 81–82.

[6] Suffolk County, Probate Records, XCVIII, 696.

[7] Francis Hyde Bangs, *John Kendrick Bangs: Humorist of the Nineties*, p. 4. See also Dudley, *The Bangs Family*.

but now he realized that the Spaniards had established themselves in America a century before his ancestors came. That fact still seemed strange to him, for he had believed all his life that only Virginia was known to Europeans before Massachusetts was settled.

He knew by tradition that at the beginning of the century in which he was born—the eighteenth—while Texas was merely a Spanish outpost and Saltillo and Monterrey were only small settlements far distant from the stately viceregal capital of New Spain, his family was represented in Boston by sturdy, industrious artisans, merchants, and seamen, who were respected by their fellow citizens and, in some cases, honored by them. Among those honored was his grandfather, who was repeatedly chosen for more than thirty years as one of Boston's "sealers of leather"; in that capacity he inspected and certified to the quality of leather sold there from 1765 to 1795.[8] The young printer remembered that his mother had often repeated to him some of his grandfather's tales of his early married life. How he and Mary Fleming had settled down in a small house on Mackeral Lane, where the fringe of the great fire of 1760 reached them and destroyed some of their very few but highly prized furnishings, and how they rejoiced when the government reimbursed them in part for their loss.[9] Aside from public duties his grandfather was by vocation a "cordwainer"—that is a boot- and shoe-maker;[10] and his popularity was such that he was able to support his family of four daughters and one son,[11] to employ a servant, Crispin, who was married to a free Negro woman,[12] and also to accumulate some savings, which he invested in property. By

[8] *Report[s] of the Record Commissioners of the City of Boston, 1758–1769* and *1784–1796* (*BTR*, XVI and XXXI) show that he served from 1764 to 1795.

[9] *A Volume of Records Relating to the Early History of Boston* (*BTR*, XXIX), pp. 9, 10, 89, 124; *BTR*, XXX, 369, gives marriage entry of Samuel Bangs (the fifth) and Mary Fleming as June 19, 1755.

[10] Suffolk County, Probate Records, XCVIII, 696; *Boston Directory* for 1789, 1796, 1798.

[11] Dudley, *The Bangs Family*, pp. 81–82.

[12] *BTR*, XXX, 433.

1790, as his immediate family had by then been reduced by marriages to four,[13] he had increased his investments substantially. In his last years troubles a-plenty had come to the thrifty man. A fire in 1794 gutted a considerable section of Boston and completely destroyed some buildings he owned on Purchase Street. Then the city, in order to widen and straighten the streets in that section before permitting rebuilding, took twenty-seven small pieces of land, for which it paid him only seventy-seven pounds.[14] This condemnation, in addition to the award of his public office to a younger man, and his wife's death,[15] stunned him. He bought the three-storied, many-windowed house on Prince Street, in which he had been living, and shared it with his daughter Sarah, who was married to Daniel Rea and had several children. In spite of his losses cordwainer Bangs was in comfortable circumstances, for he still owned his shop and a rent house on old Mackeral Lane—Samuel remembered it as Kilby Street—and another on Prince Street.[16] Then his only son, Samuel the sixth, barely thirty years old, died suddenly.

This blow the good man did not long survive, but before his death he made a new will leaving to his grandchildren, Harriet and Samuel, their father's share of his property.[17] And Samuel well remembered a neighbor, Mr. Hawes, who had been their guardian for a while;[18] later others served. His mother as well as Mr. Hawes had told him that his grandfather had authorized his executor to sell their property if he thought best, and to invest the money in public securities; but he had kept the property intact and paid their mother the income each quarter. Now Sam-

[13] "Census of 1790" in *Report of the Record Commissioners of the City of Boston, BTR*, XXII, 501.

[14] *BTR*, XXXI, 377, 380–381.

[15] Dudley, *The Bangs Family*, p. 81, says "Mary" (Fleming) was living in 1793 but dead in 1798. Samuel may not have known his grandmother's name when he was baptized. At any rate he seems to have been mistaken, as no Lucy Sprague has been located in the *Boston Town Records*.

[16] "Tax Records of 1798" in *BTR*, XXII, 70, 122, 164, 305.

[17] Suffolk County, Probate Records, XCVIII, 696.

[18] *Ibid.* William Hawes was appointed guardian for Samuel and Harriet on December 23, 1800.

61

uel wondered whether the property had been sold, and what had been done with his share. Would his mother still be alive? She had seemed very young and pretty to him as a boy, but he knew she had been married ten years when he was born. Still it was hard to realize that she must be over fifty. And what of Harriet and her children?

At last the trip of months was over and he looked at the water front of Boston with new eyes. Facing it were new buildings and businesses, and dozens of ships from all over the world were in the harbor. The city seemed smaller than he remembered it, and everybody seemed much busier than in Saltillo or Monterrey. Yet, even before he turned into Kilby Street, he knew he was back home. Again, for the moment, he was the lighthearted Samuel Bangs.

The next few hours, to which he had looked forward so eagerly during seven long years, sobered him. His sister, the curly-haired Harriet, who had taken such good care of him as a small child and whom he dearly loved, was dead, but had left four children. His mother no longer lived in Boston and had long since given him up as dead, as had also his brother-in-law, who had quietly appropriated the property that belonged jointly to Harriet and Samuel. But, thought the lone survivor, surely he will give an accounting and make a settlement now.

When he finally realized that his brother-in-law had no such intention and that no division of the property could be peaceably arranged and no accounting for the money he should have received on reaching legal age could be had from John Marshall, only one resort remained—to the courts. It was hard to take that step, for Marshall and Harriet's children were living on land in which Samuel had a half-interest. Finally in May, 1824, the disillusioned Samuel asked the court to partition the property.[19]

---

[19] "Upon petition of Samuel Bangs, printer, of Boston, Chas. P. Curtis of Boston was appointed by the court to partition land on the east side of Fort Hill, to the moiety of which Samuel Bangs was seized in fee simple" (Deed Records, Suffolk County, CCXCI, 226, May 12, 1824). On May 28, 1824, the Court ordered one-half the land awarded to Samuel (*ibid.*, pp. 228–229).

That allotted him he immediately sold,[20] for he wished to have no part in the bitterness aroused by the suit. The proceeds were small and he was unable to recover the income which had accumulated, as he had no means of proving what Marshall had collected during his long absence. Only inability to give a clear title had prevented Marshall from disposing of the property. And he was the father of Harriet's children! After finding his mother, to whom he now seemed almost a stranger, he turned his back on New England and, with his small patrimony, sailed for New York. Boston had left a bitter taste in his mouth, which he wanted to forget.

In New York he hunted up a cousin, Nathan Bangs, a devout but intelligent minister in the Methodist Church. Nathan had lately been made the book steward, editor, and agent of the Methodist Book Concern, a publishing house which proposed to issue educational and religious works.[21] In the printing office which opened in 1824, he readily found a place for his young cousin, who gave evidence of intelligence, industry, and ambition. At the end of the next year Samuel joined with Thomas McElrath, who had been the head salesman of the book department of the Methodist Concern, as a partner in establishing a separate publishing business.[22]

Then his thoughts turned to another type of partner. In Baltimore, years before, he had met an attractive dark-haired girl from lower Virginia. She was as retiring as the boy who secretly admired her, and the matter went no further. Now, with a business and prospects for a successful future, there was no need to hesitate. He hunted up Suzanne Payne, told her of his experiences, set forth his plans, and married her.

Although he worked hard in New York and the new business prospered, he was never entirely happy in the atmosphere about

[20] Deed of Samuel Bangs to Abraham Fuller of a part of the Fort Hill property, June 11, 1824 (Deed Records, Suffolk County, CCXCI, 229).

[21] Abel Stevens, *The Life and Times of Nathan Bangs*.

[22] W. F. Whitlock, *The Story of the Book Concern*, pp. 26, 38, 152; *National Cyclopaedia of American Biography*, III, 456.

him. He had lived too long in a Latin world—one in which hurry, rush, and push did not enter. Even before his marriage he had realized that he wanted to go back to Mexico, which had cast her peculiar spell on him, and had written to Monterrey offering to return as government printer at thirty-five pesos a month.[23] The offer was accepted by the governor of Nuevo León, who wrote that as the press Bangs had operated was reported to be worn out he had ordered a new one to be bought in the United States and suggested that Bangs might be commissioned by Richard Pearse, to whom the transaction had been entrusted, to make the selection and purchase before returning.[24] There were many complications and resultant delays; not until May, 1826, did the press finally reach Monterrey.[25] By that time Bangs was in business with McElrath and could not withdraw on the spur of the moment without considerable financial loss. At the end of the year, finding that his cousin Lemuel, who was acting as secretary of the Book Concern, was interested in becoming part owner of the McElrath business, Bangs sold Lemuel his interest.[26]

During the recent years spent in Boston and New York he had studied the presses then manufactured in both places, especially New York. The type that had been in most general use was known as the "Peter Smith invention," but this was being rapidly replaced by the "Washington"—then the best of hand presses. As the English press he had used in Mexico had been a small affair with type limited both in style and quantity, he began to toy with the idea of taking some good up-to-date presses to Mexico for use and for sale. If it took Nuevo León almost two years to get a press, one right at hand should readily be salable. He investigated costs and shipping possibilities and found the idea

[23] José Manuel Bangs to the "Comandante General de las quatro Provincias de Oriente," New York, April 20, 1825. AGE.

[24] José Antonio Rodríguez, Governor of Nuevo León, to José Manuel Bangs, [from Monterrey], September 19, 1825. AGE.

[25] Cossío, *Historia de Nuevo León*, V, 130–132.

[26] Dudley, *The Bangs Family*, p. 251. Thomas McElrath became, with Horace Greeley, the publisher of the New York *Tribune*, with which Bangs later had business connections.

feasible. Using a part of his inheritance that he recovered from the sale of his interest in the McElrath publishing business, he purchased two presses and all the most improved equipment and made arrangements for their shipment to Tampico.

With Suzanne, who had proved a devoted and understanding wife, and their young son, James O., Bangs sailed again for Mexico. This time he was the master of his fate. He knew where he intended to go and had the means to procure transportation for himself and his family; he was prepared for the conditions he was to meet; and he was no longer alone. The old saying "Once you know Mexico you'll be going back" was happily coming true.

FOUR

The Lure of Land in Texas

N HIS RETURN to Mexico in the early spring of 1827 José Manuel—for again he assumed his baptismal name—did not go back either to Monterrey or to Saltillo. Instead, he accepted the position of government printer for the state of Tamaulipas. He settled his family and set up his own press at the capital, long known as "Aguayo" but after the Revolution renamed "Victoria" in honor of Guadalupe Victoria, an insurgent leader who became in 1824 the first constitutional president of Mexico.

Not far from Soto la Marina, which had become a port, Victoria was pleasantly located on the eastern slope of the Sierra Madre, almost in the tropical zone. Small and compact, the old town nestled in the midst of semi-tropical vegetation on the bank of a branch of the Purification River, whose well-watered valley provided an abundance of food. Fruits and flowers were plentiful and cheap, especially during the rainy season, which often lasted from June to September, when growth was luxuriant. In typical Spanish style all activity of the town centered about the plazas. On the main plaza were the church and government buildings; some blocks away was a smaller plaza—the market place—to which the Indians daily brought their garden produce and handiwork before dawn, spread them on the ground or on improvised stands, and spent the morning trying to wrangle from their customers an extra *cuartillo* or two.

Fortunately for Bangs, his wife was a pleasant young woman, blessed with unusual good sense and the ability to adapt herself readily to Mexican living conditions; these were, after all, not as dissimilar to those of her home in Virginia as those of Monterrey had been to her husband: Indians filled the place of Negro servants; late meals were not entirely novel; and the quiet and leisure were familiar. The thick stone walls, which made for coolness, more than compensated for the absence of windows in most of the rooms, and the delightful patios, which were veritable garden spots, took the place of yards. On the walls hung baskets of trailing vines; large urns held tropical plants; beds of wine-colored or deep purple verbena gave color to the whole. Usually the music of water spattering on the stone base of the fountain in the center contributed to the restful atmosphere. In their simple but comfortable home Suzanne extended a warm welcome to her husband's growing list of local friends, and graciously received the English-speaking strangers, usually from the United States or Texas, who occasionally passed through. Although for quite a while she could carry on a conversation in Spanish only haltingly, her command of the language was soon adequate for the bargaining of the market place and the supervision of her household, but her young son James in a few months chattered happily and fluently with his Indian nurse. Life in Victoria offered a peaceful and pleasant outlook.

The placid atmosphere of the town by no means stifled the ambition or curbed the activities of Bangs. He arrived just as the fourth session of the First Legislature of Tamaulipas was approaching its close, but as soon as his press was set up he assisted with the printing of a few of the last laws passed by that body. These were regularly published in that state under the caption of "Circular," but carried no imprint.[1] He immediately realized that in printing later decrees he would have to refer frequently to earlier laws, of which no complete printed collection existed. He therefore busied himself during his first summer in Victoria in collecting and printing the *Colección de Leyes y Decretos* which had been passed by the First Legislature of that state; of this the imprint read: "Ciudad-Victoria. 1827. Imprenta del Gobierno del Estado. Dirigida por el C. José Manuel Bangs."[2] The "C" did not denote another change in his name; it was simply the abbreviation of "Citizen." This production, good evidence of his intelligence and willingness to work, won him the lasting friendship of the governor, Lucas Fernández. The same imprint appeared on a *Report* from a standing committee to the Junta of Deputies, dated August 14, 1827,[3] shortly before the opening of the Second Legislature. But even while that body was in session the volume of work required of him was small in comparison with his output in Saltillo in 1822.

The fall of 1827 brought with it one sad note. Father Mier died in Mexico City on November 3, leaving a large and widely scattered family and many citizens in several states to mourn his loss. He faced death as he had lived—bravely; at the end he called in a large group of friends to be present when extreme unction was to be administered, at his request, by Miguel Ramos Arizpe of Saltillo, whom he had regarded as a political rival and a clerical archenemy. In his passing, Bangs lost a revered and much-loved friend.

While he attended faithfully and efficiently to the work assigned him as government printer, he was relieved of much of the manual labor it involved when he began shortly after his

---

[1] The *Circular* of March 2, 1827 (Appendix II, No. 168) bears a notation, apparently in the hand of Bangs, "Se publicó en 13 de Abril." P.

[2] *Colección de leyes y decretos de la primera Legislatura Constitucional del Estado Libre de Tamaulipas.* Yale. Appendix II, No. 175.

[3] Appendix II, No. 186.

arrival to accept Mexicans as apprentices. It was thus possible for him to carry on at the same time another line of business in which he saw a future—the importation and sale of presses, type, and other printing supplies. In this connection his earlier contacts in Monterrey and Saltillo proved exceedingly helpful, and the moment was highly propitious, for right at hand was an undeveloped market for a type of goods with which his stay in Boston and in New York had made him thoroughly familiar. The governments of the four states which had earlier constituted the Eastern Interior Provinces had initiated such purchases. In Texas, at San Antonio de Bexar, the governor, José Felix Trespalacios, purchased one in 1823; this was brought out and operated for a time by a printer named Asbridge, but was soon sold to the Provincial Deputation at Monterrey. When that body ceased to exist the press was sold to the City Council of that city.[4] Tamaulipas had a press when the state government was formed in 1824, with Godwin Brown Cotten as one of its early printers; Coahuila secured a press from Mexico City in 1825; and Nuevo León ordered one from the United States in 1824, but it did not arrive until 1826.[5] During those years independent printers were coming into the region, and some of them, like Bangs, bought their own presses and did contract work. The state of Nuevo León, while waiting for the press it had ordered, had its work done by Arrese and Company, a local firm.[6] Once the efficiency of the press was demonstrated, the demand grew, and Bangs was

[4] Specimens of the products of this press are in the Bexar Archives and in the Bancroft Library (CBC). Luciano García, governor of Texas, in writing to Felipe de la Garza, commandant general at Monterrey, July 9, 1823, says the press and equipment were sold to the Provincial Deputation for 3,500 pesos (MS Letter Book of the Collector of Customs at Matagorda, 1821–1826, Austin Papers, TxU). Cossío (*Historia de Nuevo León*, V, 130) says 2,348 pesos were paid for it later by the City Council of Monterrey.

[5] Early imprints in the Prieto Papers and in the Matamoros Archives (photocopies), Vol. 9, TxU. "Actas del Congreso del Estado de Coahuila y Texas," I, 172 (June 23, 1825 and I, 207 September 6, 1825), typescript, TxU; Cossío, *Historia de Nuevo León*, V, 130–132. The press ordered by the governor of Nuevo León reached Monterrey on May 19, 1826—Notation of Governor Parás on letter to him from the *ayuntamiento* of Montemorelos, May 16, 1826. AGE.

[6] By decree of September 2, 1824, the governor of Nuevo León was authorized

kept busy demonstrating, ordering, and delivering presses and printing supplies.

Although the Legislature of Tamaulipas was called to convene on August 1, 1827, it did not get down to work for several weeks and the first session was brief; less than thirty laws and decrees were passed and few other documents required printing. In the second session, from mid-January to mid-February, some fifty decrees were passed, of which copies of fewer than twenty of the original printing survived. The small number of documents he printed in the early months of 1828 were largely concerned with the financial problems that faced the state.[7]

Before Bangs' contract with the state of Tamaulipas expired he was offered a position at Saltillo by the state of Coahuila and Texas, for under the national Constitution of 1824 these two provinces were united to form one state, to which the printer was trying to sell a new press. As there had been constant trouble with the one shipped there from Mexico City,[8] some of the officials who remembered the excellent work Bangs had earlier done on the Mina press suggested that he do the government work on a press of his own, as he had been doing in Victoria. While he was happy in Victoria, and to a degree contented, his recollections of both the cooler climate and the genial people of

by its legislature to purchase a new press and, until its arrival, to contract with Arrese and Company for government printing. José María Parás and Juan B. Arizpe to Governor Rodríguez, Monterrey, September 3, 1824. AGE.

[7] For extant decrees of the First and the Second Legislature of the state of Tamaulipas, Appendix Nos. 176–185, 192–208; for other documents connected with the government of Tamaulipas, 1827–1828, see Nos. 169–174, 186–194, and 209–214.

[8] After Bangs left Saltillo there was no government-owned press until one arrived from Mexico City late in 1825. The printer seems to have been José María Práxedis Sandoval. It was operated in 1826 by Jacobo Peters. In 1827 fifty copies of the "parte legislativo de la Constitución" were printed. Insufficient type for rapid printing caused the Constitution as a whole to be printed in Mexico City. See "Actas del Congreso de Coahuila y Texas" (typescript), Vol. II, pp. 236 and 304 ff., TxU; and correspondence of the governor and the Constituent Legislature relative to the printing of the Constitution of 1827, ACC.

Saltillo were very pleasant; besides, he realized that its location would bring him into closer contact with other larger interior towns and, hence, with more prospective customers for presses and printing supplies. The outcome was the sale to the state of Coahuila and Texas of a new press, which he engaged to operate. He then sold his press at Victoria to the government of Tamaulipas and moved his small family by the tedious route of San Luis Potosí to Saltillo. The name of that city had, in the meantime, been changed to "Leona Vicario" in honor of a revolutionary heroine whose birthplace it was, and this name appears on many of Bangs' imprints from the time he began printing there in 1828. The townspeople never accepted the new name, and in 1831 "Saltillo" again became official.[9]

In that city he turned out with his up-to-date press a steady stream of decrees, circulars, and pamphlets, ranging from broadsides to brochures of eighty-odd pages. Decrees were not termed *circulares* but were clearly labeled "decrees," and numbered. Number 54 (promulgated on May 2, 1828), which fixed the fees various governmental employees might charge for specific legal papers and services, seems to have been the first Bangs printed there after his move from Victoria. The heading on its first page, "Gobierno Supremo del Estado de Coahuila y Texas," reappears on a number of the decrees he subsequently printed; on his reprint of Decree No. 16, the colonization law of March 24, 1825, is his imprint which became more or less standard: "Leona Vicario: 1828. Impreso en la Imprenta del Gobierno de Coahuila y Texas. Dirigida por el C. José Manuel Bangs."[10] In printing the condensed regulations of the federal government concerning passports (May 1, 1828) in parallel columns of Spanish, English, and French, he varied this imprint to read "Reim-

[9] Coahuila and Texas, First Constitutional Legislature, Decree No. 29, November 15, 1827. Translated into English in H. P. N. Gammel, *The Laws of Texas, 1822–1897*, I, 85. The name "Saltillo" was restored by a decree of April 2, 1831 (Gammel, *Laws of Texas*, I, 177).

[10] See Appendix II, Nos. 215 and 216.

preso," as he had formerly done with issues of official organs from the capital.[11]

While pleasantly engaged in supervising the work under way on the press, for he now had not only apprentices but some capable printers under his direction, Bangs was disagreeably surprised by the notification that a suit had been filed against him on October 16 in the name of Henry Henricksen, an itinerant vender. The plaintiff claimed that he had lent the printer ninety-eight pesos the previous year at Refugio [Matamoros] to enable him to get some goods out of the customhouse there. Henricksen's lawyer, J. J. Vidaurre, went further and accused Bangs of fraud and malice, and demanded payment not only of the bill, but also the court costs and attorney's fees. Bangs went directly into court and frankly acknowledged the debt; in addition he explained that his only reason for not paying it was that he knew of no one authorized to accept the payment. Upon being shown a power-of-attorney held by Vidaurre, he promptly paid the amount he had borrowed. In regard to the charges of fraud and malice brought against him, Bangs stated that although they furnished ample justification for a libel suit, he would simply let the matter drop, because everybody in Saltillo knew him and realized the complete falsity of the terms used. He added that he was not moved by malice.[12]

The following year was a busy and a happy one for the Bangs family. On February 27 he was authorized by the Legislature to print three hundred copies of the state constitution. This was a large order and Bangs asked for more help in carrying it out. His request was granted: Laureano Rangel was added to his staff at a salary of 96 pesos a year and Melchor de la Garza, a more experienced man, was raised to 120 pesos.[13] This—the first printing

[11] See Appendix II, No. 219.

[12] *Expediente sobre pesos* contra Don Manuel Bangs *promovido por el ciudadano* José Jesús Vidaurri, *como apoderado de don Enrique Henricksen.* Alcalde. 2º Año de 1828. Court records (MSS). Archivo del ayuntamiento, Saltillo, 1828, Carpeta 73, Documento 17. AS.

[13] Coahuila y Texas, "Actas del Congreso," V, p. 1075, Typescript, TxU.

in the state of that fundamental document—was an exceedingly important piece of work, for few copies of the Mexico City printing in 1827 were by that time available, and no proof of that edition had been read in Saltillo.

While that work was under way his second son, Samuel the eighth, was born on March 24, and on April 5 the baby was baptized at the Sagrario with the name of Samuel Salvador. The grandparents were given as Samuel Bangs and Hannah Grice; on the mother's side as John Payne and Lincetta Jones. The godparents were Joaquín Barragán and his wife, María de la Luz.[14] But the proud father had little time just then to devote to his namesake. As the Legislature was in session, decrees, messages, and circulars had to be promptly printed. Among the pieces of greater length were the municipal ordinances of over a dozen towns in the state. Of these the thirty-six–page ordinances for the government of San Antonio de Bexar, the forty-four–page ordinances for Goliad, and the twenty-six–page regulations for the Villa of San Felipe de Austin were among the works issued in June. The imprint of each concluded with "a cargo del C. José Manuel Bangs."[15]

Barely was the printing of the Constitution completed before Bangs was faced with an unexpected chore. By Decree No. 12 of the Constituent Congress, early in 1825, the publication of an official government organ had been authorized. As the press at that time had not arrived, the paper did not materialize. Bangs knew nothing of such an organ until May 30, when he was notified that its appearance was expected. As a result, on Thursday, September 3, with the opening of the next session of the Legislature, he began a weekly four-page folder whose prescribed title was *Gazeta Constitucional de Coahuiltejas*. It bore the imprint of "la oficina del Supremo Gobierno del Estado en Palacio, a cargo del C. José Manuel Bangs." The price to nonresidents was

[14] Saltillo, Catedral, Libro de bautismos, Vol. 23, fol. 151 v. (April 5, 1829).
[15] The first two of these ordinances are at TxU; the third is at Yale. Appendix II, Nos. 249–251.

five reales for four issues, in advance. Extras and supplements were also issued from time to time.[16]

Even this comparatively small publication brought with it additional problems and worries. Not only did he have to select much of the material that went into it, but he was held responsible for all of it. Hardly was the issue of January 28 off the press before he was hailed into court to answer a charge brought by Francisco Salas that he had been insulted and offended by its *Supplement.* In reply Bangs exhibited to the Board of Censors the manuscript of the article in question; it was signed by Juan Francisco Fuentes. When asked how many copies of that *Supplement* he had printed and what disposition he made of them, he replied that he printed two hundred; eighty were furnished the government—the rest went to the author, except nine copies he turned over to the court. Fuentes was then ordered to bring in all his copies. Not until late in February was Bangs cleared; eventually Fuentes was also, and his copies were returned to him.[17]

In the meantime Bangs' mind was occupied by other matters which he regarded as of greater importance to him. As Saltillo was the capital of both Coahuila and Texas, it felt strong repercussions from the rapid increase in colonists from the United States after Moses Austin secured the first grant in 1821 to settle Anglo-Americans in Texas. Bangs had come into close contact with most of the promoters of colonization, as his command of both English and Spanish and his knowledge of the customs and laws of Mexico made him extremely useful to colonizers. He

[16] See Appendix II, No. 297. A circular letter soliciting subscriptions signed by José María Ibarra and dated September 5, 1829, is at TxU, as are Nos. 1–3, 14, 28, and 29, 1 extra, and three supplements. At Yale are Nos. 32–40 (April 8 to June 3, 1830). Nos. 11, 16, and 22 are in private hands.

[17] El C. Francisco Salas denuncia ante el Juez de Imprenta por insulta y ofensiva el *Suplemento* a la *Gazeta del Estado* y tiene razón lo pone en ridículo su autor. *Suplemento* a la *Gazeta del Estado*, de hoy 28 de enero de 1830.— Saltillo, Carpeta 75, No. 10. Año de 1830. (AS). Salas had formerly been an *alcalde.*

heard constantly of vast tracts of land being granted to families who agreed to make their homes in the province of Texas. Since Mexican citizenship was a prerequisite to securing such a grant, on January 1, 1830, Bangs filed an application for such citizenship. On the fifteenth, by Decree No. 112, the printer José Manuel Bangs, a native of the United States, was formally declared a citizen of the state of Coahuila and Texas by its Legislature.[18] He had laid his plans so carefully in advance that in less than two weeks, on the twenty-seventh, he filed a petition for a grant of six leagues of land on the Colorado River in Texas, as this was the amount to which a man with a wife and two sons was legally entitled. In this petition he recited his services with the Mina Expedition, his imprisonment and forced labor without recompense during four years, and his work on the provincial press until 1823. He also recorded his return with his family and press to Tamaulipas in 1827 and his later employment in Saltillo.[19]

The petition was referred to the City Council of Saltillo for verification of facts; it replied on February 18 that Bangs was married to a North American lady, that he had two sons, that his conduct and that of his lady was entirely proper and had never aroused any unfavorable criticism. As to his work as a printer, the governor and the Legislature who employed him were in a better position to judge his ability than the Council.[20] On May 21, 1830, the petition was granted, and he was authorized to have the land (265,370 acres) surveyed and the survey recorded.[21]

Busy as Bangs had been with his printing and plans for becoming a colonist, he was completely unaware that the moment he chose to settle in Texas was most unpropitious, for Texas at

---

[18] Coahuila y Texas, Congreso, "Actas," V (January 1 and 14, 1830), 1104 and 1120; Decree No. 112 (January 15, 1830), BA, photocopy, LMS; Appendix II, No. 262.

[19] Spanish Grants, XXX, fols. 200–200 v (TLO).

[20] *Ibid.*, fols. 200 v–201.

[21] *Ibid.*, fol. 201, but the date the petition was granted is given as March 11 and so recorded in Bastrop County Deed Records, Book C, p. 99.

that very moment was making her first bow upon the broad international scene. Settlers in that province from the United States had increased so rapidly and had shown themselves so enterprising and independent as to justify the fear of the Mexican government that the United States proposed to add Texas to its own territory. This belief was greatly strengthened at the end of 1829 by the arrival in Mexico City of a new chargé d'affaires from the United States, Anthony Butler, a confidant of President Andrew Jackson and a proprietor of Texas lands. His mission, it was widely rumored, was to buy Texas for five million dollars, and to move its boundary from the Nueces River, where it had been from the time of the founding of the first Spanish settlements in Texas, to the Rio Grande, which flowed through the Province of Tamaulipas before entering the Gulf of Mexico. At once the Mexican Secretary of State, who had felt concern about Texas for some years, alerted his diplomatic representatives in Washington, London,[22] and Paris; and on April 6, 1830, the Mexican Congress, at his behest, cut off further colonization from the United States,[23] although a few empresarios were permitted to complete the number specified by earlier contracts. In May the Mexican minister in London, Manuel E. de Gorostiza, who himself had given the colonization question serious study and had sent the Mexican government a forty-page "Memoria" on the subject,[24] reported the suspected intentions of the United States to the British Foreign Minister. The matter was promptly

[22] México, Secretary of Foreign Affairs Lucas Alamán to Manuel E. de Gorostiza, Mexico City, January 28, 1830, Confidential No. 2, MS. ASRE. Printed in México, Secretaría de Relaciones Exteriores, *Lucas Alamán, El Reconocimiento de nuestra independencia por España y la unión de los países hispanoamericanos,* p. 43 (Archivo Histórico Diplomático Mexicano, No. 7).

[23] *Colección de los decretos y órdenes . . . que ha expedido la soberana Junta provisional gubernativa y soberanos congresos generales de la nación mexicana,* V, 100–102.

[24] The original was enclosed with Gorostiza's letter to México, Foreign Office (Alamán), London, June 22, 1830. MS. Expediente 3305, Núm. 63. ASRE. For further details, see Lota M. Spell, "Gorostiza and Texas," in *HAHR*, XXXVII (November, 1957), 425–462.

brought before the House of Commons. England had two reasons for objecting to such a scheme. Although slavery had been abolished by the laws of Mexico, the colonists in Texas had been permitted to bring in slaves, and the extension of the United States boundary toward Mexico would further expand slave territory, to which England was bitterly opposed. Besides, she had commercial interests in Mexico which would be threatened. So definitely did the British Prime Minister express himself in the House of Commons and the British press voice its strong disapproval on May 21[25]—the very day Bangs' petition for land was granted—that the United States minister at the court of St. James wrote to the Secretary of State of the United States that the extension of the United States toward Mexico through the purchase of Texas would not, under any circumstances, be favorably viewed, and might be directly opposed, by Great Britain.[26]

Entirely unaware of the newly awakened international interest in Texas and moved instead by visions of ownership of extensive and valuable lands, Bangs, now a man thirty-three years old, prepared to leave for Texas to select and perfect title to the six *sitios* allotted him. He discontinued the *Gazeta* in June,[27] and the next legislative session would not convene until September.

Getting off for Texas was not so easy. Others in Saltillo had secured grants to land there, and when Bangs' plans became known he was besieged with commissions to select land, to perfect titles, and to arrange leases. One such commission was en-

[25] *The Times* (London), Editorial, May 21, 1830.
[26] Louis McLane to [Martin Van Buren], London, May 21, 1830. United States, Department of State, MSS Dispatches from U.S. Ministers to England. NA.
[27] The last issue known is No. 41, June 10, 1830. See a pamphlet signed by Ignacio Sendejas, June 18, 1830, which refutes an editorial in No. 41 of the *Gazeta*: "Este comunicado correspondía a la *Gazeta* del jueves, que se suspendió por orden del Supremo Gobierno." The pamphlet, with the following mutilated title, is at TxU: "[   ] les Coahuiltejanos / [   ] a esta vindicación / su honor ultrajado / la gratitud / de uno de sus conciudadanos." See Appendix II, No. 316. BA.

trusted to him by a legislator, Ignacio Sendejas, who had been granted eleven *sitios*; he gave Bangs, in addition to a power-of-attorney, a lease on the whole tract. Similar authority was given him to handle fourteen *sitios* of a seventeen-*sitio* grant by Pedro Pereira and his partners, J. J. and Mariano Grande. But the preparation of these and other documents detained Bangs in Saltillo until the last days of July.[28]

The trip tested both his patience and endurance. Northern Mexico, especially as far as the Nueces River, was an arid region; at the peak of summer, when he started, the heat was excessive; and only the trees that bordered the few rivers and smaller streams offered any relief from the scorching sun. The small scattered villages offered poor accommodations, if any. Some eighty miles beyond the Nueces he stopped at San Antonio de Bejar, which had been the capital of Texas before that province was joined with Coahuila into one state by the Mexican Constitution of 1824. From there the landscape became more promising; rivers were more numerous; shrubs and trees, more general; and the road he traveled, following the base of foothills of mountains far to the west, was much more interesting. The Colorado River proved a broad, deep stream which promised facilities for irrigation and transportation. Its banks were lined by many tall pecan trees which yielded delicious nuts. On the west bank of the river, at a bend where a new town called Mina had lately been laid out, he found a very desirable four-league tract facing the San Antonio Road and adjoining one owned by Ben

---

[28] Bexar County, Records of the Probate Court. Estate of James Bowie, deceased. In the inventory made by the administrator appointed in September, 1837, are the following papers:
Contract for leasing 11 leagues of land between Ignacio Sendejas et al and Manuel Bangs, dated July 27, 1830.
Power of attorney for locating and taking possession of said 11 leagues granted by Sendejas to Manuel Bangs, July 27, 1830.
Contract for lease of 14 leagues of land granted to Pedro Pereira et al made between Pereira et al and Manuel Bangs, dated July 23, 1830.
Power of attorney from same to Manuel Bangs for locating and taking possession of aforesaid 14 leagues, dated July 27, 1830. TSA.

Milam.[29] On it were many beautiful live-oak trees whose wide-spreading branches furnished cool and inviting shade. With this tract he was entirely satisfied, but it was not enough. After diligent search convinced him that no additional two leagues were available in that vicinity, he rode some seventy miles to the east to San Felipe de Austin on the Brazos River to confer with Stephen F. Austin, who had been the first empresario in Texas and was still the most influential. They had already become acquainted in Saltillo, where Austin frequently went on business connected with his colony. He suggested to the printer that he take his other two leagues on the Brazos River, a section that was developing rapidly, perhaps in the Nashville Colony. By August 14 Bangs was authorized by the agent of that colony to select the amount of land he needed from any as yet ungranted;[30] but he found none that he regarded as desirable. He next went to the colony of Robert Leftwich, where he found a well-watered and heavily timbered tract he decided to consider. Meanwhile he did his best to carry out the various commissions entrusted to him.

In November he was still trying to have the Colorado River tract surveyed, as a recorded survey was a prerequisite to establishing legal title. Finally, disgusted at having spent so much time and accomplished so little, he started for Saltillo. At San Antonio de Bejar he stopped long enough to sign a contract to accept the two leagues offered him on the east side of the Brazos and across the Little Brazos.[31] Authorization from the agent for that colony to take possession of the land and to have it surveyed did not reach him until he was back in Saltillo.[32] There he was to be disagreeably surprised again.

---

[29] See Bangs, José Manuel, application for grant of land, Spanish Grants, XXX, fol. 215. TLO.

[30] Hosea H. League, agent, authorization, August 14, 1830, for Bangs to make selection in Nashville Colony, Spanish Grants, XXX, fol. 203. TLO.

[31] He signed this on November 3, 1830 (Spanish Grants, fol. 202. TLO).

[32] Thomas Barnett, agent for the Leftwich Colony, to Bangs, San Felipe de Austin, November 17, 1830, Spanish Grants, XXX, fol. 204. TLO.

As he was still absent from his post as government printer when the Legislature convened and bills to be printed began to pile up, the governor very unwillingly appointed Antonio González Dávila to take charge of the press. When Bangs did arrive it was to find his position gone. For him there remained no choice but to push his Texas claim by every possible means, to devote himself meanwhile to merchandising, and to help on the government press as occasion offered.

Fully convinced that the red tape involved in acquiring legal title to land in Texas, even after it had been officially granted by the state, was beyond him, Bangs engaged Thomas J. Chambers, a lawyer living in Texas who had lately been granted citizenship, to represent him in the formalities incident to perfecting the title and taking formal possession of the lands granted him. The power of attorney he gave Chambers in 1831 was witnessed by Stephen F. Austin, who was at that time a representative from Texas to the state Legislature.[33] The land was finally surveyed in 1832 by Thomas P. Borden, the surveyor whom Bangs himself had engaged two years before; but even with that accomplished, title and possession were still lacking. Neither did Sendejas have title although Bangs had given a power of attorney to S. M. Williams at San Felipe and he had transferred that authority to Isaac Doneho.[34]

Even Bangs' means of livelihood—merchandising—was threatened that year by a decree which limited retailing to native Mexicans.[35] He immediately appealed to the Legislature, which, as he had many good friends among its members, declared him exempt from the application of that decree on the ground of hav-

[33] The power of attorney which Bangs gave Chambers was dated May 8, 1831 (Spanish Grants, XXX, fol. 206. TLO).

[34] Bexar County. Records of the Probate Court. Estate of James Bowie, deceased. Power of attorney granted in San Felipe de Austin by S. M. Williams to Isaac Doneho, dated July 2, 1831, conferring the power to act as a substitute for power of attorney given Williams by Bangs, relative to locating and taking possession of Sendejas' eleven leagues of land. TSA. See n. 28.

[35] Coahuila and Texas, Laws, Decree No. 183, April 9, 1832; Gammel's *Laws of Texas*, I, 185.

ing a family in the state and one son born there.[36] Having cleared this hurdle, he began importing more presses and a greater variety of supplies. One of his agents who was quite active in the business was Alejandro Uro in Monterrey, from whom he had borrowed in times of need. Don Alejandro not only sold presses and accessories but he collected for them—a more difficult matter—and remitted the funds to Bangs from time to time as occasion offered.[37]

Political shifts and changes were the order in Mexico in 1833, but none affected Coahuila and Texas more than the ascendancy of Antonio López de Santa Anna to the presidency. Among the changes was the transfer of the state capital from Saltillo to Monclova,[38] which had several times earlier been the seat of government. It was an insignificant and comparatively inaccessible place and offered no inducement of any kind to Bangs, who still had his eyes on Texas. But before the government press finally left Saltillo in April, Bangs had decided to return to Victoria to print for the state of Tamaulipas. Governor Francisco Vital Fernández was his friend and promised him a contract, and from there he planned to expand his merchandising.

Not until late in the year did the contract materialize; then the government was authorized to contract for all state printing, including the treasury reports and one or two periodicals. The press was to be either bought or rented; the periodicals were to be the responsibility of the empresario, the state to furnish the paper, and the editor to be approved by the government, which was to be furnished one hundred copies free. With legislative approval of this agreement on November 5,[39] plans were set on foot to establish a new official organ, *Atalaya*, which appeared in January, 1834.

In this new semiweekly, which was priced at first at nine pesos

[36] Coahuila and Texas, Laws, Decree No. 195, April 28, 1832; *ibid.*, p. 196.
[37] See the Bangs-Uro y Lozano correspondence, 1821–1835. CBC. Photocopies, LMS.
[38] Coahuila and Texas, Laws, Decree No. 13, March 9, 1833. AHE.
[39] See Appendix II, No. 345.

ATALAYA

CUIQUE
SUUM.

ACADA
UNO LO
SUYO.

PERIODICO OFICIAL DEL GOBIERNO

TOM. I.   VICTORIA, (TAMAULIPAS.) MARTES 18 DE MARZO DE 1834.   **NUM. 11.**

Heading of an 1834 issue of the official organ of the State of Tamaulipas.

annually but later reduced to six, the decrees of the Legislature and the messages of the governor and committees appeared in the official portion, but in addition Bangs included excerpts from the leading papers of Mexico City and New Orleans and a variety of other articles. In the early numbers he advertised for three boys from fourteen to eighteen years as apprentices and for a *mozo* for the press. In April he reported the ceremonies attendant upon the opening of a girls' school in Tampico. In September he printed a "Canción" in honor of Santa Anna and the prospectus of a newspaper, *La Balanza de Astrea,* in San Luis Potosí. In a good editorial *Atalaya* regretted the decree closing the port at Soto la Marina in the absence of Santa Anna from the presidency and hoped for its repeal; in another it described conditions in Victoria and criticized the city officials for tolerating them; and, in a later issue, pointed out possible improvements in election procedures. From time to time during the year the paper was suspended because of press of other work, and occasionally it was reduced to weekly issues.[40]

In regard to his Texas grant no progress had been made since the completion of the survey in 1832, but in the summer of 1834

[40] See Nos. 11, 15, 43, 45, 46, 48, and 57 (March to December, 1834). TxU.

the special commissioner, Ira Lewis, who had been appointed by the governor of Coahuila and Texas to clear up pending grants in Texas, issued title and gave possession of Bangs' tract to Chambers.[41] It was then arranged that the two would meet in Saltillo to settle the business, and there in December the lawyer placed in Bangs' hands the papers covering what he claimed was the perfected title to the six leagues of land (two-thirds [176,913 acres] on the Colorado; one third [88, 457 acres] on the Brazos). Even with the papers in his hands Bangs could hardly believe that his dream of becoming the owner of a vast tract of land in Texas had come true.

It was as well he could not. Next came the question of settling with Chambers for his services. Bangs was himself an honest man and a trusting soul; he had thought about the fee but had felt sure the lawyer would be fair. When he put the question, Chambers handed him a deed ready for signature. After a preamble reciting that Chambers had rendered a service to Bangs and had paid "out of his own purse all the expense incurred in obtaining aforesaid title," the document transferred to Chambers three of the four leagues on the Colorado which had been granted to Bangs.

Had the sky fallen the printer could not have been more shocked! He simply could not believe that the man before him, whom he had befriended, would make such a demand. Without question the fee was exorbitant, yet Bangs saw no avenue of escape from the trap set by the wily lawyer. Had the terms been stated in cash and equally exorbitant Bangs knew that he could not readily have raised the money. As there had been no written agreement and Chambers had left him no ground for argument, on December 15, 1834—almost four years after he applied for the grant—he signed the deed which transferred to Chambers the three choicest of his four leagues on the Colorado.[42] Sick at heart he rode wearily back to Victoria, hating to have to tell Su-

[41] Granted by Governor Vidaurri, July 30, 1834; Spanish Grants, XXX, fol. 216 v.
[42] Bastrop County, Texas, Deed Records, Book C, pp. 217–218.

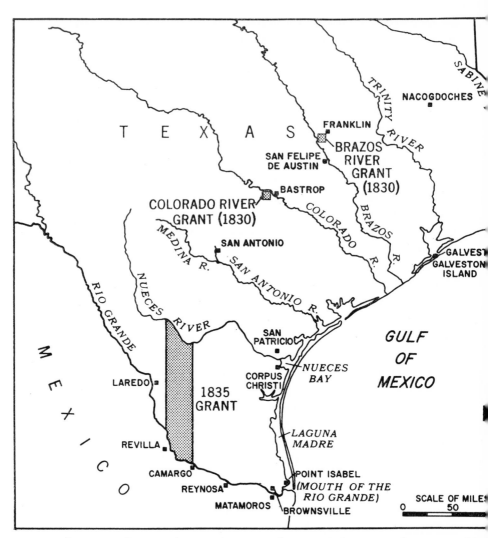

Grants Made to José Manuel Bangs. The size of the map makes impossible completely accurate indication of size and shape of the 1830 grants.

zanne how their dream of a home on the Colorado had faded. With only one league it was impossible to carry out their earlier plans.

Putting aside as well as he could his bitterness toward Chambers, he turned his energy to his merchandising. In this he was ably supported by his old friend Uro. Although business in the Monterrey area was hampered by distance and sometimes by unreliable messengers, Bangs kept Uro in close touch with the business in general. Most of the presses and printing supplies he handled were ordered from New York and shipped to Tampico. From there some were dispatched directly to the purchasers; others were brought to Victoria for distribution as needed. By 1834 the territory he covered included not only Nuevo León and Coahuila but San Luis Potosí, Aguas Calientes, and Zacatecas. The goods were delivered by pack mules, and cash was transmitted by trusted employees or friends.

Athough differences sometimes arose between the two men, the friendly relations of the early Monterrey days generally prevailed. At one time when the closing of a sale in the vicinity of Monterrey was unusually slow Uro charged Bangs for storage of the press. Bangs was shocked at this unprecedented procedure and wrote the offender to that effect. Uro nevertheless stood his ground, and Bangs ultimately yielded, considering, as he said, that friendship was more valuable than money. Once the bill was paid, the pleasant relations were reestablished. Each man was his own secretary, and both the letters and bills of the two were those of honest, hard-working men, happily absorbed in the many details of promoting the printing business.[43] *El Atalaya* served Bangs as an advertising medium for, as a government organ, copies were sent to each of the other state governments. In it he advertised, in addition to presses, forms and dies for casting type, and instruction in such work when needed.[44]

Neither the move back to Victoria, his experience with Chambers, nor his merchandising induced Bangs to abandon his

[43] See the Bangs-Uro y Lozano correspondence, 1821–1835. CBC.
[44] *Atalaya*, II, No. 1 (January 17, 1835) and later.

dream of becoming a great landed proprietor. As his attempts in Texas had involved him in so many difficulties, he turned his attention next to Tamaulipas, in which there were vast stretches of land open to settlement and colonization. The regulations regarding colonization had lately been broadened,[45] and the governor at the moment was a good friend. By early 1835 he had ready a petition for a grant of land on which to settle 250 families. This was approved on February 27, 1835, the tract assigned him being described as extending from "the left bank of the Rio Bravo del Norte beginning opposite Camargo and following the bank of the river till opposite Revilla, thence toward the Nueces, until a sufficient quantity of land should be found to satisfy the claims of all the settlers and the empresario."[46]

His next problem was to get the stipulated number of families on the land, for such grants were subject to nullification if the conditions were not promptly fulfilled. Almost at once, as if in answer to his prayers, a solution presented itself.

About two weeks before the grant was approved, Bangs had received a visit from Benjamin Lundy, a rabid abolitionist, who was seeking a grant of land on which to establish a colony of free Negroes and escaped slaves. In his diary[47] Lundy recorded the events that transpired:

Feb. 8, 1835 [Matamoros]. This morning I paid my friend Richard Pearse a visit, and obtained from him a letter of introduction and recommendation to the government printer at Victoria, whose name is Samuel Bangs. He is a native of Boston, but has resided long in this country, and is said to enjoy, in a high degree, the confidence of the Mexicans.

Feb. 16 [Victoria] . . . I called on Samuel Bangs, the Bostonian . . . and presented to him my letter from Richard Pearse. I found him

---

[45] See Tamaulipas, Decree No. 44, November 17, 1833. AGT.

[46] James Ogilvy to Richard Pakenham [British minister to Mexico], New Orleans, August 20, 1839; George P. Garrison, editor, *Diplomatic Correspondence of the Republic of Texas*, I, 597–599.

[47] Benjamin Lundy, *The Life, Travels and Opinions of Benjamin Lundy, including his journeys to Texas and Mexico* (Thomas Earle, compiler, pp. 154–172.

polite and disposed, in every way, to befriend me. I . . . inquired where I could obtain a room, to occupy during my stay in town. He thereupon kindly offered me the use of a comfortable apartment in his printing office, which I accordingly took. He also sent my horse, by one of his boys, into the country to be taken care of. In the course of our conversation I learned from him that he is a relative of the editor of the *Christian Advocate and Journal,* a well known periodical of the Methodist Episcopal faith, published in New York.

February 22. I spent most of this day in the company of my friend Bangs, and his interesting little family. His wife is a native of lower Virginia, and is a very pleasant and agreeable woman.

Feb. 23. . . . Friend Bangs is inclined to do something in the way of colonizing, and wishes me to assist him. It is probable that we shall agree upon terms in relation to it.

Feb. 26. Bangs says that he has presented his petition for permission to colonize 250 families. . . . I expect to introduce the families on his behalf, upon this grant.

Feb. 28. I prepared today, a draught of an agreement between Bangs and myself, relative to my colonizing his grant of land. We are told that both his papers and mine are ready for the governor's signature.

March 2, 1835. My funds having again become exhausted, and my friend Bangs having offered, some days since, without solicitation, to accommodate me in case of need, I took from him today a loan of eight dollars. He went with me to the governor's secretary.

March 6. Accompanied by S. Bangs, who went as interpreter, I had a considerable conversation with the governor.

March 10. [For stamped paper] I was thus placed under the necessity of borrowing more from friend Bangs, who now furnished me with nine dollars.

March 11. I took leave of the governor. I informed him that . . . my friend Bangs would call upon him for instructions as to the mode of procedure in commencing my colony. I then went and took leave also of S. Bangs and his hospitable lady. She insisted upon my taking with me a fine roast fowl, some bread and cheese, etc. My gratitude to this worthy family cannot be expressed, much less, I fear, can their hospitality ever be reciprocated.

87

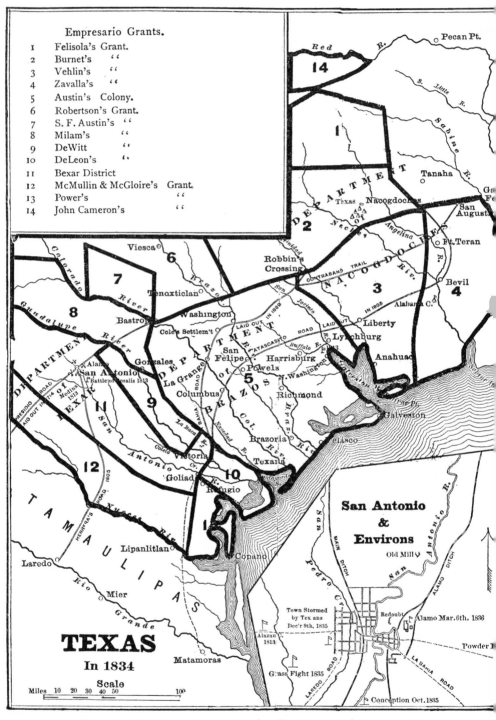

TEXAS

In 1834

Scale
Miles 10   20   30   40   50   100

San Antonio & Environs

Texas in 1834. From Homer S. Thrall's *A Pictorial History of Texas.*

March 21. I got a letter from S. Bangs, containing the governor's answers to the questions I left. From these answers it appears that I cannot locate my grant of land until I bring on a part of the settlers. This information . . . will render it necessary for me to hurry home and expedite the migration as fast as possible.

Events in Texas were moving faster than Lundy; its boundaries were also undergoing changes undreamed of by either man when Lundy sailed for New Orleans at the end of the month.[48] When these men parted in the spring of 1835 the Nueces River was the western boundary of Texas on all the maps which included that province. Its colonists, however, were actively taking control, clearing it when possible of Mexican troops, and preparing to set up their own form of government. *El Atalaya* reported on August 15 that the Texans had run the Mexican custom officials and soldiers out of Galveston. With the approach of autumn the Mexican government realized that drastic measures were necessary if such open rebellion was to be halted. In November an army, with the president, Santa Anna, at its head, was on the way to "pulverize" the "bad colonists" in Texas; and Congress, in an attempt to halt military aid from the United States to that province, passed a law that all armed foreigners who entered Mexico would be treated as pirates, as would any who imported arms or ammunition for those hostile to its government.[49] In spite of this drastic legislation, arms, supplies, and men were pouring into Texas and the revolution was on.

Bangs, torn between his landed interests in Texas and those in Mexico, made a trip to Matamoros to try to find out the real state of affairs. There he ran across a friend of many years standing, James Ogilvy, a Scotchman who had been active in land matters in this region and had befriended Lundy.[50] After discussing the

[48] *Ibid.*, p. 173.
[49] México, Laws and Decrees, *Legislación mexicana o Colección completa de las disposiciones legislativas desde le independencia de la republica.* Law of December 30, 1835. III, 114.
[50] Lundy, "Diary" (March 30, 1835), in *Life, Travels and Opinions* (p. 173), said he was from the Shetland Islands.

matter of the Tamaulipas grant and the pressing need of bringing in colonists without further loss of time, Bangs gave Ogilvy a general power of attorney with full authority as agent to carry out the original terms of the grant.[51] He himself returned to Victoria and his work.

After General Santa Anna reached Texas, Mexican troops soon captured Goliad, Brazoria, San Felipe, and Matagorda, and the extermination of the retreating Texan army under Sam Houston —the only one left—was momentarily feared by Texans and the friends of Texas, including the President of the United States. Instead, early in May, the outside world was startled by news that the Mexican troops had been defeated on April 21 on the San Jacinto River, and the President of Mexico had been captured. In the treaty that followed, and that Santa Anna signed, all Mexican troops were to be withdrawn beyond the Rio Bravo del Norte [the Rio Grande], thus accomplishing the mission of Anthony Butler without the payment of a penny by the United States. Through this shift the land that had been granted to Bangs by Tamaulipas was no longer in that state; it, like his earlier grant, was in Texas, but neither he nor Lundy had any authorization from the government of Texas to settle colonists within its boundary, and Lundy well knew that he, an abolitionist, would never have it.

Discouraged as Bangs was over the turn of affairs, he still had hopes that Texas, if able to maintain its independence, which certainly seemed doubtful, would confirm his grant. Even more

[51] Ogilvy makes this statement in his diary under date of December 25, 1838 (*SWHQ*, XXX [1926], 145), and repeats it, with a full description of the grant, in his letter to Richard Pakenham, New Orleans, August 20, 1839, cited in n. 46.

The MS diary of James Ogilvy (November 25, 1838, to January 20, 1840) was published in installments in *SWHQ*, XXX, 139–155, 219–232, 305–324, as part of the "Diary of Adolphus Sterne," as its editor did not realize until after Vol. XXX was in print that the portion already printed was the work of Ogilvy. Ogilvy died at Sterne's house in Nacogdoches in 1840, and when Sterne, as administrator, went through Ogilvy's papers he was so much impressed with the importance of the diary that he decided to continue it, as he did beginning September 28, 1840 (Vol. XXXI, p. 63).

discouraged was the government of Tamaulipas at seeing a vast stretch of its territory snatched away at one stroke of the pen, but it firmly refused to recognize the claim of Texas and looked forward to the reestablishment of the Nueces as the permanent boundary. In that case Bangs felt sure his grant would stand. As there was nothing he could do to settle the matter, he turned his attention to the establishment of another paper. On August 25, 1836, *El Telescopio de Tamaulipas*, a news sheet, began to appear each Thursday in Victoria.[52]

Not only his grant but his merchandising was suffering from the Texas revolution, as it was difficult, if not impossible, to get shipments through the customhouse at either Tampico or Matamoros without long delays. Mexico was shaken by the outcome of the Texas campaign, but was as unable to accept the situation as it was unprepared to change it. For the whole country the year that followed the battle of San Jacinto was a hard one.

For Bangs it was a tragic year. Yellow fever scourged the region. Before he fully realized the danger, his faithful wife, his solace in all times of trouble, was one of its victims. He laid her body tenderly in the earth of Mexico, which she had loved;[53] but for him it was the end. He must take her children to the United States.

The last issue of *Atalaya* which he supervised was that of March 25, 1837, and with Number 32 on March 30 he suspended publication of *El Telescopio*;[54] the government printing he

[52] A weekly of which the first issue was dated August 25, 1836. No. 6 (September 29, 1836), Yale, photocopy, LMS. Nos. 21 and 28–32 (January 12 and January 26–March 30, 1837) are in the Matamoros Archives, Vol. 25. Photocopy, TxU. Appendix II, No. 347.
[53] In the burial records of the Parish of Santa María of Ciudad Victoria (Vol. III, 1829–1837) there are no entries between February 27 and the end of March, 1837, and no later record of the burial of Suzanne Payne de Bangs, as her name would have been written. Possibly the epidemic carried off the priest and he was not immediately replaced, or the dead were buried in such numbers that no record was attempted.
[54] This issue and also the last of *El Telescopio* are in the Matamoros Archives. Photocopy, TxU.

turned over to Francisco García, a capable Mexican. He sold his household goods, and packed only a few clothes and keepsakes. Then he said farewell to his friends in Victoria and to a country which had regarded him for a decade as an honest and deserving citizen and had been good to him.

He would have to begin again, sometime, somewhere.

FIVE

The Press in the Island City

HE NEW BEGINNING a year later was, by a strange stroke of Fate, on that same low, flat, almost treeless island in the Gulf of Mexico which the young printer had first sighted with great disgust from Mina's brig more than twenty years before. Then he thought it looked "like a piece of prairie that had quarreled with the main land and dissolved partnership," and it had not changed much since, except in name, for it was no longer San Luis but Galveston Island—an anglicized form of the name of the earlier settlement.[1]

At the eastern end, instead of Aury's array of thatched huts,

---

[1] The settlement was named for Bernardo de Gálvez, who was appointed governor of Louisiana in 1776 by the Spanish government. Aury and other corsairs had their headquarters there in 1816, authorized by the insurgent government of Mexico. Lafitte established himself on the island directly after Aury left, and was there from time to time until 1820, when he was notified by the United States government to vacate. (*The Galvestonian*, March 27, 1839, reprinting an article entitled "Name of Galveston," originally published in the *Commercial Intelligencer*).

93

was a customhouse which had been built in 1825 by the Mexican government when it provisionally established a port there.[2] That building had also served two years as a customhouse for the Republic of Texas and one year as a courthouse for Galveston County. Along the harbor front was a row of rough-looking buildings—a hotel, stores, and a blacksmith shop—and behind them were scattered a few poorly constructed frame dwellings suggesting little more of permanence than those of Aury, which had been burned on the departure of the "Commodore." The streets still needed only a shower to convert them into veritable marshes. But now on the wharves were many immigrants with lots of baggage—wagons, plows, horses, guns, and clouds of black servants—all of which gave evidence of Galveston's growing importance as a port of entry for those intending to till the soil of Texas.[3] Across the bay other towns had sprung up, among them the capital city of Houston, which had been named for the victor at San Jacinto, Sam Houston, who at this time was the President of the Republic.

Several matters, but especially the hope of capitalizing on his land grants, had brought Bangs back to Texas. He had clear title to the league of land on the Colorado River, across from the town that was originally named "Mina" but now was "Bastrop," but he had made the discovery through Ogilvy that the field notes to the two-league grant on the Brazos lacked a legal requisite, the signature of the surveyor, Isaac Cummins, and the grant had not been recorded according to the laws of the Republic of Texas. And this after Chambers had taken more than half of the land on the Colorado for securing what he claimed was a "gilt-edged" title to each piece of land! Nor had any progress been made in the matter of securing validation of the Tamaulipas grant to lands now within the borders of Texas, for which he had given Ogilvy authorization in 1836 to act as agent.

The late spring of 1838 found Bangs trying to validate these

---

[2] Mexico, Congress, Decree of October 17, 1825. *Colección de Decretos,* IV, 6.
[3] *The Weekly Picayune* (New Orleans), March 5, 1838. Hereafter cited as *Picayune.*

claims. As a step toward securing title to the land covered by the Tamaulipas grant, he filed suit against Sam Houston, President of Texas, demanding its validation;[4] in this he had the advice and backing of Ogilvy, whom he had met again in New Orleans in 1837. He was also occupied with publishing the prospectus of the Island City's first newspaper, the *Commercial Intelligencer*, which proposed to devote itself to the commercial and agricultural interests of the young republic.[5] With him were two brothers-in-law, George H. and Henry R. French, both newspaper men, with whom his interests were to be closely linked. During his stay in the United States, Bangs had not only placed his boys in school, inspected the presses in Baltimore and New York, and worked on others in Cincinnati and Mobile, but he had also found a young and very clever wife in Caroline H. French, who was to follow from Kentucky as soon as he was settled and had a house for them to live in.

So effective was the prospectus which Bangs issued early in June that the editor of the New Orleans *Weekly Picayune*[6] called the *Intelligencer* to the attention of his readers as the seventh newspaper in Texas, and predicted that, if well conducted, it would be a great public benefit and would be well patronized both in Texas and in the United States. He added that Galveston, which would certainly be for a long time the principal commercial town of the republic, was a most suitable place for the enterprise, and he wished it success. This comment Bangs regarded as a feather in his cap, for the *Picayune* was rapidly becoming the most influential paper in the Southwest.

The second issue of the Galveston paper, which appeared on July 27,[7] announced that the *Commercial Intelligencer* was

[4] Houston, Harris County, 11th Judicial District Court, Book A, which includes the record of filing, could not be located, but Book B (p. 55) records the case of José Manuel Bangs vs. Sam Houston, President; on December 28, 1838, the case was continued; and on p. 89 is the record (May 3, 1839), that leave was granted to amend pleadings.

[5] *Picayune*, June 18, 1838. See Appendix II, No. 348.

[6] *Picayune*, June 18, 1838.

[7] This issue was among the papers of the Texas Historical Society in the

"published weekly by Samuel Bangs for the proprietors," whose names were not given; but that of the editor, John Evans, was known. This issue included poetry, an historical and a biographical article, several columns of anecdotes, the tariff rates of the republic, and a few political documents, including a letter of Mirabeau Lamar, then a candidate for President, in reply to one of J. W. J. Niles and Samuel Whiting suggesting that he was ineligible for office.

The reception accorded the pioneer journal by other editors was very cordial. "A new paper styled the *Commercial Intelligencer* now published in Galveston is printed on an imperial sheet, and its numbers thus far do much credit to its conductors," said the Houston *Telegraph and Texas Register* on July 28 and again on August 11. The *Picayune* announced the arrival of the first number on August 13—"a large and well-conducted paper"; and on October 1 again recommended the *Intelligencer* to those who had business connections in Texas.

It was soon evident, however, that interests other than agriculture and commerce inspired the journalistic enterprise, and that one of the proprietors was Moseley Baker, who was then waging an active campaign for election to the Third Congress of Texas as the representative from Galveston. During the campaign the fact that he had lately cleared off some $32,000 of financial obligations left unpaid when he absconded some years before from Tuscaloosa, Alabama, was made known through the July 23 *Picayune* and quickly copied by Texas papers. The result was much comment unfavorable to the candidate. Especially strong in its denunciation of him was the Houston *Telegraph*, the most influential newspaper then published in Texas. It characterized him editorially as a "fugitive from justice" and as "wholly unworthy to hold any office of profit or trust within the gift of the people of Texas."[8]

After Baker was elected, according to returns which the *In-*

Rosenberg Library, Galveston, but has disappeared. Photocopy at TxU and in library of writer.

[8] *Telegraph and Texas Register*, August 18, 1838. Hereafter cited as *Telegraph*.

telligencer published and the *Telegraph* copied but questioned, the Houston editor, Francis Moore, commented on September 8 that the Galveston paper appeared "to have been upheld wholly for the purpose of securing the election of Moseley Baker." He also charged later that Baker had spent $3,000 on the election and that more than half of the votes were illegal.

The situation thus created was more than distressing to Bangs, for he soon realized that the future of the paper was very uncertain. Even more painful to him was the implication when Moore, in welcoming the first issue of a rival paper, the *Civilian and Galveston Gazette* on October 6, rejoiced that the Island City could at last "claim a respectable public journal." The further exchange of comments between the Houston and Galveston editors, which became both personal and acrimonious, continued to embarrass him. Before Congress met on November 5 the editor of the *Telegraph* recalled that his paper, the oldest in Texas, had been the first to greet and welcome the *Intelligencer*, but that after its editor was found associating with "loafers" he and his brother editors determined to leave him to his fate. "Loafers" was a term applied to men who felt it beneath them to dig and were ashamed to beg, but not borrow. Their means of securing a livelihood consisted of loitering about bars and hotels to meet or make acquaintances who might invite them to a drink. By skillful timing of their appearance they sometimes secured a free lunch of meat, bread, and pickles, which was served at noon to all drinkers. Of these Galveston had more than its share.[9] By November Evans listed himself as "editor and proprietor" and Bangs had bought a lot in Houston[10]—that is, he had accepted the lot in payment of advertising.

Bangs' employer, Moseley Baker, was a thirty-six–year–old Virginian who had edited the Montgomery [Alabama] *Adver-*

[9] *Ibid.*, October 13, 1838. See Sheridan, *Galveston Island or a Few Months off the Coast of Texas: The Journal of Francis C. Sheridan, 1838–1840*, pp. 34–36. Edited by Willis W. Pratt.

[10] Harris County, Deed Records, Book C, October 24, 1838, pp. 132–133 (George Everett to S. Bangs).

tiser and had been speaker of the House of Representatives of that state. After taking "French leave" for Texas, he located his family at San Felipe on the Brazos, and in 1835 bought a league of land on the east shore of Galveston Island.[11] He had personality and a persuasive tongue, which he used both publicly and privately to his own advantage. Before leaving Galveston to serve in the Third Congress, he succeeded in persuading Bangs, who was as honest as the day was long, that there was nothing to the charges afloat against him, and in selling him for $1,350 the lot on which stood not only the printing office and a dwelling, but also a blacksmith shop owned by Charles L. Lewis.[12] But scarcely was the deed recorded when Bangs learned that the name of a Houston newspaper, the *National Banner,* had been changed to the *National Intelligencer,* and that Evans, now the sole proprietor, had gone to Houston. With the Galveston paper in the resulting precarious state, Bangs received word that his wife was on the way and would expect him to meet her in New Orleans. He left the newspaper in charge of his brother-in-law and was in New Orleans by the first of December, expecting to return by the next boat.

This he was unable to do, as his wife was wrecked twice in coming down the Mississippi River and did not arrive until the end of January. The happenings in Texas, so far as his affairs were concerned, while he was fretting in New Orleans over his protracted stay, are recorded in the following diarial jottings of James Ogilvy, the methodical Scotchman to whom he had entrusted the handling of his Tamaulipas grant.[13]

Wednesday, Dec. 12, [1838. Houston]. Conversed with Mr. Royall about the Grant—mentioned the agreement which Mr. Bangs had been drawn into, & Mr. Royall asked what sum I asked, told him I had the offer of one hundred thousand dollars in 1835

---

[11] *The Handbook of Texas,* I, 100–101.
[12] Galveston County, Deed Records, Book A, p. 5. Moseley Baker to Samuel Bangs, November 3, 1838, by John Evans, who held power of attorney.
[13] Ogilvy Diary, *SWHQ,* XXX (1926), 142–145, 219–232, 305–324.

Thursday 13th   Wrote letters to . . . Bangs . . . to go pr "Cuba."

Friday 14th   Wrote to Mr. Bangs enclosing R. Pitkin's receipt for 2 certificates No. 339 and 340 for 640 acres of land; and for a Draft on the Treasury for $233.20.

Thursday 20th   Wrote to . . . Bangs

Tuesday 25th. Christmas day. Mr. W. H. Jack came up to me at the City Hotel and asked to speak with me—took seats on a bench out-side—He enquired what was to be done with Bangs grant? I asked what point he alluded to—the business he put in his, Jack's hands— I told him that I considered any arrangement Mr. Bangs had been drawn into unauthorized by me and consequently null and void in-asmuch as he had no power to make contracts, he having delegated me, irrevocably, to be the active agent of the Grant as far back as March 1836. That he had been deluded into the transaction and had, when he discovered it, declared the agreement with him, Jack, as null and void. He said he did not care for more business than he had, but he did not like to be treated so—that Mr. Bangs came to him and proposed the business—this I did not believe & defended that point by illustration. I told him the suit was foolish in the extreme—that we were not in the same situation as those whose Grants emanated from the Govt. of Coahuila and Texas, whose suits, even, would not get a hearing this Session—that our grant was from the government of Tamaulipas, who might call on us to fulfill soon—and that I did anticipate favorable intelligence on this point pr the Cuba tomorrow or next day.—that I had not spent the last three years in inactivity as to the various views of contending parties and that I felt myself quite competent to manage all the points at issue alone—and if I saw hereafter any necessity for taking the advice of a professional man that I would do so.

Three days later Bangs' suit against Sam Houston was called but, because of his absence, continued.[14] In the meantime Bangs had written Ogilvy, in great distress, that Lewis had taken pos-session of his house in Galveston and that he had asked Mose-ley Baker to have him evicted. Ogilvy noted the steps he took in the matter.

---

[14] Harris County, 11th Judicial District Court, Book B, December 28, 1838, Bangs vs. Houston.

Friday [December] 28. Delivered Gen¹ Moseley Baker's letter from Mr. Bangs to Captain Wright.

Saturday 29.   Wrote answers to Mr. Bangs and to Mr. Leplecher and put the whole under cover to Mr. Bangs.

Wednesday, [January] 9th [1839]. Wrote to Mr. George French respecting Mr. Bangs' house on Galveston Island.

Monday 14—Wrote to . . . Mr. Bangs pr the "Cuba"

Tuesday 15   Spoke to Mr. Evans about Mr. Bangs' house who said that Lewis had taken possession in consequence of a misunderstanding with Reed, and that when Mr. Bangs came there would be no obstruction in the way, but for any other person to begin with pistols and Bowie Knives would be a piece of folly.[15]

One of the things Bangs fretted over while held in New Orleans was that he was thereby prevented from pushing the validation of the Brazos River grant. Finally he placed this business in Ogilvy's hands also.

The lawyer's diary continued:

Jan. 19, 1839   Lent Capt. Bredall all the Powers and contract between Mr. Bangs and myself, to take copies thereof (which he afterwards returned to me)

Monday 21 Jan   Went to the Land Office to meet Mr. Borden on the subject of Mr. Bangs 2 leagues of land on the Brazos—was introduced to a Col. Pierson, who was appointed Surveyor in Sept. 1834. We examined the title and found the plat to be above Webb and Morrow's grant-leagues, and on a survey of old Mr. Robinson, but there being no Surveyor's name to the field notes, and the Title not recognized by any one in that Quarter, it was looked upon as spurious . . .

Saw Gen¹ Chambers on this business, who expressed his sorry [*sic*] at the publicity I was giving to the affair, that as soon as Mr. Bangs came here he would give him the papers and forever after shake his hands clear of him. . . . That the defect in the Titles arose from Mr.

---

[15] Ogilvy Diary, December 28, 1838, to January 15, 1839, *SWHQ*, XXX, 146–221.

Bangs long absence from the country and not being here at the struggle & &—A title that cannot bear the light is not worth saving, and the sooner it is exposed the less trouble will attend it.—

Tuesday 22   Met Capt. Longscope of the "Empresario" who told me Mr. Bangs could not get off this trip from N. O. as his wife had not come down the river yet—that she had been twice wrecked on her way.

Saturday 26 January 1839 Wrote to Mr. Bangs to go pr Empresario.[16]

Thereupon came a letter from Bangs telling Ogilvy that the *Intelligencer* was definitely to be discontinued and asking him to find out whether the editor of the Houston *Telegraph* could use him. It would be hard to have to tell his new wife that he was without work after she had come so far and faced so many difficulties.

Ogilvy's jottings continued.

Feb. 8, 1839. Mr. Fisher told me there were some letters for me in his office—There were—one from Mr. Bangs and a parcel of Papers from D. McLeod. I went immediately in search of Mr. Moore, to get an answer respecting the employing of Mr. Bangs, but did not find him, left a message with Mr. Nicholson on the subject. . . .

Saturday 9th   Spoke to Mr. Moore, who informed me he had a Spanish compositor in his employ, and for the present did not need another— . . . Wrote to Mr. Bangs.

Monday 11   Closed my dispatches . . . to Mr. Bangs at Galveston. Saw Genl. Baker on Mr. Bangs' business—who would do nothing more. . . . Sent off Mr. Bangs' trunk also

Saturday 16th   Wrote to Mr. Bangs enclosing my last letter pr Empresario to him pr Mr. Borden of Nacogdoches

Friday 26th   Wrote Mr. Bangs pr San Jacinto to inform him that Mr. Belden was enquiring after a League of land & said that the late Mr. Rossio's title was dated only the day after Bangs' That a widow was on the land—nevertheless he seemed anxious to buy with all these clogs.

---

[16] *Ibid.*, January 19–26, 1839, pp. 223–224.

Wednesday 27th   Mr. French also came up from Galveston to hunt up Evans for money &

Again Ogilvy busied himself with the title of the land on the Brazos. Bangs was back in Galveston.

Tuesday March 5 1839. Wrote Mr. Bangs and sent down the Title to his Lot in Houston also the Title to his 2 leagues of land on the Brazos pr R. Putnam—Wrote also pr "Friend" stating the above and answering his letter of the 2d Inst just received—

Wednesday 13th March 1839   Wrote Mr. Bangs pr Mr Sandusky— Sent Mr. French's letter to him pr Mr. Hammeken

Thursday 14th   Wrote to Mr. Bangs to send up Title and translation of the 2 leagues on the Brazos.

Friday 15th   Wrote to Mr. Bangs pr "Sam Houston" to send up the translation of the Deed properly executed against tuesday first—Nap and . . . spoke to Genl Chambers who said he had seen Mr. Bangs at Galveston.

Tuesday 19th   Paid the dues on the Land at the Secy of the Treasury's Office—Met Mr. John Teal there, who lives at Tinoxtitlan & sold some land to Webb or Morrow—Knows the tract granted to Mr. Bangs. Showed him the title and agreed to exchange ideas when I came to his house.

Friday 29th March 1839   Crossed the Brazos at Tenoxtitlan and proceeded toward Franklin the County Seat of Robertson County reached that at sunset—Called at the County Clerk's Office—engaged a person to record Mr. Bangs' deed. This produced great excitement in the town.

Tuesday Apr. 2   Heard of Isaac Cummings intended departure set off in pursuit immediately & overtook him he recollected all about running the lines of Bangs 2 leagues. Had the original letter of Genl Chambers respecting the survey in his possession would look for it until next time we meet . . . Offered his best services in the matter . . . Proceeded to Washington . . . Waited on Mr. Hemphill and conversed on the subject of Mr. Bangs titles

Saturday April 6th 1839   Wrote Mr. Bangs after seeing Genl Chambers who said he had got an order from the Comr of the Land Office for the delivery of the original of Bangs titles in said office—which he expected to recover soon—I told him the object of my trip to Franklin & Made a proposal to Mr. Bangs about his 2 Leagues of land.

Sunday 7th   Wrote to Mr. Bangs to say I had sent the Title pr "the Rufus Putnam" in charge of the clerk[17]

On his tardy arrival in Galveston with his wife, Bangs found, as Ogilvy had reported, that his house was occupied by Charles Lewis and that John Belden was indeed interested in acquiring the land on the Colorado. This interest grew out of the belief that the new capital of the Republic would be established at a piont on that river only thirty miles above Bastrop. Population was moving westward, and land values were soaring. Bastrop itself was on the main route between Houston and the proposed capital, and also on a post road from San Antonio to Nacogdoches. On this, Bangs' land faced. The future of the town and the surrounding region seemed assured.

Bangs' interests—in contrast with Belden's—centered in the coastal cities of Galveston and Houston. He had heard only vague rumors of the proposed location of the new capital, and besides he needed money. As Belden was insistent, an agreement was soon reached. On March 4, Bangs parted with his Colorado league for a price stated as $5,000 in New Orleans money. Of this amount he received only $100 in cash and a Galveston City lot (Lot 8, Blk. 124) valued at $1,500; the balance was secured by notes—one for $150 payable in a month and another for $1,000 payable in eight months; the third was for $2,250 payable in two years; and all were to bear 6½ per cent interest. In this deed his new wife, Caroline, joined.[18]

With these securities in hand, Bangs bought a printing press and the necessary equipment for a printing office from J. W. J.

---

[17] *Ibid.*, February 8 to April 7, 1839, pp. 227–231, 306–314.
[18] Samuel Bangs to John Belden, March 4, 1839, in Bastrop County Deed Records, Book C, pp. 84–85.

Niles,[19] who had been publishing a paper at Matagorda but was at that time establishing himself at Houston; he had there secured a contract for the government printing and was starting a new paper.

By this time Galveston was sixteen months old and had grown rapidly both in area and in population. It now boasted some 2,000 inhabitants and around 250 houses sprinkled over more than two square miles, parts of which were still rising "above the reach of overflow." It looked "something like a lawyer's blank before the filling up," but gave an idea of the "prophetic spirit of enterprise among its founders."

It had two wharves, a courthouse, a new customhouse, a jail, a naval station, and an arsenal. Near the wharves were several large warehouses and lumber yards; and close by were over a dozen general retail stores, in addition to a market, a drug store, a confectionery, a fruit store, a bakery, and several oyster houses.

For the accommodation of both residents and visitors there were two hotels already finished and doing a flourishing business, and three larger ones under construction. One of the first group was the "Marine," which was formerly the steamer *Warsaw*; on its main deck guests were accommodated and in the hold merchandise was stored; the other was the "Galveston," which occupied the lower floor of the old Custom House. Within easy reach were also six licensed taverns or coffee houses, a number of boarding houses, some private homes which accepted temporary guests, and a hospital for the incapacitated. Tailors, dressmakers, milliners, cordwainers (shoemakers), and barbers ministered to the personal appearance of the citizens, while a wide variety of artisans engaged in the construction and repair of everything from watches and trinkets to ships and buildings.

Consuls, lawyers, doctors, notaries public, magistrates, and printers had their offices in or near the business center.

For those not interested in taking advantage of Galveston's reading rooms, Grignon's Dancing Academy offered entertain-

[19] Samuel Bangs to Henry R. French, November 14, 1840, in Galveston County, Deed Records, Book A, p. 651.

ment and instruction to both adults and children; and Charles I. Cummens was proposing to establish a Classical Academy for the instruction of the youth of the city.[20]

For communication with the outside world four boats were plying regularly between Galveston and New Orleans. Others came irregularly; an English boat with cargo had arrived, and German boats were not infrequent. Four boats were running between Galveston and Houston—one, the *Sam Houston* with T. W. Chambers as master, made two trips a week.

Toward the end of March two advertisements—one dated March 18, offering for sale the press on which the *Intelligencer* was formerly printed, and the other announcing that Evans had disposed of his interest in the paper and requested settlement of all accounts—appeared in a new and "trifling little paper"[21] called the *Galvestonian* and priced at "one bit." It was edited by "Plain John" Gladwin; and, although of rather small dimensions, evinced, in the opinion of the editor of the *Picayune*, "a good degree of talent, spirit, and industry."[22] In it Mrs. Bangs made her journalistic debut in Texas under the pseudonym of "Cora" by offering suggestions on how religious services might be regularly maintained even without a minister. It was the intention of Gladwin to issue it tri-weekly and to devote its pages, not to foreign news, but to matter derived from "Texian journals and correspondence and from the editor's pen."[23] "Plain John" was also a printer and a friend of Bangs, whose press he utilized. The office of the *Galvestonian* was at the old Custom House (late Court House) above the Galveston Hotel. Bangs had by this time regained possession of his house, and had filed suit against Lewis for damages. The case was tried at the May, 1839, term of the court, but the jury disagreed and the case was continued.[24]

---

[20] *Galvestonian*, I, No. 2, March 27, 1839. Appendix II, No. 349.
[21] *The Morning Star*, Houston, Texas, April 15, 1839.
[22] *Picayune*, April 8, 1839.
[23] *Galvestonian*, I, No. 2, March 27, 1839.
[24] Galveston County, District Court, Minutes of 1839–1840, Book A (May, 1839 Term), p. 6.

Pioneer Printer

The early issues of the *Galvestonian* were favorably regarded by most editors, many of whom reprinted extensively from its columns, as the *Galvestonian* already had done from the demised *Intelligencer*; and for seven months the subscription list continued to lengthen, in spite of uncomplimentary remarks about its editor and his publication as "a miserable excuse for a paper" by the *Morning Star* in Houston.[25] During this period Bangs engaged in book and job printing and assisted Gladwin in various ways.

The future of the little paper was first seriously threatened when Gladwin died in October,[26] and repeatedly during the period in which the editorial chair was held by his successor, Henry R. French. In spite of the uncertainty of its future, in March, 1840, the *Galvestonian* became a daily, the first in Galveston, and within the next two weeks the demand necessitated the printing of over a hundred more copies daily,[27] the printing being now entirely the work of Bangs. Such success was brief, as in April a new paper, *The Courier,* began publication[28] and soon managed to secure the official printing of the county, thereby reducing the *Galvestonian's* income considerably. Bangs' generally optimistic spirit was for the moment further depressed when, through the absence of his attorney, his case against Sam Houston was dismissed by the Houston court. This action closed conclusively that legal avenue to his Rio Grande land title.[29]

Besides, to his dismay, he found that Henry French could not command the respect of other editors. The *Picayune* contented itself with reporting in a bantering tone that when the 1840 New Year's ball was in prospect Editor French had been able to borrow a pair of dress shoes for the occasion, but was unable to raise

[25] *Morning Star* (Houston), May 8, 1839.
[26] *Telegraph*, October 30, 1839.
[27] *Galvestonian*, April 4, 1840. Issues of April 3–4, 1840, are at the Library of Congress. Photocopies at TxU.
[28] *Austin City Gazette*, May 6, 1840.
[29] Harris County, Minutes of the 11th Judicial District Court, Book B (May 9 and 12, 1840), pp. 278, 284.

enough from his subscribers to buy a ticket.[30] Others were by no means so mild. The Houston *Weekly Times*, in particular, did not mince words about him. "The poor fellow down at the Island," its editor, Augustus Tompkins, wrote, "owed his education to no one, not even himself, for he never had one; his head was always like a piece of steel; common sense could not be beat into it."[31] The same editor reported that French had once been found asleep in a wheelbarrow, and on another occasion under an old work bench on the prairie—implying a drunken condition —and that he had been taken home and put to bed by the assistant editor of the *Times*, who was on a visit to Galveston.[32] Shortly afterward the publication of the *Galvestonian* was suspended, but French still had a "light heart and a thin pair of 'Oh, no, we never mention 'ems'" and "calculated" on "coming up with renewed vigor." In the meantime he went into the horned-frog business.[33]

Bangs, an entirely different type of man, needed the newspaper work, as job printing alone did not provide an adequate living for his family. Ogilvy had died, leaving the Tamaulipas grant pending;[34] but Bangs still cherished hope that a way would be found to secure confirmation. While waiting the outcome of his damage suit against Lewis, he sold half of the lot on which his house stood;[35] then to avoid any personal difficulties with Lewis, he bought a lot on the Strand for a home and another from the Galveston Company as an investment.[36] It was fortunate that he moved, for Lewis had no hesitation about shoot-

[30] *Picayune*, January 13, 1840.
[31] *The Weekly Times* (Houston), April 30, 1840.
[32] *Ibid.*, June 4, 1840.
[33] *Picayune*, June 29, 1840.
[34] "Ogilvy died some time ago," wrote Sterne in his diary entry of September 28, 1840, at the same time referring to a shipment Ogilvy had made on April 30 (*SWHQ*, XXXI, 63).
[35] Galveston County, Deed Records, Book A, p. 286.
[36] Galveston City Company to Bangs, Lot 8, Blk. 732, and Lot 11, Blk. 436, February 10, 1840, Galveston County, Deed Records, Book F, p. 619.

ing a man.[37] Bangs' suit against him for damages was not tried again until October 12 of that year; the verdict then rendered assessed Bangs' damages at $1,983.83, which Lewis was ordered to pay.[38]

During the summer the *Galvestonian* had been brought to life through the sale by French of a half-interest to David Davis, but Bangs saw little future for himself as its printer. Several months before the suit against Lewis was finally tried he had relocated in Houston to become the printer of a small but "spirited and independent" tri-weekly called *The Musquito*, and the "agent of the proprietor" of a job printing shop at "No 12 Congress Street, below Main." This paper, which borrowed its title from a Mexico City publication similar in size, contained some "pretty good articles" and was, on the whole, cordially received. The editor of the *Telegraph*, however, felt some misgivings about it from the first. "The neat little sheet styled the *Musquito* made its appearance in this city last Sunday, edited by G. H. French," he wrote on July 15. "The *Musquito* buzzed about quite harmlessly on its first appearance, but if we are not mistaken in the animal it will show its sting before many weeks." In contrast the *Picayune* enthusiastically called it "one of the most witty and spirited little prints read for a long time. . . . We'll exchange; you're the only *Musquito* we ever saw that was worth anything."[39] Such an exchange was a distinct compliment, for the *Picayune* had for some time declined exchanges with other southwestern newspapers.

After the Lewis suit was settled Bangs, who planned to remain in Houston, sold to Henry French, still busy with the publication of the *Galvestonian*, its Washington-type printing press and equipment, the half-lot on which the office stood, and his home on the Strand. In lieu of the specified price of $1,000, he had

[37] *Picayune*, April 20, 1840.
[38] Galveston County, District Court, Minutes, 1840–1843, Book B, p. 33.
[39] *Picayune*, October 5, 1840. Appendix II, No. 356.

French give him a general power of attorney covering all this property, but he did not immediately record it.[40]

As the year 1840 closed, all was going well with Texas, the city of Houston, the *Musquito*, and Bangs, who was now writing humorous poems and articles for the little paper. Subscriptions were increasing; property was being rapidly improved; and better order prevailed in both the city and the Republic. But the New Year brought a shock to both editor and printer. The "Honorable" A. B. Shelby, who presided over the district court in Galveston and acted in a like capacity in Houston, had been in the habit of dealing pretty rigidly with those guilty of disrespect toward either. As a penalty for some animadversions upon the Houston court which the *Musquito* had published on January 6, 1841, its editor was fined a thousand dollars and sentenced to a year in jail. French was arrested and lodged in the county jail, where he would have had to serve out the specified time had not a friend interposed. Through the intercession of Thomas Johnson he was brought into court on January 8. After having "purged · himself of the contempt heretofore offered the court," as the judge expressed it, by an explanation and apology, he was ordered released and the fine remitted. Only a few days later the same judge imposed a fine of two hundred dollars and a sentence of ten days in jail upon the pro-tem editor of the Galveston *Courier*, who had published an editorial on "His Honor." This aroused the Galveston public, who demanded a reversal, and imprisonment was stricken from the penalty.[41] The two cases served to call to public attention the weakness of Texas law which permitted a district judge, without recourse to a jury, to assess such penalties. "His Honor," however, did not long enjoy such a privilege. In the *Musquito* of February 10 French an-

---

[40] Galveston County, Deed Records, Book A, p. 651.

[41] Harris County, Minutes of the 11th Judicial District Court, Book C (January 1, 1841–May 24, 1842), pp. 27–28, 45. *Telegraph,* January 15, 1841, quoting from the *Morning Star; Picayune,* September 28, October 5, 1840, and January 25, 1841.

nounced, with much pleasure, that Judge Shelby had been replaced by "Colonel Johnson."

News from Galveston was also disconcerting. Henry French had made no payment on the press or the property, and the future of the *Galvestonian* was seriously imperiled by the appearance of another daily, *The Morning Herald*.[42] The upshot of the matter was that by the end of March, 1841, both George French and Bangs were back in the Island City, where French took over the editorship of the *Galvestonian,* while Bangs announced himself as its "Printer, Publisher, and Proprietor,"[43] and Mrs. Bangs became a contributor, under the pseudonym she had earlier used, "Cora." To these 1841 issues of the *Daily Galvestonian* Bangs gave the same volume and issue numbers that the *Galvestonian* of 1839, an irregular tri-weekly, had carried. On May 8 he began to publish the *Weekly Galvestonian and Ladies Saturday Evening Visiter* [*sic*]; this included a story by "Cora," the prospectus of the *Daily Galvestonian,* and an advertisement of Bangs' printing office. "With regret" it announced the demise of the spicy little *Herald,* to which Henry French had transferred his services. Under him, on that paper, Bangs' two boys, James and Samuel, were introduced to printing.[44]

Up to this time Bangs had felt that Texas had been advancing in every respect. During the three-year administration of Lamar as President the Republic had been recognized by the United States, England, France, and Holland; favorable treaties had been signed with various other powers; badly needed loans had been effected; Mexico had been kept at bay; and the nation had become respected abroad.[45]

But as Lamar's term of office drew to a close in 1841, conditions began to change drastically. By September, when Houston

---

[42] *Picayune,* December 7, 1840. S. S. Callender was the editor.

[43] Issues of Vol. I, Nos. 2–3. Vol. I, No. 3, has a story by "Cora." Issues of March 31 and April 1, 1841, are at the Library of Congress; photocopies at TxU.

[44] Issues of May, 1841, TxU. Letter of F. R. French, Woodward, Oklahoma, to *Galveston News,* February 6, 1910.

[45] *Picayune,* May 3, 1841.

was again elected, business was dull and money scarce; credit was dead; politics were running high; the weather in Galveston was excessively hot; mosquitoes were plentiful; and many people felt their condition was quite unendurable.[46] Even before the campaign reached its climax two more of Galveston's newspapers—the *Courier* and the *People's Advocate*—had ceased to exist, but a new *Intelligencer* supporting Burnet had been established with A. J. Yates as its editor.[47] The *Galvestonian*, supporting Houston, survived; and, after only a brief suspension in December, Henry French was added as coeditor of what was claimed to be "the largest daily paper in Texas."[48] Bangs still owned and printed it.

With the opening of 1842 a definite rift between Bangs and his brother-in-law Henry became evident. On January 3 Bangs recorded the power of attorney Henry had given him in 1840, and exercised it by deeding to his own son James the property he had earlier deeded to Henry.[49] In the document he merely stated that he had the authority to make such a conveyance "as the said Henry R. French [had] not complied with his agreement verbally entered into as a man of honor with Mr. Samuel Bangs." The *Galvestonian* continued, but without the services of Henry, who announced, through the advertising columns of the paper on February 28, that he had "cut the business of catering for the literary tastes of his friends" and had "taken up the more agreeable one of providing for their appetites."[50] He had, in fact, opened a confectionery in a "shanty" at No. 3 Tremont Street, and Bangs ceased to have further journalistic dealings with him.

George French remained with the *Galvestonian* as editor, and early in the year married Catherine Crosby, an attractive girl from Mobile. In view of the claim that Henry still asserted to the

---

[46] *Ibid.*, September 13, 1841.
[47] *Telegraph*, July 21, 1841.
[48] *Daily Galvestonian*, December 6, 1841.
[49] Samuel Bangs to James Bangs, January 15, 1842, press and property in Galveston County, Deed Records, Book B-2, p. 120.
[50] *Daily Galvestonian*, February 28, 1842.

Galvestonian, a change in name was found expedient. After another brief suspension, extending from March 21 to April 10, it reappeared on April 11, 1842, as the *Daily News,* and advertisements which had been given to the *Galvestonian* in October, November, January, February, and March and carried the printer's symbol *tf* ("till forbidden" or "until further notice") were continued in the April 19 issue of the *News.*[51] The relationship between the two papers is well established not only by the fact that the two papers had the same editor and by the continuance of the same advertisements, but by a half-column advertisement in the *News* of the *Daily* and the *Weekly Tribune* of New York, then being published by Horace Greeley and Thomas McEmrath [McElrath], the latter the McElrath with whom Bangs had been associated in the Methodist Book Concern. In the columns of the *Daily News* Bangs announced himself as book, job, and newspaper printer, and gave the location of his shop as the *"Galvestonian* office on the Strand." In another advertisement "To Printers," Samuel Bangs offered for sale a good screw press and an iron printing press with type and stands, all very little used. In the same column appeared a "Public Notice" signed by José Manuel Bangs, which had been inserted in the *Galvestonian* on February 1; in it he revoked all powers of attorney authorizing anyone to represent him in the Republic of Texas in the matter of a grant of land made him by the state of Tamaulipas; this he described as "situated on the east side of the Rio Grande, embracing a portion of the salt lake." The seventeenth issue of the *News* (Saturday, April 30, 1842) also carried the advertisement of Bangs' printing office—the same as that of the *Galvestonian*—on the Strand.

In the meantime the capture of San Antonio by a Mexican army had stirred the whole Republic. Houston, on assuming office, had advocated peaceful tactics with the Indians, rigid

[51] *The Daily News,* April 19, 1842 (No. 8), is regarded as the earliest extant issue. Original in the office of the *Galveston News;* facsimile in possession of the writer. A study of the *tf's* shows that many of the ads were dated months earlier than April 11. Appendix II, No. 352.

economy, and moderation in dealing with Mexico, as the empty Texas treasury made an invasion of that country impossible. Now a Mexican army was *in* Texas! The response was swift; hundreds of men volunteered; but before they were organized the Mexicans withdrew across the Rio Grande. Congress then authorized Houston to act, but because of lack of funds he refused to consider a war. Such a state of affairs, with Texas left at the mercy of Mexico, made the blood of many a citizen boil.

Among these was Bangs. He could not justify Houston's attitude. Neither was he in sympathy with the editorial policy of French in the *Daily News,* although he continued to share his shop with him for eight dollars a month and to rent him the use of a press for four dollars.[52] To give voice to his opposition he established a paper of his own, the *Commercial Chronicle,* which he both edited and published. In size it corresponded with the lately demised *Intelligencer,* which Yates had been publishing; but the *Chronicle* carried more reading matter. Its office was at the "East end of Church Street," where he also did job printing. His policy he stated clearly at the outset.

The course we shall pursue in political matters will be such an [*sic*] one as to give no offence [*sic*] to those to whom we are opposed, while it shall be directed with an eye to the interests of the great mass of the people. As we esteem it the duty of every good citizen to sustain the Executive in all cases where he conceives his policy to be founded on right and justice, we shall always be found ready to support such of his measures as are calculated to benefit the people; and, on the contrary, we shall express our disapprobation of any and all measures which are calculated to oppose or conflict with their rights.

As our name implies, we shall *chronicle* all matters of commercial interest, and care will be paid to the selection of such matter as we shall deem important and amusing, toward the accomplishment of our undertaking.

Local matters which tend to the benefit, instruction or amusement

---

[52] Ben C. Stuart, "History of Texas Newspapers," p. 37, unpublished MS in the Rosenberg Library, Galveston. While not, as a whole, reliable, some facts are correct. See *Galveston Daily News,* April 11, 1917.

of our patrons, will be carefully noted and all communications of general interest will receive due consideration.

This statement was carried by the *Telegraph*, whose editor added a few lines indicative of the regard in which Bangs was generally held. Moore remarked that although Bangs was commencing his new editorial career "in the dullest of dull times," he seemed well aware of the difficulties to be faced; and that if industry, perseverance, and unremitting application could ensure success, he would eventually surmount every obstacle. The *Telegraph* heartily wished him success.[53] Even Houston supporters were pleasant to him. The *Red-Lander* mildly commented that he "bangs away at every measure of 'Old Sam's' just as the member from North Carolina opposed every measure advocated by his colleague; and when asked his reason for so doing, he replied, 'It is enough for me to tell my constituents . . . that I spoke and voted against every bill that he supported.'—You had best save your squibbs, old fellow."[54]

Before the sixth number of the *Chronicle* was off the press another Mexican army had invaded San Antonio and captured some of its leading citizens. Three hundred mounted men rushed to its defense and within a week the Mexicans had begun to retreat, but not before they had battled with a small group trying to join the defenders. And still Houston organized no retaliatory army!

With excitement over the situation still running high, a tropical storm swept Galveston. The wind played havoc with buildings in every part of the island, and the combined force of wind and water swept the margin of the bay. Water stood three to four feet deep in the Tremont Hotel and extended a quarter of a mile further. Two churches, the Episcopal and the Catholic, were blown down. Nearly half of the Strand was more or less destroyed. Some of the stores were torn to pieces; others simply floated to a new landing. The cotton press was nearly destroyed;

[53] *Telegraph*, August 10, 1842.
[54] *The Red-Lander* (San Augustine), September 8, 1842.

the "Social Hall" of José Arce floated away; not a vestige was left of Matossy and Soussan's restaurant; Benedict's shoe store was damaged by water; the houses adjacent to the García store were blown to pieces and the roofs of many others were lifted off; a large number of boats were grounded. The loss of property was over $50,000, but there was no loss of life. After the water receded, the region of the Strand was so unhealthful that congestive fever caused several deaths, and bilious fever was general. Fortunately the upper or eastern portion of the city remained entirely clean and healthful,[55] and among the residents of that section was the Bangs family, which gave refuge to friends for several weeks. Through it all every issue of the *Chronicle* appeared according to schedule and gave to the world the detailed story of the happenings on the island.

While the debris was being cleared away and buildings were being returned to their original sites, the first issue of the *Texas Times* appeared in Galveston. Only the title was new. Since September, 1840, there had been printed at San Luis, a town on a small island near the western end of Galveston Island, a newspaper called the *San Luis Advocate*, which had been edited by unusually competent men and was favorably known for its scholarly historical articles.[56] Among these, in installments from November 11, 1840, to February 5, 1841, was the story of the Mina Expedition, based on Robinson's account and the tales of survivors, among whom Bangs and his assistant were mentioned. As the location of San Luis did not favor news gathering, the projected removal of the weekly to Galveston was announced by the *Telegraph* on March 30, 1842. The owner and editor was Ferdinand Pinkard, a capable and well-educated man, who had been "one of the nabobs in the flush times at Vicksburg." The *Times* was about the size of the *Civilian*, but as much of the paper was printed in small type, it offered more reading matter. The first eleven weekly issues of the *Times* printed in Galveston,

[55] *Telegraph,* October 5 and 12, 1842, reprinting from the *Chronicle.*
[56] Twenty-four scattered issues of Vol. I (1840–1841) of the *Advocate* are at TxU. See also "The old newspapers," *Galveston News,* February 17, 1878.

which completed the first volume of the *Advocate*, were offered gratis to new subscribers. In policy the paper was independent.[57] With the *Civilian*, the *Commercial Chronicle* and the *Texas Times* each publishing from one to six issues a week, the *Daily News* found, in less than a year,[58] that competition was too stiff and finally suspended publication. For Bangs business had been good, as the *News*, as well as the *Chronicle* and the *Times*, were issued from his presses. In the spring of 1843, after a lengthy suspension, George French sold the *News* to Michael Cronican, and, with G. L. Hamlin, took charge of the *Texas Times*, as Pinkard was planning to join an expedition to Yucatán, then in a state of revolt against the Mexican government.[59] French's connection with the *Times* proved brief; he was stricken with yellow fever and died. The last issue of that paper that he published (Volume II, No. 17) was dated April 22;[60] and the *News*, when it resumed publication under the new management, was generally regarded as its successor. With the discontinuance of the *Times*, Bangs leased to Cronican, and later his partner, Wilbur Cherry, the press and type he had formerly leased to French.[61] In the death of that gentleman Bangs lost a business associate whom he respected and a brother-in-law who had been a much loved member of his own family.

The Yankee printer's voice was not the only one raised against the Houston administration. The series of expeditions of Texans against Mexico and the treatment accorded the men who fell into Mexican hands inspired many anti-Houston protests. Letters from members of the Santa Fe Expedition, who were driven like animals overland from New Mexico to Perote, brought tales of suffering, starvation, and torture which aroused cries for ven-

[57] *Telegraph*, October 19, 1842. A clear copy of the prospectus of the *Times* is in its issue of December 14, 1842.
[58] MS (undated), p. 13, in Dyer Collection, Rosenberg Library, Galveston, says first *News* lived a year.
[59] *Texas Times*, March 11, 1843 (II, No. 11).
[60] *Handbook of Texas*, I, 647.
[61] Stuart, "History of Texas Newspapers," MS, pp. 34, 37. See *Galveston Daily News*, April 11, 1917.

CANCION PATRIOTICA

, al desembarcar el general Mina y sus tropas en la Barra de Santandér, compuso Joaquin Infante, auditét de la division.

Acabad, Mexicanos,
De romper las cadenas
Con que infames tiranos
Redoblan vuestras penas.

De tierras diferentes
Venimos á ayudaros
Y á defender valientes
Derechos los mas caros.
En vuestra insurreccion
Todo republicano
Toma gustoso accion,
Quiere daros la mano.
Acabad, &c.

Mina está à la cabeza
De un cuerpo ausiliador :
El guiará vuestra empresa
Al colmo del honor.
Si Españoles serviles
Aumentan vuestros males,
Tambien hay liberales
Que os dén lauros á miles.
Acabad, &c.

Venid, pues, Mexicanos
A nuestros batallones :
Seamos todos hermanos
Bajo iguales pendones.
Forzad con noble zaña
Ese yugo insolente
Que os impone la España
Tan indebidamente.
Acabad, &c.

Nuestra gloria ciframos
En que seais exâltados :
Veros, pues, procuramos
Libres y emancipados.
De nuestros sacrificios
No queremos mas premio :
Los sucesos propicios
Serán, si hacemos gremio.
Acabad, &c.

Abajo los partidos
Y toda vil pasion :
Estando siempre unidos
Formarémos nacion.
Independencia, gloria,
Religion, libertad,
Gravense en vuestra historia
Por una eternidad.
Acabad, &c.

Los mozos, los ancianos,
Las mugeres tambien
Esfuerzos sobre-humanos
Hagan hoy por su bien.
Y si los opresores
No huyeren arredrados,
Por vuestros defensores
Serán esterminados.
Acabad, &c.

oto la Marina 1817. SAMUEL BANGS, impresor de la division ausiliar de la republica mexicana.

1. A patriotic song—printed on landing on the Mexican coast.

DON XAVIER MINA, GENERAL EN

GEFE DE LA DIVISION AUSILIAR DE LA REPUBLICA MEXICANA.

Soldados españoles del rey Fernando,

Si la fascinacion os hace instrumentos de las pasiones de un mal menores ó de sus agentes, un *** patriota vuestro que ha con agrado *** mas preciosos dias al bien de la patria viene á desengañaros s.. otro interes que el de la verdad y la justicia.

Fernando, despues de los sacrificios que los Españoles le prodigaron, oprimo á la España con mas furor que los Franceses cuando la invadieron. Los hombres que mas trabajaron por su restauracion y por la libertad de ese ingrato, arrestran hoy cadenas, estan sumidos en calabozos ó huyen de su crueldad. Sirviendo, pues, á tal principe, servis al tirano de vuestra nacion; y ayudando á sus agentes en el Nuevo-Mundo, os degradais hasta constituiros verdugos de un pueblo inocente victima de mayor crueldad por iguales principios que los que distinguieron al pueblo español en su mas gloriosa epoca.

Soldados americanos del rey Fernando,

Si la fuerza os mantiene en la esclavitud y hace que obligueis á seguir en ella á vuestros hermanos, tiempo es de que salgais de tan vergonzoso estado. Un esfuerzo ahora basta a a sacudir el yugo que os encorva y realizaros á la dignidad de hombres de que estais privados ha *** siglos. U i *** vosotros que venimos á libraros sin mas fin que la gloria que rodea la de las generaciones. El suelo que os vio que poseeis, no debe ser eternamente el patrimonio del despotismo y de la rapacidad. No interrumpais la carrera de vuestros destinos. Si perdeis esta ocasion, contrariais á las miras de la Providencia que os proporciona en ella la mejor coyuntura para cambiar vuestra suerte con y miseria en elevacion y prosperidad ¡ Que triste experiencia teneis de la metrópoli y que dolorosas lecciones habeis recibido de los malos Españoles que para oprobio de los buenos han venido hasta aqui á sujuzgaros ó á enriquecerse á costa vuestra!

Si entre vosotros hay quienes abanderizados con ellos, hacen causa comun para oprimiros por cobardia, interes ó ambicion, abandonadlos, detestadlos y aún destruidlos. Son peores que los tiranos principales á quienes se juzan; pues degeneran de su naturaleza y sacrifican sus mas sagrados deberes á tan rastreras pasiones.

Soldados españoles y americanos,

Dejad á esos viles caudillos y acudid con nosotros al campo del honor donde tremola el lucido estandarte de la libertad. Vosotros sereis felices contribuyendo á la emancipacion de este pais ; y los laureles que ceñirán vuestras cienes en defensa de la mas justa causa, seran un premio inmarchitable superior á todos los tesoros.

Cuartel-general de Soto la Marina á 18 de mayo de 1817.

XAVIER MINA.

2.   A Proclamation of Mina issued at Soto la Marina.

HABITANTES DE LAS QUATRO PRO-

INCIAS DE ORIENTE DE ESTA AMERICA SEPTENTRIONAL: Vuestro Comandante General y efe superior politico acaba de recibir noticias de oficio, de que el Coronel Don Agustin de Yturbide que andaba una corta division cerca de la Costa de Acapulco, ha concebido el anti-constitucional proyecto de irar la Independencia de esta America, para separarla de lo demas de la Monarquía Española, comenzando is operaciones por apoderarse de un comboy de platas y efectos.

El solemne juramento que hemos prestado de ser fieles á la Constitucion de la Monarquía, al Rey, y á s leyes que nos goviernan, ahora mas que nunca grita en nuestros oydos, la precisa obligacion en que esta- os constituidos de no faltar á el, de mantenernos firmes y fieles subditos de tan desgraciado como virtuo- Monarca, y de acreditar con nuestros hechos el ser unos verdaderos ciudadanos Españoles, iguales, y uidos á nuestros hermanos los Europeos dependientes de la misma nacion y Monarquia.

Estas Provincias que tengo el honor de mandar, me han acreditado en el tiempo mas critico de la revolu- on pasada, su docilidad al Govierno y á las leyes, su decidido patriotismo por la justa causa, su grande frimiento en medio de las mayores escaceses, y su imponderable valor para pelear contra los enemigos del ey y de la Nacion: Estas virtudes nos condujeron á la mas perfecta felicidad; por que cuando las mas de s poblaciones de las Provincias de afuera se vieron saqueadas, muchas de ellas reducidas a cenizas, destruidas is Haciendas, talados todos sus campos, y llenos de sangre y de cadaveres; en nuestros terrenos disfrutaba- os de una perfecta paz y tranquilidad, hasta en terminos de transitar por los caminos despoblados hombres sarmados, y mugeres sin siquiera un niño que las acompañase. ¿Y será posible, que no sean suficientes tos datos tan verdaderos para quedar convencidos de lo dañosa y perjudicial que es una revolucion? No eo que vosotros cerreis los ojos á unas verdades tan claras y manifiestas, y por lo mismo estoy cierto, y con segura confianza y satisfaccion de que desechareis todo mal pensamiento, y sugestion que os indusca á pararos de vuestros deberes. Pues qualquiera que con perversidad entente alterar el orden y tranquili- id de vuestras familias, Domicilios, y Poblaciones, será refrenado y contenido en su deber por las legiti- as autoridades: y estas deben contar siempre con que hallarán en su Gefe Superior quien á todo trance roteja y sostenga las providencias que dicten y practiquen de conformidad con la Ley.

Si la Revolucion llegare á aproximarse á las fronteras de nuestros terrenos, que es muy dificil por las ctivas providencias que está tomando el Govierno, no os dé cuidado; que el mismo que os exorta, sabrá)nerse al frente de las tropas, y salir á libertaros de su furor. Monterrey 13 de Marzo de 1821.

Joaquin de Arredondo.

3. Arredondo announces the defection of Iturbide.

D JOAQUIN DE ARREDONDO MIOÑO PELE

GRIN, Bravo de HOYOS Y VENERO, CABALLERO DE LA ORDEN DE CALATRAVA, BR
GADIER DE LOS EXERCITOS NACIONALES, GOBERNADOR, COMANDANTE GENERAL Y GEF
SUPERIOR POLITICO, DE LAS QUATRO PROVINCIAS INTERNAS DE ORIENTE EN ESTA AME
RICA SEPTENTRIONAL, GENERAL EN GEFE DEL DE OPERACION EN ELLAS, SUB INSPECTO
DE SUS TROPAS, Y SUB DELEGADO GENERAL DE CORREOS EN LAS MISMAS, &c. &c.

EL Sr. Coronel Don Agustin de Yturbide Primer Gefe del Exercito Ympe

rial con fecha de 20 de Junio proximo pasado en la Hacienda del Colorado se há ser

vido expedir la Circular que sigue :

Estando probado por los *Economistas* politicos, y demostrado por la experiencia que el recargo d
contribuciones publicas, sobre los efectos de Comercio, y de la Yndustria, al paso que entorpecen el gire
y progresos de estos dos importantes ramos de prosperidad, no producen al fondo nacional el aumento qu
con el quiere darsele, sino que por el contrario lo empobrece, y aniquila ; y siendo justo que desde ahor
comienze el Pueblo à sentir los beneficios justos de su Yndependencia, con el alivio de las exhort
tantes pensiones que lo gravan, he tenido por conveniente, que interin las Cortes Mexicanas establece
el sistema de Hacienda que en adelante haie regir, queden abolidos los derechos de subvencion tempora
y contribucion directa de guerra : el de comisoy : el de diez por ciento, sobre el valor, y alquiler de casa
el de sisa ; cuyo nombre solo horroriza, y da idea de su arbitrariedad ; y en una palabra todos aquello
impuestos estraordinarios con que el Govierno de Mexico, ha oprimido al Reyno en estos ultimos di
años ; quedando reducido el de Alcabala al seis por ciento, con cuya proporcion se cobraba antes de co
menzada la rebulucion. Ya advertira V. S que al dictar esta providencia, no me anima otro espirit
que el de la felicidad general, à cuyo servicio me he dedicado ; y espero que penetrado V. S. de igu
les sentimientos, ejercitará su zelo, y patriotismo haciendo que con la mayor rapidez, se circule y ejec
te para que sin demora experimente la Provincia de su cargo el alivio que deseo proporcionarle con ell
Dios guarde à V. S muchos años.=Hacienda del Colorado 20 de Junio de 1821.=Es copia.=Yturbid
Es copia.=Echavarri."

Y a fin de no retardar en las Provincias de mi cargo tan benefica y util de

terminacion, mando se publique por Bando en esta Capital y en los demas Ciudad

Villas y Lugares de la comprehension de este territorio, dirijiendose los correspo

dientes exemplares a los Gefes y demas autoridades para su cumplimiento y observa

cia. Dado en Monterrey a 27 Julio de 1821.

Joaquin de Arredondo.

Por mandado de S. S.

4. Arredondo's last official act—the publication of a Circular of
   Iturbide.

LOS CAPITULADOS

DE ZARAGOZA.

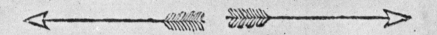

DESARMADOS.

POR EL

§R CORONEL DON FELIPE DE LA GARZA

GOBERNADOR DEL NUEVO SANTANDER.

Y

OBLIGADOS A

EMBARCARSE POR TAMPICO

Ymprenta de la Comandancia General.

Saltillo Año de 1822. Segundo de la Yndependencia del Ymperio.

5. Title page of the first pamphlet Bangs printed in Saltillo.

Sôr: D.or D.n Servando Mier.

Saltillo Julio 13.822

Mi benerado Padre y Sôr. de mi
respeto: desde que V.S. se separó de nosotros
Quando la expedición de Mina, no ha
via tenido noticia de su paradero hasta
ahora con certeza), cuya noticia ha sido
para mi de mucha Complacencia), de
cuyo incomparable gusto é fuerso esta
para demostrarle mi gratitud, siempre
reconocida à la que V.S. me manifesta-
va desde que fui su impresor

Yo me hayo bueno
en esta Villa desde hace tres meses
Que bine con el Comand.te Gral.

6. First and last pages of Bangs' letter in which he explains his change
   of name.

Vicente Allen, su hermano, y dador de esta, ó por el Correo.

Dios Nuestro Señor Guarde la importante Vida de V.S. m.
años, para Consuelo de este extrangero, pues hasta lo pide su Afecto. S.
Q. Atento B.S.M.U.

Samuel Bangs

Participo á V.S. que me llamo
Manuel, para que me ponga en la
Cubierta de la Carta. Este fué el
Nombre q.e me pusieron en el Bautismo. lo pide Samuel, y S.r q.e haú me
conoció V.S.

HABITANTES DE LAS QUATRO PROVINCI.

Quando os dirijó la palabra, quisiera mas bien poder manifestaros mi corazon; para que siend╱
╲otros testigos de los sentimientos que lo animan, el lo fuese, teniendo parte en cada uno de los lugares de mi interino m
del gozo en que os contemplo inundados al recivo de esta.

Los habitantes de la populosa Mejico, juntos con el Ejercito que la guarnece, levantaron por fin la barrera que del
parandonos para siempre de la esclavitud ó de una bien temida anarquia, evitar que la divergencia de opiniones nos simese c
ciadamente en una guerra destructora. Si caros compatriotas, aquellos hombres decididos y valientes, han obligado en
modo á que empuñe el cetro aquella mano misma que con asombro del mundo supo manejar la espada en favor nuestro.
mismo acabo de resibir por medio de un extraordinario esta feliz nueva; y quando repasaba con plaser las muestras de re
échas por tan feliz acontesimiento en la capital del Imperio, se me presentó el Ylustre Ayuntamiento, oficialidad cuerpo de en
dos, clero, vecindario y pueblo todo de esta villa, con quienes recordando los acaecimientos todos ocurridos desde Iguala ó
drid, lo que somos, a quien lo devemos, y el estado actual de la Nacion, proclamamos por nuestro Emperador al grande
tin, jurando al mismo tiempo sostener sus derechos.

La satisfaccion de comunicaros tal noticia es mia, resta que me deis la de solemnisarla como se merese y vosotros se
empero sin abandonar las hueyas que nos ha enseñado nuestro Libertador, y sin olvidar que la union y nuestra obedienc
el taliman de la felicidad. Espero que ninguno de vosotros querrá ser el ultimo en decir poniendo á la voca por interprete
pecho, viva la sagrada Religion cristiana, vivan las Cortes Mexicanas, viva, viva viva nuestro Emperador Agustin Pri╱
Saltillo 27 de Mayo de 1822, Segundo de la Independencia.

7. A Proclamation announcing Iturbide's assumption of imperial
power.

PROCLAMA
DE S M. EL EMPERADOR
AL EXERCITO TRIGARANTE.

SOLDADOS Trigarantes: nunca os dirigiera la palabra con mas necesidad ni con mayor importancia que cuando se empeñó en extraviaros de la senda del bien y cuando la Patria se interesa grandemente en el acierto de vuestros pasos. Yo estoy seguro de la rectitud de vuestras intenciones, y os amo cordialmente como á hijos los mas beneméritos, porque vosotros cambiáis momentaneamente y sin estragos el gobierno español en mexicano, haciendo Independiente nuestro suelo, del dominio extrangero; porque sois los primeros Soldados del mundo, que sabeis reunir al furor en la batalla, la compasion con el vencido y débil, á la fortaleza la generosidad; porque soy testigo de vuestra resignacion en las privaciones y fatigas. Os amo finalmente, que me amais, y porque siempre habeis unido gustosos vuestra suerte con la mia.

Si, Soldados, mi suerte y la vuestra estan hoy intimamente unidas á la de la Patria: las desgracias de ésta, son nuestras, en su prosperidad y bienes, tendrémos la mejor parte; porque nadie nos quitará la gloria de haberla dado libertad, consolidado el gobierno que deseaba y precavidola de males incalculables, á costa de sacrificios y fatigas, que sabrá apreciar la posteridad.

Soldados: libertasteis por dos veces á la Pátria de la anarquía; estais en el caso y obligacion de hacerlo la tercera. La division en los pueblos es causa precisa de su desolacion; esto es lo que procura el gobierno español para dominarnos de nuevo, esto es por lo mismo, lo que mas cuidadosamente debemos evitar. Sabed que las intrigas inhumanas y astutas del gabinete Madrid, son causas de las guerras intestinas de Buenos-Aires, aunque la España no haya sacado otro fruto que el triste sacrificio de cien mil hombres. El mismo empeño tienen en Columbia, y en el Perú: sepámos, pues, en México frustrar sus miras, imitando el carácter firme y constante de los Chilenos.

Mi voz debe ser para vosotros el norte mas seguro. He llegado á la última dignidad (aunque contra mi voluntad y deseo;) no tengo á que aspirar, y por lo tanto no necesito hacer escala de cadaveres, como otros quieren para subir. Acordaos que siempre os dirigí á la victoria, siempre en favor de la Patria, siempre por el camino del bien, y siempre evitando la efusion de sangre, porque para mi es de mucha estima la de cualquier hombre.

Sabeis que cuando algunos representantes del pueblo, extraviados en el Santuario mismo de las leyes, á tiempo que trababais de establecer la representacion nacional, os llamaban carga pesada, é insoportable, asesinos pagados, y se empeñaban hacer desaparecer el ejército, yo fuí quien lo sostubo á todo trance, y lo sostube porque vuestros servicios inestimables os hacian acredores á ello, y porque era preciso para conservar nuestra Independencia, precaver las convulciones interiores y consolidar nuestro gobierno en su mismo establecimiento. Considerad con atenta circunspeccion la conducta y las operaciones de los que os hablan, que es lo que tienen que perder, y á lo que pueden aspirar, y esta regla os será muy útil para evitar el engaño.

Finalmente, Soldados, tened presentes vuestros juramentos, la denominacion de trigarantes os los recuerdan. Debeis tener la Religion cristiana, mantener la Independencia de nuestro pais, y conservar la Union entre sus habitantes. Jurasteis tambien mantener la Monarquía moderada constitucional, por que así es conforme al voto unánime de los pueblos del Septentrion.

Yo estoy ligado con iguales juramentos, los hice en Iguala, y los he ratificado solemnemente ante el Dios de la verdad, á la mayor efusion de mi corazon, por que estoy plenamente convencido de haberlo hecho con la mayor justicia y necesidad. Me vereis siempre á vuestro lado para desempeñar mis deberes, por los cuales haré sacrificio gustoso de mi comodidad, de mi reposo, y de mi existencia: ni un Padre anciano, mucho hijos tiernos, ni una esposa amable, ni cosa alguna me servirá de obstáculo para obrar conforme á mis principios; por el contrario, en todas esas caras prendas de la naturaleza, descubre mi honor nuevos estímulos. No salga de vuestros labios, ni se aparte de vuestros corazones el deseo de sacrificaros conmigo, si es preciso, por la Religion Santa que profesamos, por la libertad de nuestra Patria, por la Union y órden entre todos sus habitantes y por la Monarquía moderada constitucional, pues que así lo jurasteis, así es conveniente, y ésta es la voluntad de la Nacion. México 11 de Febrero de 1823.

AGUSTIN.

Reimpreso en el Saltillo á 22 de Febrero de 1823. Imprenta de la Comandancia General de Oriente. José Manuel Bangs, Impresor.

8. Iturbide's last appeal to his army for support.

EL SUPREMO PODER EJECUTIVO
DE LA NACION
A SUS COMPATRIOTAS.

LA Patria se presenta con dignidad segunda vez á ocupar el lugar que le corresponde entre las má grandes naciones. Si algunos momentos se vio esclavizada; si sirvió á los Estados que la rodean d objeto de desprecio, de ridiculés ó de compasion, pasaron esos dias aciagos, y hoy da un ejemplo qu no tiene semejante en las historias antiguas y modernas.

La reaccion contra la tirania jamas ha sido tan pronta, tan activa y tan eficaz como en nuestr suelo. No bien acababa de asomar la cabeza esta espantosa hidra cuando fue sepultada para siempr por vuestros heroicos esfuerzos. Los dignos gefes que han dirigido la gloriosa empresa de nuestra l bertad, no han hecho mas que aprovecharse de vuestras virtudes para lograrla Una mano opresor atentó contra vuestra Representacion nacianal; pero aun no bien habia cometido el crimen; cuando distéis el condigno castigo. El Santuario de las leyes aparece entre vosotros Los Representantes d la Nacion ocupan las sillas de donde los arrojára el despotismo Ellos ejercen sus funciones en vuestr beneficio con entera y absoluta libertad en medio de un ejército protector los que asegura: su prime ensayo ha sido encomendarnos el ejercicio del Poder Ejecutivo, si acaso se han engañado en la ilu tracion y aptitud de los individuos, han acertado ciertamente en el patriotismo y deseo de vuestra fel cidad de que abundan.

Reimpreso en el Saltillo á 20 de Abril de 1823, Tercero de nuestra Independen cia y Segunda de la Libertad. José Manuel Bangs, Impresor.

---

9. Address of the Supreme Executive Power to the nation, 1823. Heading, closing, and imprint.

INFORME

Que la Comision Permanente, dio a la Junta de Diputados para el Congreso Constitucional en 'a sesion de 23 del corriente, sobre las credenciales de los Ciudadanos Diputados Eleno de Vargas, y Dr. Jose Eustaquio Fernandez, segun lo acordado en la sesion de 14 del mismo.

————◆◁◯◯▷◆————

C UMPLIENDO la Comision permanente con el encargo del articulo 94 de la Constitucion del Estado, ecsaminó las credenciales de los Ciudadanos Eleno de Vargas, y Dr. Josè Eustaquio Fernandez, nombrados Diputados por los partidos de Palmillas y Escandon. En la primera se vee que los Electores de Infantes no concurrieron á la Junta de partido, y este defecto vuelve nulo el acto; pues era necesaria su concurrencia y votacion, à menos que constase imposibilidad de hacerlo. Es tambien notorio

Imprenta del Gobierno del Estado,

Dirigida por José Manuel Bangs.

10. Decoration of the imprint of an *Informe* of 1827.

[*Tom. 1.*]   [*No. 1*]

GAZETA CONSTITUCIONAL DE COAHUILTEJAS.

*El buen juicio forma á los hombres capaces, y
amor propio es el viento que soplando las velas co
duce el bajel al puerto.* =Max. de Nap.

LEONA-VICARIO, JUEVES 3 DE SEPTIEMBRE DE 1829.

CONGRESO DEL ESTADO.

*Sesion del dia 31 de Agosto de 1829. Presidencia
del Sr. Balmaceda.*

El H. Congreso del Estado, convocado á sesiones extraordinarias para acordar las providencias que sean conducentes á fin de cooperar á la comun defenza de la república, que nuevamente se haya invadida por sus antiguos opresores los españoles, ha dispuesto la publicacion semanaria de esta gazeta con el principal objeto de comunicar á todos los pueblos del Estado los partes oficiales que se recivan, incertando igualmente las providencias que se dicten por parte de sus respectivas autoridades, por las demas de la federacion, y por las supremas de la union, dando lugar por último entre sus columnas, á las proclamas, comunicados ó cualesquiera otras producciones incertas en los periodicos que hoy circulan y que deben contribuir á formar el espiritu público de la nacion, y esté la fuerza moral de ella que la ha de hacer inespugnable contra todos sus agresores.

SECRETARIA DE GUERRA Y MARINA.—SECCION 1.ᵃ

Division de operaciones de la cuarta seccion de Veracruz.

Escmo Sr.=El 31 del pasado julio á las cuatro de la tarde llegó el enemigo en número de tres mil da con direccion á esta fortaleza, segun se le tei prevenido, y despues de haberle hecho al espresa enemigo un destrozo de mas de 300 hombres, y e tre ellos, segun dice el ya citado prisionero, fué m erto el general en gefe Isidro Barradas : el enemi en el resto del dia permaneció en aquel citio, echa do al agua sus muertos y levantando sus heridos seis lanchas cañoneras que le ausiliavan por el m A las seis y media de la tarde se me dió parte por oficial de la guerrilla, que estaba á su vista, de q el referido enemigo continuaba su marcha por el p citado paso, y que debia ir á salir á Tampico el A ó Pueblo Viejo, yo replegué mis fuerzas á la forta za, porque presumí ser atacado en la noche,tanto p los de tierra, como por siete belas que inmedia mente aparecieron en el mar, y hasta esta hora hallan situadas frente á la barra, y muy poco fue de los tiros nuestros. El citado enemigo hasta e hora se halla situado en Tampico el Alto en el atr de la Iglesia, y yo le he puesto para que le incomo en retaguardia una partida de 250 caballos para q lo hostilize en cuanto sea posible, no siéndome a quible volver á tomar la retaguardia que abando el enemigo por tener que estar organizando la fu za batida, pues su mayor número consta de gei bisoña, por ser cívica. En la madrugada del 2, i puesto de las posisiones que guarda el enemigo, d puse trasladarme con toda la fuerza à este punto c lo mas de la fuerza que está á mis órdenes, y es m ó menos de 800 hombres, de ellos 300 permanent y el resto de milicia civica, dejando guarnecid los baluartes con 60 infantes, y yo á la vista con indicada fuerza, pareciéndome mas oportuno la m dida tomada para conservar la defensa de este inter

---

11. Heading of the first issue of the *Gazeta Constitucional de Coahuiltejas.*

ORDNANZAS

MUNICIPALES

PARA

EL GOBIERNO Y MANEJO IN-
TERIOR, DEL AYUNTAMIENTO
DE LA CIUDAD DE

SAN ANTONIO DE BEJAR.

1829.

CIUDAD DE LEONA VICARIO.
~~renta del Supremo Gobierno del Estado,
á cargo del C. J. Manuel Bangs.

12. *Municipal Ordinances governing the City of San Antonio.* Title page.

Gobierno Supremo

DEL ESTADO LIBRE DE

COAHUILA Y TEJAS.

El Gobernador del Estado de Coahuila y Tejas á todos sus habitantes, SABED que el Congreso del mismo Estado há decretado lo siguiente.

Decreto Numero 112.

El congreso Constitucional del Estado libre, independiente y soberano de Coahuila y Tejas, ha tenido á bien decretar lo siguiente:

Se declara ciudadano Coahuiltejano á José Manuel Bangs, natural de los Estados Unidos del Norte América.

Lo tendrá entendido el Gobernador del Estado para su cumplimiento, haciendolo imprimir publicár y circulár. Dado en la Ciudad de Leona Vicario à 15 de Enero de 1830 — Jose Maria Balmaceda, *Presidente.*—Ignacio Sendejas, *D. Secretario.*—Vicente Valdez, *D. Secretario.*

Por tanto mando se imprima, publique, circúle, y se le dé el debido cumplimiento. Ciudad de Leona Vicario, 15 de Enero de 1830

José Maria Viesca.

Santiago del Valle
Secretario.

13. Bangs made a citizen of the state of Coahuila and Texas.

LA CATORCENA JUDITH PIENSA HACER VIDA PRIVADA.

...TIMA CONSERVACION QUE TUBIERON EN CATORCE JUANA Y PASCUALA, QUE ESCRIBIO UN CURIOSO QUE LAS ESTUBO OYENDO.

---

cuala. HEMOS quedado preciosas
Todo lo que hablamos Juana
Anda con letra de molde
Leyendose por la plaza;
Y tambien nos representan
En sus tertulias las Damas :
¿Que curioso, ó que demonio
Escucharia nuestra parla
Que no á faltado una letra?
na. Lo que yo siento Pascuala
Es que esté tan enojado
Por aquello de las naguas
Que oficiosa le ofresiste
A D. Vicente Miránda.
cuala. Le suplico me perdone
Yo se lo dije por chanza.
Mas antes que conversemos
Observa querida hermana
Si nos hoye algun soplon
Que interprete las palabras.
na. Solo miro á Betancourt
Que está parado en la plaza
Atisbando lo que dicen.
Callate por Dios Pascuala;
Mas yá se vá calle abajo
Habla cuanto te de gana.
cuala. ¿Con que estaremos seguras?
na. No nos escucha ni una alma.
cuala. Pues hoye: muchos impresos
Han venido esta semana.
El Mechoacano y el Sol
Como una calandria cantan.
Los impresos de Agualulco
Y de Morelia retratan
A Vicentillo Romero
Con sus pelos y sus lanzas
Este á hecho formal renuncia
(Dios sabe con cuantas ancias)
De el poder ejecutivo
Por qué le han benido ganas
De hacer en lo subsecivo
Una vida muy privada.
Se le admitió la renuncia
Pero han sido desechadas
Las justas iniciativas
Que pedian se castigara

Al delincuente Romero;
Mas tenemos esperanzas
El que oigan nuestros clamores
Las camaras soberanas
Que con arreglo al articulo
Treinta y ocho, parte cuarta
De la carta federal
Se le debe formar causa
A Romero, pues es justo
Sus crimenes satisfaga,
Si acaso para el las leyes
No se buelven telarañas.
Juana. Si para hayá me lo dejas
Hechame aca lo que falta.
¡No estas mirándo á Victoria?
¡Ya no vimos á Zavala.
Ellos salen desdorados
Pero á nadie se desplata.
Pascuala. Allá biene Betancourt,
Silencio, silencio Juana.
Juana. A imitacion de Romero
Voy hacer vida privada:
Al Jordan pienso marcharme,
Y alli al compas de sus aguas
Cantaré con triste plectro
De mi pátria las desgracias.
Me haré amiga de los dioses
Cargaré la hermosa aljava
Sirviendole por los montes.
A la casadora diana.
Las hijas de Mnemosine
Que dulces arietas cantan
Al compaz de el suave ruido
De la Hiprocrene y Castalia,
Las haré mis compañeras;
Y las Nayades y Driadas
Harán todo mi consuelo
En consorcio con las gracias.
Caliope me inspirará
Y cantaré con la flauta
De Euterpe en Epico estilo
De un grande Heroe las azañas.
Pascuala. No entiendo Mitelogia,
Hablame mas claro Juana.
Juana. Quiero decirte que voy
A hacer vida solitaria
Para componer un poema;
Y si acaso no me engaña

Mi amor propio, le hade dar
Grandes zelos á la Iliada.
Y si la escucha Voltaire
Se mudará con su Henriada
A esconderse en el averno.
Pascuala. ¿No podrás decir hermana
Como se hade titular?
Juana. Se nombra la Romeriana.
Pascuala. Luego Romero es el Heroe.
Juana. Esa es una verdad clara:
Algo cantaré de Sousa
De Villanueva y Oajaca,
De Garcia, de Betancourt
Y otros que mi pluma guarda,
Pascuala. Quieres que te dé una regla
Para que tu puema salga,
Algun tanto razonable?
Juana. Yo lo apreciaré Pascuala.
Pascuala. No eleves mucho el estilo
Si de cera son tus alas,
Que el Icaro Potosino
Ha dado una grande caida,
Ni cantes *risco tramonto*
Que ese lenguage se usaba
Allá en la *epoca altanera*
En que Gongora cantaba,
A medio buelo y al grano
Economia en las palabras,
Consicion en los conceptos
Exprecion sencilla y clara.
Si en tu poema figurares
De Santiago alguna dama,
No quieras que sea hechisera
Pues los encantos se husaban
Cuando Tasso escrivió la
Jerusalen Libertada.
Cual el Heroe, tal el poeta
Dicen por hay las muchachas
Y yo quiero hacer ver
Que este adagio las engaña,
Ya no quiero detenerte
Ve á disponer de tu casa,
Y en tu solitaria vida
Acuerdate de Pascula.
Juana. Pues dale el último habrazo
A tu fina amiga Juana.

El Curioso,

CIUDAD DE LEONA VICARIO 1820.

Impreso en la imprenta del Supremo Gobierno de este Estado, á cargo del C. José Manuel Bangs.

14. Bangs issues satirical poetry with a political slant.

INSTRUCCION

FORMADA PARA MINISTRAR

LA VACUNA.

*Como único preservativo del contagio de las viruelas, y
en defecto de su fluido inocular con el pus de esta;
del modo de conocer y distinguir las cali-
dades de las naturales, y el metodo de
curarlas.*

REIMPRESA POR DISPOSICION DEL HONORABLE CON-
GRESO DE COAHUILA Y TEJAS, A COSTA DE
LOS FONDOS PUBLICOS PARA REPARTIRLA
GRATIS EN TODO EL ESTADO.

1830.

CIUDAD DE LEONA VICARIO.

Imprenta del Estado, á cargo del C. J. M. Bangs

15. *Instructions for administering vaccine against smallpox.* Title page.

geance. The capture of the members of the Matamoros Expedition and George Fischer added new coals to the fire. The "black bean" treatment applied to those in the Mier Expedition inflamed the hearts of even the most indifferent, but not until July, 1843, was there a promise of an armistice which would, for a time at least, put an end to further invasions from Mexico without notice.[62] But Bangs' persistent demands for adequate defense and for action against Mexico won for him many firm friends.

His career as editor and publisher, though marked throughout by a kindly personal feeling toward him by all, was not without incident. In the early summer of 1843, an extremely dull season, the *Chronicle* was suspended for a time, but on August 1 publication was resumed in the form of an Extra—a single sheet, printed on both sides. Its immediate purpose was to discredit President Sam Houston, who had declared E. W. Moore, the Commander of the Texas navy, an outlaw who had engaged in a piratical cruise and who had also accused Moore of flagrant disobedience of orders. Bangs and many citizens of Galveston resented this action—the Navy meant more than a defense to them—and arranged a dinner in honor of the "disobedient" Commander and his officers. The address in which Moore refuted the charges against him was printed in full in the Extra, as was also the statement of James Morgan, who was one of the commissioners Houston had sent to New Orleans to convey his orders to Moore. The various toasts offered, including one by Bangs to Dr. Levi Jones, the president of the organization which sponsored the dinner, were also included.

In this issue Bangs took occasion to call attention to the change in the title of the *Chronicle* from "Commercial" to "Independent," as his paper was entirely independent of party affiliation or influence. At that time he planned to issue, during the next few weeks, similar "Extras" which would "embrace the most important matters of the day." Later, after private business (in

[62] *Proclamation* of Sam Houston, July 29, 1843. Original in the Huntington Library, San Marino, California. See Texas, Republic.

which he was then engaged) was transacted, he planned to reappear on a firmer foundation and "as formerly, fearlessly and independently, to advocate the rights and echo the voice of the people." In this same issue he called attention to the fact that his office, although "somewhat out of the business way"—he was then at the east end of Church Street—was well supplied with materials for job printing and for both book and pamphlet work "in the neatest manner and at the lowest possible prices."[63]

With the circulation of this Extra, which carried both volume and issue number, it seemed that Texas was experiencing an "age of resurrection," at least as far as newspapers were concerned. The Houston *Telegraph* reported the revival of the *Chronicle* without reference to the change in name, and added that the defunct *Times* seemed to be "embodied in the form of the *News*."[64]

In the prospectus of the *Independent Chronicle*, which was still being carried in the issue of October 15, Bangs announced himself as editor, printer, publisher, and proprietor, and clearly set forth his policy in the opening paragraphs.

The undersigned proposes to establish *permanently* in the City of Galveston, a Weekly Family News-Paper, to be styled the *Independent Chronicle*, being rather a continuation of the "Commercial Chronicle," the publication of which was suspended only for a time; to be devoted to Politics, Literature, Commerce and Arts. The leading feature in our political department, will be a *firm* and *decided* stand against the prominent measures and policy of the present administration; believing, that from a *fair* and *impartial* presentation of *facts*, without personal or rancourous abuse of party, that we will be able to convince an honest and intelligent People, that such measures and such policy, are not only in opposition to the best interests of our country, but subversive of the fundamental principles on which our government is founded.

Our columns shall be open, at all times, for well written Comuni-

[63] See *Extra*, August 1, 1843. Vol. I, 2nd Qta., No. 1. By Samuel Bangs, Galveston. Editor, Publisher and Proprietor. AAS. Appendix II, No. 353.

[64] *Telegraph*, August 9, 1843.

cations, in which the public good may be concerned; and our controversies shall be conducted in a courteous and temperate manner.

In the mechanical part of our paper, no exertion shall be wanting to make it, at least in appearance, equal to any of its contemporaries; and to the merchant, business man and general reader, the *Chronicle* shall be both useful and entertaining. And in conclusion we ask only of a generous public, a portion of that patronage, to which they may think we are justly entitled.[65]

The contents of this issue are representative of Bangs' idea of the "useful and entertaining." In the "Poetry" section are two poems, one written expressly for this paper—"The Lock of Hair" —which is signed "Cora"; the other is based on the line "Wherefore should I fear in the days of evil" from the *Psalms*. The "History of the Mina Expedition" was in course of installment publication, as it had been in the *San Luis Advocate* in 1840. In the narrative here presented, Mina was advancing in 1817 from the Valle de Maíz to San Luis Potosí, a critical march. On the editorial page, the date is given as October 16; the motto of the paper as "Go ahead—Never give up the Ship." At the head of the editorial column is a "full rigg'd ship, under a press of sail," bearing the motto "Conquer or Sink for Lone Star, the People's Rights and our Navy." "To Correspondents" he courteously makes known the reasons for the nonappearance of some of their communications. "Truth being a libel" in the state of society then, he declines "Sketches of Characters in Galveston," although it "possesses wit and perchance some truth." While he cannot offer his columns to the author of "A Political Squib," as it is of too personal a nature and too full of errors, he suggests that if the author would give to the study of "grammer and authography" [*sic*] as much attention as he had spent on satire and abuse, he would be a wiser if not a better man. He then discusses a report in the *Civilian* that a naval expedition was in preparation at Veracruz. There is a modest reference to a letter from General Thomas Green complimenting him on his edi-

---

[65] *Independent Chronicle*, Vol. I, 2nd Qta., No. 8, October 15, 1843.

torials for "the country's weal" and wishing him success. Under "Communications" is one entitled "The Yucatan Message," written expressly for the *Independent Chronicle* and signed "Crito," but beside the heading in Bangs' clear handwriting is the notation "By D. G. Burnet." Another, signed "Texas" on "The Proclamation and our poor Prisoners" was also written expressly for this paper. Under "Extracts" is news from Victoria of Mexican traders; a report on the crops, the weather, and the price of whiskey; a brief excerpt from Senator Benton's description of the Columbia River Valley; and an item on British influence abroad, especially the British attitude toward Texas. At the end of official notices and other advertisements is Bangs' own, as "book, job and newspaper printer." At this "Office East end of Church Street," he is prepared to print "at the lowest possible rates, for cash or trade," such items as customhouse blanks, bill heads, auction bills, "phamphlets" [*sic*], bills of lading, business cards, magistrates' blanks, steamboat bills, and checks, "&.&.&." The last page quotes the rates of insurance at New Orleans to Texas and foreign ports, rates of passage and freight from that city to Texas points, the prospectus of *The News* of Galveston and of the *Western Advocate* at Austin, the tariff of the Republic, a list of the "Post Towns" and the distance of each from the capital, a Proclamation of the President concerning martial law between the Frio and the Nueces Rivers, and the "ad" of a "fashionable hairdresser and barber" who keeps in stock "a choice collection of Perfumery, Chewing Tobacco and Spanish Segars," and of John P. Davie, "a coppersmith, tin plate and sheet iron worker and stove dealer." In the prospectus of the *News*, which had been inserted on August 9, is the statement that that paper was then on such a permanent basis that on October 1 it would change from a semi- to a tri-weekly. Among the fillers are a notice of custom-house blanks for sale at the *Chronicle* office, reminders of job printing neatly done there, and of the location, for the convenience of his patrons, of his Advertisement and Communication Box at the Fulton House, care of Mr. G. H. Kidd, where copies of the *Chronicle* could be obtained "on application at the bar, every Monday evening, price 12½ cents." A few proofreader's corrections, in the hand of Bangs, are in the margin, as are his fingerprints.

Realizing that many Texans were at heart with him, Bangs continued his attacks throughout the next year on the administration policies, and could smile at some of the editorial darts, such as those of the *Red-Lander*, directed at him. Typical was one in 1843 when its editor, who had not seen a copy of Bangs' paper in some time, noticed the change in title.

The *Independent Chronicle* is the title of a new weekly journal commenced in Galveston by Samuel Bangs, Esqr., Editor, Printer, Publisher, and Proprietor. The *Chronicle* promises that "the leading feature in its political department will be a *firm* and *decided* stand against the prominent measures of the present administration!"

Now that is an awful sentence. Shocking!—positively shocking! As a travelling John Bull declared to be the manners of all the foreigners he saw in making the tour of Europe. The man of the "Chronicle" has got a full rigg'd ship, under a press of sail, at his mast head, as a signal that he is a champion for the Navy and Com. Moore and ready to *Bang* daylight out of the President if he persists in his pacific policy.

Though he has got the "wrong Bull by the horns" Bangs is nevertheless "a right down clever fellow—but his wife is the smartest of the two." At least so said their old friend Ogilvy. . . .

We wish him success; partly because we have an idea that he is a bit of an old salt; for all of whom we have a kindly sympathy, and partly because we don't believe he will do any harm.[66]

Early in 1844 the *Red-Lander* was lamenting that the *Independent Chronicle* was "banging down everything . . . calculated to promote the interests of the country. What a pity it is that his [Bangs'] enthusiasm is not accompanied with a discretion and sense of propriety consonant with the dignity of the station he has assumed. He is a good fellow, but suffers his passions to get the better of him."[67]

[66] *Red-Lander*, October 7, 1843.
[67] *Ibid.*, January 13, 1844.

121

By February the *Chronicle* ceased to be "Independent" and resumed its original title—the *Commercial Chronicle*. By that time Bangs was generally recognized in Galveston and in the press as "The Commodore," and the *Chronicle* was known as a "small lively, humorously edited sheet" which went in strongly for the Navy in particular and for patriotism and the Constitution in general.[68]

The ship at full mast was still prominently displayed at the head of the editorial column!

[68] *The Northern Standard,* Clarksville, February 10, 1844.

SIX

Between the Nueces and the Rio Grande del Norte

HE ANNEXATION of Texas was the main topic of the press and of general discussion in Texas, the South, and many other sections of the United States during the year 1845, for it was widely believed that such a step would entail war with Mexico. After the Congress of the United States passed a bill in February providing for such action and the retiring President signed it, orders were issued to General Zachary Taylor to place his troops in a state of readiness to defend Texas. In July, following a favorable vote on annexation by both the Congress of Texas and a convention called to consider the matter, he was ordered to proceed to Texas and there place his army in position for such action as circumstances might render advisable. By the end of that month he and a part of his troops were on the Texas coast, prepared to establish an encampment west of the Nueces River, which Mexico still insisted was the western boundary of Texas.

On the bay at the mouth of that river was a small settlement known as Corpus Christi, which had served as a point of departure for traders bound for northern Mexico, but after the Mexican invasions of San Antonio the place had been almost abandoned.[1] With annexation looming, early in 1845 it began to improve, and by May some fifty families had gathered there, about thirty houses and stores were completed and occupied, and trade with northern Mexico was reopened.[2]

From the moment that United States troops arrived at that site, annexation was generally regarded in Texas as accomplished; in the United States more and more eyes were turned toward the Mexican border; and representatives of the press from various parts of the United States began to gather in Texas. Almost overnight the comparatively unsettled border regions of the Republic became the scene of action. Federal troops and supply trains en route overland from St. Louis to Corpus Christi blazed trails through vast uninhabited stretches and established camps in somnolent villages peopled sometimes entirely by Mexicans.

Throughout 1845 Bangs watched with great interest the steps leading to annexation, and, in spite of the repeated disappointments[3] he had experienced in the past, saw for himself a brighter future. By August his plans were taking form, and shortly afterward he was in Corpus Christi looking over the situation. He found the place enjoying unprecedented prosperity. The number of troops was increasing daily; a regular steam packet was running between that port and Galveston carrying United States mail; four to six vessels were arriving daily; and their cargoes were finding a ready sale.[4] He was easily convinced that a good newspaper would not lack for subscribers, but he needed local backing. This he secured by forming a partnership with George

[1] *Telegraph,* April 10, 1844.
[2] *Telegraph,* May 14, 1845.
[3] On February 10, 1845, Bangs released to the estate of John Belden eight Galveston City lots which had been transferred to him as security for the unpaid balance due on the Bastrop County land on the Colorado River (Galveston, Deed Records, Book E, p. 112).
[4] *Telegraph,* December 24, 1845.

124

W. Fletcher, a Corpus Christi physician, and engaging José de Alba, one of the most influential members of the Spanish-speaking colony, to edit the paper he proposed to publish. Back in Galveston in November, he placed the *Chronicle* in the hands of B. F. Neal, formerly an editor of the *Galveston News*, who at once began the publication of the *Daily Globe and Galveston Commercial Chronicle*. Owned and published by Samuel Bangs and Company, the *Globe* was a "neat little sheet," somewhat smaller than the Houston *Morning Star*, but its editorial department, as the *Telegraph* kindly remarked, "displayed a considerable degree of talent."[5]

Bangs then appeared before the Board of Land Commissioners of Galveston County, proved that he was entitled to a grant of land by the Republic, and was awarded, on December 1, 1845, a Galveston County land grant for 1,280 acres. Through the sale of this certificate, which he transferred immediately to Charles Frisbee for cash,[6] he was able to have a new press and the necessary equipment shipped to Corpus Christi.

The prospectus of the projected paper announced that it would be both useful and entertaining and that it would devote its columns to the interests of the army and the region about Corpus Christi. A summary of the foreign, political, and commercial news was promised, as was strict neutrality in politics.[7]

On Thursday, January 1, 1846, the "most western journal in the English language on the American continent"[8] came into existence on soil still vigorously claimed by Mexico. Its slogan was

[5] *Telegraph*, November 19, 1845; La Grange *Intelligencer*, November 25; *Red-Lander*, December 11, 1845.

[6] The land, situated in Pleasant Valley on a branch of the Colorado River about 140 miles north from the City of San Antonio, was not surveyed until March 16, 1847. (Texas, General Land Office, File No. 164, Bexar County 2nd Class. TLO.)

[7] The *Texas Democrat* was still carrying this prospectus on May 6, 1846.

[8] Much of the following account of the *Corpus Christi Gazette* was included in my article "The Anglo-Saxon Press in Mexico, 1846–1848" in the *American Historical Review*, XXXVIII (October, 1932), 20–31. Appendix II, No. 357.

"Be sure you are right, then go ahead." This first war newspaper, the *Corpus Christi Gazette*,[9] was no "two-by-four" paper, but an imperial sheet with four pages to the issue.[10] The type was new and good; woodcuts adorned the advertisements; and the whole paper bore evidence of the hand of an experienced printer, which Bangs certainly was.

Life in Corpus at the opening of 1846, with more than 4,000 troops stationed there, furnished Bangs ample material for the weekly issues of the *Gazette*. For, in spite of its remote location and the persistent winter rains that kept the men much indoors, the little Mexican town was gay beyond belief. With the choice, for instance, of the "Ethiopian Serenaders" or *Richard III* at the Army Theater and *Blackeyed Susan* at the Union, and all the "comforts, conveniences, and luxuries" of which Corpus Christi was "susceptible" offered by the Kinney House, while the Kilgore Oyster Parlor was a lively competitor in the "vinous" line, none needed to be dull. Bakers, butchers, and candlestick makers were at hand; lawyers, doctors, barbers, and hairdressers offered their services, while the confectioner and photographer supplemented the list. Everything from hair mattresses, carved furniture, music boxes, and jewelry to shoestrings and handkerchiefs was offered to the public in the pages of the *Gazette*. It also contributed news of the outside world through excerpts from the New York *Sun*, the *National Intelligencer*, and the *Daily Picayune*.

During two months the *Gazette* fulfilled Bangs' every dream, for it was the principal medium of information for the outside world concerning events in the region. But before the printing

---

[9] The *Picayune*, January 6, 1846, announced the arrival of the first issue of the *Corpus Christi Gazette* of January 1, a "new and spirited paper just started by Bangs and Fletcher."

[10] An Extra of March 8 is at TxU. No. 7 (February 12), Wisconsin State Historical Society, Madison; photocopy, TxU; No. 12 (March 19), Archivo de la Secretaría de la Defensa Nacional, Mexico City, (see H. E. Bolton, *Guide to Materials for the History of the United States in the Principal Archives of Mexico*, p. 293); and No. 14 (April 2, 1846), AAW. Others are in the reports of General Taylor to the Secretary of War, U.S. War Department Papers, NA.

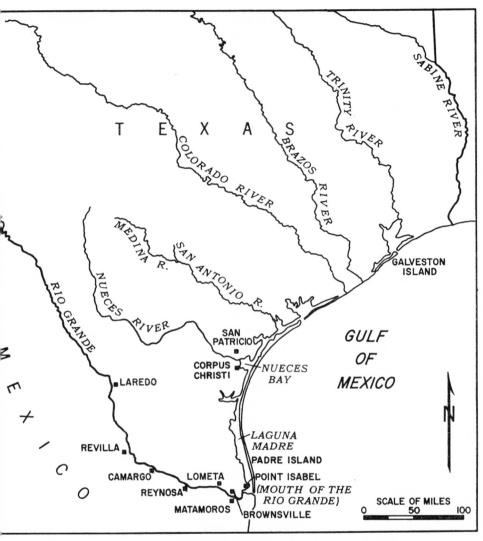

Texas in 1846.

business in Corpus had gotten into full swing, for Bangs also did job printing for both the army and civilians, General Taylor recommended the advance of the troops to the Rio Grande. Upon receipt of orders to move forward, preparations for the march were set in motion early in February, 1846. On the twelfth Bangs issued an Extra reporting the advance of a large body of Mexicans toward Texas.[11] In spite of the excitement this aroused, preparations for the evacuation of Corpus Christi went steadily forward. No Mexican army materialized; and by the end of the month all was in readiness for departure. Even before the first detachment took up the line of march toward Matamoros, it was predicted that a new paper, to be styled the *Rio Grande Herald*, would be immediately established near the future encampment.[12] On March 8, as the troops began to move, General Taylor had Bangs publish his order No. 30 in the form of an Extra, commanding his men, much as Mina had done forty years before, not to molest any person or property while advancing, and forbidding civilians to accompany them.

Day by day the military population of Corpus Christi dwindled; by the eleventh almost all the troops were under way. With them gone, civilians who had done a brief but thriving business left for other parts. Bangs remained for two reasons: many of his subscribers had paid for six months, and there was still a possibility that the troops would return. Each Thursday the *Gazette* continued to appear. But by April 2, when the fourteenth issue was published, General Taylor had reached the Rio Grande and reported conditions which daily made war more imminent and the return of the troops to Corpus more unlikely. The presidential proclamation of a state of war definitely turned all eyes to the Rio Grande.

Even earlier Bangs had read the writing on the wall. While he knew the Corpus bonanza had ended, he was not discouraged,

[11] William L. Marcy to Zachary Taylor, Washington, March 2, 1846, in 30th Congress, 1st Session, House of Representatives, *Executive Documents*, No. 60, p. 92.
[12] *Telegraph*, March 4, 1846.

for he had made other plans. By March 26 he and Fletcher had dissolved partnership and had turned the paper over to De Alba, who continued its publication.[13] Before long Bangs found another partner and jointly they issued the prospectus of the *Rio Grande Herald*. It reached the editor of the *Picayune* before the middle of June;[14] he thereupon announced the *Herald* as shortly to be published at Matamoros by Bangs and Gideon Lewis, of the Galveston *News*.

Lewis, a lean, humorous individual known as "Legs" in the Island City, was a young and daring but shrewd business man. Once, when left in charge of the *News* while its owner made a business tour of the Republic, he bought out the local theater and operated both paper and theater with considerable profit to the firm.[15] An adventurous fellow, he had followed the army to Corpus Christi, and there persuaded Bangs to take part in a new journalistic venture where the army was making news.

By the time they reached the scene of action General Taylor had crossed the Rio Grande and was occupying Matamoros; all Mexican troops had been hastily withdrawn and many officials had fled. The site the General had originally selected for his headquarters was on a high point of land known as Fronton, but later called Point Isabel. Like a pediment it jutted out into the Gulf near the mouth of the river and was readily accessible to the steady stream of vessels bringing troops and supplies from the United States and Texas ports. Matamoros, although some twenty miles further inland on the west bank of the river, had served northeastern Mexico for many years as a port, under the name of "Refugio." At this time ocean-going vessels were unable to go up the river to that point and their cargoes had to be unloaded at its mouth, but river boats docked close by.

At this town, long since familiar to Bangs, he and Lewis decided to establish the new paper. It was another typically Spanish town. Near the center were two large plazas; on one were

13 *Corpus Christi Gazette*, No. 14, April 2, 1846. AAW. Photocopy, LMS.
14 *Daily Picayune*, June 14, 1846.
15 *Galveston Daily News*, April 11, 1917.

the government buildings, and on the other stood the "capilla" or church. Clustered closely about these squares were flat-roofed adobe houses which had few windows, and those few were sturdily barred by iron grills; but the patios they enclosed were, as in Victoria and Saltillo, luxuriant with flowers. The narrow streets, in contrast, were usually dry and dusty. Beyond the town toward the Gulf were fields and gardens watered from the river and outlined in many cases by rows of tall palm trees.

All of the business section had been taken over by North Americans and a motley assortment of establishments were being opened. Hotels, cafes, livery stables, dry goods and grocery stores were carrying on business; more troops were daily crossing the river; and prospects for the new paper seemed good. The promised *Herald* did not materialize; in its stead on June 22 the prospectus of the *Matamoros Reveille* was ushered into being by Bangs and Lewis;[16] but under conditions far less propitious than had greeted the *Gazette* in Corpus, for the *Reveille* had active competition from the first issue.

This came from a company of Louisiana volunteers, composed almost entirely of printers, who had accompanied General Taylor to the Rio Grande but whose terms of service expired before the army crossed the river.[17] On entering Matamoros immediately after its occupation, an enterprising New Orleans printer, J. N. Fleeson, secured the use of a Mexican press—for the town had boasted a dozen different newspapers in the preceding decade—and on June 1, 1846, he and a partner, Hugh McLeod, issued from the press of the former *Boletín* the first number of a proposed semiweekly entitled *The Republic of the Rio Grande*.[18] McLeod, who had taken part in the Santa Fe Expedition, was

16 Vol. I, Nos. 1–2, photocopy, TxU. Appendix II, No. 358.
17 *Daily Picayune,* May 6, 1846.
18 New Orleans *Weekly Delta,* June 15, 22, 29, July 13; *Daily Picayune,* June 14, 16, 21, 24, 1846. A facsimile of Vol. I, No. 3, p. 1, dated June 12, 1846, is included in Lathrop C. Harper's *Catalogue No. 12 of Books, Pamphlets, Broadsides Printed in Mexico, 1813–1850,* p. 47. No. 2 is dated June 6, 1846. The title is listed as "República de Rio Grande y Amiga de los Pueblos." LC.

the editor; Fleeson, the printer. As there were then more than six thousands troops in and about the Matamoros area, the four-page paper was in ready demand, both for local consumption and for shipment of news of the region to the United States. But the *Republic*, in title as well as in policy—its editorials advocated the formation of a northern Mexican republic under the protection of the United States and ultimate U.S. annexation— was so objectionable to the army that the name was shortly changed to the *American Flag* and McLeod withdrew from the management.[19]

The *Reveille*, which was frequently confused with the St. Louis paper of the same name, did not appear until the twenty-fourth and was at first issued, like its competitor, as a semiweekly on Mondays and Fridays in both English and Spanish.[20] Larger in size than its competitor, the *Reveille* took as its epigraph President Monroe's historic statement, "The people of this continent alone have the right to decide their own destiny," and made news of Mexico its specialty. It credited Matamoros with rain, muddy streets, lots of fleas and dogs of every size. Upon the long strings of eighteen or twenty yoke of oxen it bestowed the title of "Yankee flying artillery," but admitted that the speed attained fell far short of "greased lightning." All in all it was colorful and promised to become an important sheet. The Spanish page of the *Reveille* entitled *La Diana de Matamoros*, was soon dropped. Then a Mexican publisher issued from Bangs' press a separate paper, *El Liberal*. This practice of increasing his income by sharing his press and office with other papers was one which Bangs had long followed and found satisfactory.[21]

While Lewis gathered and edited the news, Bangs published it at his office on "Guanacuato Street" and also operated there a job printing shop which turned out many types of printing including pamphlets and small books. In the first issue of the

[19] *Telegraph,* July 29, 1846. Appendix II, No. 359.
[20] See first and second issues, June 24 and 27, 1846. TxU.
[21] *Daily Picayune,* July 26, 1846.

Reveille he announced that his establishment was "not to be surpassed by any office in Mexico" and that work would be done "at the shortest notice."

Following this practice, he published in July a "wonderful" production entitled "The Brave Ranger," which professed to be a history of Captain Samuel H. Walker, with emphasis on his exploits from the time of his appointment as captain of the Texas Rangers until May 10, 1846. So noble and valorous was the "Ranger" pictured and so marvelous were his accomplishments that a correspondent of the *Picayune* commented that he feared their northern friends would not believe them at all after a while, even if they should overrun all Mexico. To this he added: "These ridiculous puffs do no good, and make honest men doubt even the truth when told."[22] The work, however, sold well, for Captain Walker was a popular hero.

While Bangs was busily engaged in producing the Walker "puff," *El Liberal*, the Spanish paper that used his press, was voicing the Mexican viewpoint on the war so openly that the *Picayune* remarked that merely allowing it to exist was ample evidence of the American respect for freedom of the press.[23] But there was finally a limit even to that respect. As the result of an objectionable article supporting the "pretensions of Mexico" in the war, which was printed late in July, the office of the *Reveille* was closed by order of General Taylor, and Bangs was lodged in jail. When he was brought into court, he immediately disclaimed the authorship of the article in question or any part in its publication aside from renting his press, as he had not even seen the material before it appeared. *El Liberal* was permanently suspended; the *Reveille* was permitted to resume publication.[24] Bangs decided not to use this privilege. As the reputation of the paper and even his own had been questioned, sales would suffer; his partner Lewis had meanwhile joined the Rangers; and he had had enough experience to know that Matamoros could not much

22 *Ibid.*, August 9, 1846.
23 *Ibid.*, July 26, 1846.
24 *Northern Standard* (Clarksville, Texas), September 5, 1846.

longer be a profitable location for two newspapers, as the main body of the army was being rapidly thrown forward toward Monterrey.

As soon as the proprietors of the *American Flag* learned of Bang's decision, they offered to buy his printing materials and press, which would permit them to offer a larger sheet,[25] and to employ him as a printer. They also offered him the privilege of conducting a job printing office on his own account, with free rent and advertising in the *Flag*. This he accepted as, for once, he had no advance plans; and from time to time, as space was available, he inserted his "ad," announcing his readiness to print posters, steamboat bills, blanks of all kinds, sutler's receipts, and cards. He gave his address as the office of the *American Flag* on the Plaza de la Capilla.

Early in 1847 he moved with the *Flag* to Captain Smith's building on Abasola Street, known as the Steamboat House, next door west of Bigelow's livery stable.[26] And not until this date was it possible for the *Flag* to offer its subscribers the larger sheet which Bangs' press made possible, as its new proprietor was unable to obtain suitable paper. Business flourished until the seventy-sixth number was issued on February 17; then no more paper was to be had. After waiting several weeks with publication suspended and earnings cut off, Bangs returned to Corpus Christi,[27] where he was when a new supply of paper made possible resumption of publication of Number 77 on March 3. But Bangs did not print it nor did he return to Matamoros.

During the months the printer spent in Matamoros he was closely associated with Simon Mussina, whom he had known for more than a decade as an editor, lawyer, and general promoter. Mussina suggested to him, after he decided not to go on with the *Reveille*, that he locate at Point Isabel, where General Taylor had established Fort Polk and where military supplies and troops

---

[25] The *American Flag*, July 31, 1846. The file in LC continues to July 29, 1848.
[26] *Ibid.*, January 20, 1847.
[27] New Orleans *Weekly Delta*, March 22, 1847, quoting from a letter written on March 2 at Corpus Christi and published in the *Galveston News*.

were still being landed. Mussina had a personal interest in the matter as he was one of the owners of a tract of land, adjacent to the post, on which were the remains of the old town of Fronton and a newly laid-out town.

Prospects were indeed excellent that the place would become a port of importance for the newly acquired southwestern territory. Located in a semitropical coastal region which gave promise of rich returns from cultivation, protected from hurricanes to a large extent by the off-shore Padre Island, which extended from Corpus Christi to the mouth of the Rio Grande, provided by nature with an excellent beach and by the United States government with extensive wharf facilities, and washed by waters abounding in many types of fish, Point Isabel promised great possibilities. A further evidence of the importance the United States government attached to the location was the construction then underway of an army hospital—one of the largest and most expensive of that type in Texas—on a nearby elevated spot commanding a wide view and exposed to the cool, salubrious breeze from the Gulf.[28] Its facilities for caring for convalescents were unusual, as a twelve-foot gallery on all sides permitted patients to spend many hours in the fresh air and sunshine.

As an added inducement to Bangs for settlement in that town —which Mussina assured him would certainly far surpass Galveston—the promoter offered some centrally located property on which to establish a printing office and a home. Little more was needed to convince Bangs again that a bright future lay before him. On Bangs' agreement to establish himself there, Mussina transferred to him three centrally located lots—one directly facing the wharf of Front Street and two on the street directly behind it, at the corner of F and Second Streets.[29]

After a trip to Galveston to persuade his wife of the desira-

[28] *Telegraph*, June 28, 1847, quoting in part from the *American Flag* of May 26, 1847.

[29] Bangs was given Lots 1, 11, and 12 in Block 6. See the plot of the town of Point Isabel, October 24, 184[7], in Deed Records, Cameron County, Bk. A, p. 533. Fort Polk lay outside the limits of the town.

bility of the move, to borrow $400 from Perry and Flint with which to build a home and print shop, and to make arrangements to ship his furniture and the press he had left there, Bangs returned to Point Isabel and put up a frame dwelling to accommodate his family and a few guests. His wife came as soon as it was livable and together they hopefully awaited the arrival of their household goods and the press. Weeks passed. Eventually news came of what had happened. The boat carrying everything was wrecked, and all Bangs' property was lost.[30]

A man of less courage would have despaired, but not Bangs or his wife. While forced to resort to many makeshifts they accidentally found a way to make a living. As many travelers were passing through the port and they had space in the house, they began to accommodate transients and others "with the best of fare." Being near the Laguna Madre, Bangs found it easy to supply the table with fish, oysters, and fowls; and his bar soon became known for the high quality of the liquor he dispensed. Encouraged by the success of this venture, Bangs decided in the spring of 1848 to take advantage of a brick factory which had been established in the vicinity by building a large and commodious structure—a splendid hotel for its day and location.

He sold his Galveston property piece by piece: first his home, then his printing office, and finally the real estate. He and his wife transferred one lot to a trustee with authorization to sell if they were not able to pay the $400 borrowed from Perry and Flint, which would be due on January 1, 1849; all the proceeds above that amount were to be remitted to Bangs.[31] Instead, Perry bid in the property for $225 and Bangs received nothing. With the proceeds of the Galveston home he built the Brick or City Hotel of Point Isabel, but still was not able to replace the press. Both he and his wife worked hard and many friends helped them, and he worked cheerfully, confident that the revenue from the hotel would make a new printing establishment possible.

---

[30] "Printing in Galveston" in *Galveston City Directory*, 1859, p. 90.
[31] Deed Records, Galveston County, Book F (1848).

The editor of the *American Flag* announced Bangs' plans for the hotel:

NEW HOTEL—Our old friend Samuel Bangs, we learn, is about erecting a splendid hotel at our neighboring town of Point Isabel. The building is to be large and commodious, 60 by 20 ft. and to be built of brick. At present Mr. Bangs is occupying a wooden building, where he accommodates travelers and others with the best kind of fare: Being near the margin of Laguna Madre his table is always supplied with fish, oysters and fowls and his bar with the best of liquors. We rejoice in this evidence of the prosperity of Point Isabel, and trust that our friend Bangs will reap a golden harvest as a reward for his enterprise, for he is deserving of it.

Mr. Bangs, we believe, is the only survivor of that glorious band of fellows who followed the fortunes of the patriotic and chivalrous, but ill-fated Mina. It was in 1816 that he embarked his fortunes under the banner of that exiled Spanish patriot, with the rank and pay of captain of artillery, and for seven long years encountered the dangers and shared the glories of that memorable expedition with the fearless chief. He took with him a portable printing office, and the bulletins which he occasionally issued therefrom, imparted to the world the only account ever published of Mina and his exploits. To this unfortunate man and his brave comrades was Mexico partially indebted for her independence. . . .

Mr. Bangs was afterward printer to the government of Tamaulipas, and was among the pioneers who introduced the divine art into Texas. He is the very man to make any project go ahead and is seldom mistaken in his estimate of things.[32]

But while plans for the development of Point Isabel were still in the making, the war with Mexico came to an end. By the treaty of Guadalupe Hidalgo, signed in 1848, the western boundary of Texas was fixed at the Rio Grande, and the withdrawal of United States troops from Mexican territory began. By the time that those stationed in Monterrey, Tampico, and west of the Rio Grande evacuated those places, the situation on the east of the Rio Grande also was materially changed. The civilians who had

[32] *American Flag*, May 17, 1848.

been carrying on business on the Mexican side of the river located for a time at Point Isabel, Santa Rita, or some of the other towns that had been laid out on the east bank. The region certainly had its attractions. According to its promoters it offered a fertile and extensive valley watered by one of the largest rivers in America; its climate was mild and salubrious; and its soil was adapted to the cultivation of all the great staples of the Union—advantages that few other areas of the United States could claim.

But the army, which in 1846 selected Point Isabel as a port and established a fort in its vicinity, did not make Fort Polk a permanent post. Instead, it selected a site on the Rio Grande directly opposite Matamoros for a new one, which was named Fort Brown in honor of the first officer killed there in one of the early skirmishes. Once this decision became known, speculators who had earlier conducted their business in Matamoros, Mussina among them, laid out the city of Brownsville, adjoining the new post. At Fort Brown the government built quarters for some three hundred men, and a bakery and slaughter house for the use of contractors who engaged to furnish bread and meat to the troops. By August, 1848, the last detachments had retired from northern Mexico, the sick being sent to the hospital at Point Isabel.[33] The full quota of troops was then stationed at Fort Brown.

Just at this time Bangs found, among the newsmen who had returned from Mexico, a partner eager to join him in establishing a newspaper at Point Isabel. This was R. A. DeVilliers, one of the New Orleans printers who had composed the company of Louisiana Volunteers mustered out before Matamoros was occupied.[34] He had been the editor of the *Free American* at Veracruz, where he had managed to maintain friendly relations with the military "powers that be," but finally became entangled in difficulties with the governor and was ordered to depart. The

---

[33] *Telegraph,* July 13 and August 17, 1848.
[34] *Daily Picayune,* May 6, 1846.

Free American was suspended.[35] After returning to New Orleans, De Villiers came back to the Rio Grande with plans for a new paper in that region. At once Bangs saw an opportunity to re-establish himself in the printing business. By September he had arranged all details for the publication of the new paper, which was to bear the title of the *Texas Ranger*. The New Orleans *Delta*, in announcing the prospective publication,[36] said it was expected to advocate the cause of the new government called the "Sierra Madre," whose ramifications were said to extend throughout the country, including foreigners as well as Mexicans. This new government, which the *Ranger* was said to be supporting, was the same scheme as the Republic of the Rio Grande, which had been advocated in *The Republic of the Rio Grande*, whose name was changed to the *American Flag*.

Before the first issue of the *Texas Ranger* appeared it was clear that Point Isabel and most of the paper towns of the Valley had been doomed by the rise of Brownsville. Lometa, which had been laid out as the county seat of the newly created Cameron County and gave promise, for a time, of being an important trade center between Point Isabel and Laredo, was superseded by Brownsville. The *American Flag*, whose editor died the last of July, was removed to Brownsville, where E. B. Scarborough succeeded him. Already well known both in the region and also in the United States, the *Flag* left small room for a new paper which had only limited financial backing.

The effect of the withdrawal of the "war" army from the region was only slowly realized by the people who had established themselves, full of hope and energy, in the Valley; but the old dullness and apathy returned; both energy and enterprise waned. Point Isabel was slowly deserted and many of the earlier buildings were pulled down; speculators who had laid out other towns were reduced, according to a gentleman from Point Isabel,

---

[35] See Lota M. Spell, "The Anglo-Saxon Press in Mexico, 1846–1848," in *American Historical Review*, XXXVIII, 29.

[36] New Orleans *Weekly Delta*, September 4, 1848, quoting the Austin *Democrat*.

to living on cat fish and roasting ears, or "some spontaneous productions of the earth."[37] While a few troops were still left at Brazos Santiago at the mouth of the Rio Grande to attend to the shipment of army goods and stores, a storm in September reduced their number and function by washing away the storehouses and damaging the few remaining buildings.[38]

In the face of the dwindling population of Point Isabel and the established circulation in a wide territory of the *American Flag*, De Villiers and Bangs, both basically hard-headed business men, realized the futility of their intention to establish the *Texas Ranger*, and Bangs saw the end for his dream of establishing a profitable printing business in Point Isabel. De Villiers stayed on, bought some land, and became a merchant.[39] Bangs turned again half-heartedly to the hotel, although he realized that its day, too, had passed.

In December he took a definite step. In justice to his wife, who had not approved the move or the disposal of the Galveston property which would have furnished her a living had anything happened to her husband, he deeded to her everything he owned: the three lots "in the town of Frontón or Point Isabell" on which stood the "Brick or City Hotel"; a wharf kitchen and household furniture, "stables, three horses, one carriage, and one boat, with furniture, tackle, and apparel thereunto belonging."[40] This represented all that remained as the fruit of their industry through many years, especially the last two, but he gave it to her willingly and cheerfully.

Life in and about Point Isabel was, by no means, entirely dull. In the spring of 1849 there was great excitement when news came from Palo Alto, a small place midway between Brownsville and Point Isabel, that a "numerous and formidable band of Indians" had just made a descent upon that place and committed

---

[37] *Telegraph*, August 17, 1848.
[38] *Ibid.*, October 12, 1848.
[39] U.S. Census, 1850, Cameron County, Texas. Photocopy, TxU.
[40] Cameron County, Deed Records, Samuel Bangs to Caroline H. Bangs, Brownsville, December 14, 1848, Book A, p. 212.

many acts of "startling and savage barbarity." Among others, they had intercepted the stage from Point Isabel and taken prisoner the proprietor, who was no other than Mr. Bangs, and a passenger, James Lombardo, also a resident of Point Isabel. Plans were immediately made to organize a ranging company to follow the Indians, but before it got started word came that both had escaped from their captors, but had been rescued in a state of nudity, which Bangs could ill afford.[41] Friends brought him home in motley garb, but how glad the whole town, not to mention his family, was to see him!

Now he could sympathize with all the settlers on the western frontier of Texas who never knew what moment, day or night, they might be attacked, their children and cattle stolen, and their homes fired. He understood why they were demanding rangers full time to man the line from Fort Worth to the Rio Grande to drive back the dreaded threat to their peace. He wondered now why he had ever left Galveston, which was safe from them. But even there, he remembered, Nature herself went on the war path; gulf storms also came to rob and destroy. Perhaps it was so everywhere.

[41] The Corpus Christi *Star*, June 2, 1849, following the Brownsville *Flag* of May 16, 1849.

SEVEN

Beneath the Soft Blue Grass

S AMUEL BANGS was over fifty years old before he faced his situation squarely. He had realized for some time that there was no future in Point Isabel; there was not even a living. He could barely pay the taxes, small as they were. But where should he turn next?

His two sons, James O. and Samuel K.,[1] were now grown. They had been introduced to the press in Galveston when still very young and James continued to print there, but when their father left for the Rio Grande, Samuel went back to Kentucky, where he had earlier attended school and where his stepmother's family lived. When his father wrote him of the Point Isabel situation at the end of 1849, he advised Samuel, Sr., to come on to Kentucky, leaving his wife with James in Galveston until he had permanent work. The problem then was money—for his trans-

---

[1] Although young Samuel was baptized "Samuel Salvador," he signed his name later as "Samuel K." James, whose baptismal record has not been found, seems to have been named for Ogilvy, or to have adopted his name.

141

portation to Kentucky and hers to Galveston. It was his wife who solved the problem. With her unwavering faith in her husband, she bravely risked her all by borrowing $500 from Simon Mussina, to be repaid in two equal installments in May and in November, 1850.[2]

Again Bangs crossed the Rio Grande, on whose banks he had dreamed of establishing a thriving colony that would make him an independent empresario; once more he waited for a New Orleans-bound boat in Matamoros, the port through which he had returned to his native land in 1823 and later brought out presses to Tamaulipas, Nuevo León, and Coahuila. After seeing his wife off for Galveston, he visited again the Plaza de la Capilla and the Steamboat House, where he had printed the *Reveille*, the *Flag*, and the tribute to Ranger Captain Samuel Walker, who was killed during the advance of the United States troops to Mexico City. Once more he was in New Orleans, where he had waited impatiently, more than ten years before, for his young wife to come down the river.

In Kentucky it was not difficult for a good printer to find work, especially after his son had proven himself such. But his earnings, after his own expenses were paid, were too small to enable him to pay Mussina off and to bring his wife to join him. In order to earn more he gave up his position in Louisville, where Samuel K. worked on the *Courier*; instead he took a place on the *Herald* in Georgetown, where the French family had formerly made their home. Living as economically as he could, Mussina was finally satisfied.

But when typhoid fever claimed him as a victim, the small savings with which he had hoped to bring his wife back were soon swallowed up. He made a brave fight, but was long a convalescent. Far from the home of which he had dreamed, far—too far—from his loved ones, he found himself weary and worn. Without the old energy which had generated hope and created plans, he was content merely to rest, waiting for his wife to

[2] Cameron County, Deed Records, Deed of Trust, November 20, 1849, Book B, pp. 244–245.

come, as he was sure she would. But as he quietly rested, dreaming of her and of Texas, his spirit slipped away, just as the spring of 1854 was merging into summer.

Without a member of his family near, he was laid, by kindly hands, gently to rest beneath the soft blue grass. A last generous tribute was paid him by the local paper, which he had earlier helped to print.

Died—In this town, on Wednesday, the 31st of May, of debility consequent upon a protracted spell of Typhoid Fever, *Samuel Bangs*, aged 53, a highly respected citizen of Texas. His had been a remarkably adventurous and even romantic life—through all of which he maintained the character of an honest man. He bore his long and painful illness with the patience and fortitude which becomes a man and a Christian, putting his whole trust in the Redeemer, to whom, even in his dying moments, he commended his afflicted widow and orphan children. Though a perfect stranger in this community, and dying far from the home where he was known and esteemed by all, his last moments were soothed by the kind attention, and the last duties to him performed by friendly hands; deeds ever to be remembered with heart-felt gratitude by his sorely afflicted widow and orphan children. F.[3]

And thus, almost unnoticed, there passed from the scene a printer who had never appreciated his own unique accomplishments. Not only was he himself a capable printer, but under his

[3] Georgetown (Kentucky) *Herald*, X, No. 13, (June 8, 1854), 3. A file is owned by the Kansas State Historical Society at Topeka, Kansas, which kindly furnished the writer a certified copy. From the records of vital statistics of Scott County, in which Georgetown is located, the Kentucky Historical Society at Frankfort, Kentucky, supplied the following: "Bangs, Samuel. Age 55, married; died April, 1854; cause of death, typhoid fever; place of birth, unknown; place of death, Scott County; parents, unknown."

F. R. French, son of Henry French and nephew of George H. French, who died in Galveston in 1843, and of Bangs' wife Caroline, wrote (*Galveston News*, February 6, 1910) that Bangs died at his father's house at Georgetown, Kentucky, in 1850 or 1851 and his wife in 1854 or 1855, and that his father died at Ashland in 1858. He also stated that he, with James and Samuel, worked for his father on the Galveston *Herald*.

Such errors in dates are natural when dependence is placed entirely on memory more than a half century later.

instruction many young fellows were trained to print. At Saltillo he introduced the apprentice system and improved the work of the more experienced by rigid supervision and by securing better wages for them. At Victoria he trained his apprentices not only to print but to mold type. He created new openings for his fledglings through introducing presses into towns where the possibilities and advantages of the press had been unknown.

His practice of sharing his office and his presses, as well as his knowledge, made it possible for others in Galveston to publish several newspapers with which he had no direct connection. Some printers paid rent for the use of one of his presses; some paid for the use of both a press and his office; some publishers utilized his office and contracted with him for such printing as they needed. While he had difficulties with certain individuals, such as Charles Lewis, no problem arose from sharing either his office or press until the episode in Matamoros that led him to end the *Reveille* and to accept a position as printer on a paper owned and published by someone else. Without his genial temperament, his honesty, and his consideration for others, such an arrangement could never have been feasible.

Aside from his work as a printer and a teacher of printing, he developed, from his early days in Monterrey, a trade in presses and other tools of the craft. He was aware of the possibilities the region offered to a dealer in presses and in printing paraphernalia. During the ten years after his return to Mexico he was the only man engaged in the importation and sale of presses in an ever-widening territory. It was not easy to carry on such a business. Orders had to be dispatched by boat to New York; shipments were slow and uncertain; getting them through the customhouse at Matamoros or Tampico was another problem; while delivery of the goods and collection of the sales price were even more difficult. Only a man commanding the necessary capital, familiar with business methods in the United States, and blessed with an unquestioned reputation for fair dealing could have successfully accomplished his mission in behalf of the press in an area extending from Aguas Calientes and Zacatecas to Texas.

In the course of his work as a printer Samuel Bangs had indeed qualified as a pioneer. In addition to being the first printer in Texas while it was still a Spanish province, he was in turn, during the next five years, the first printer in three other Spanish provinces—at Soto la Marina in Nuevo Santander (now the state of Tamaulipas); at Monterrey, the capital of the province, and later the state, of Nuevo León; and at Saltillo, the capital of the province of Coahuila—all three bordering on Texas to the north. During the existence of the Mexican state of Coahuila and Texas he was for some years the official government printer at its capital, Leona Vicario (Saltillo), and the publisher of its first official organ, the *Gazeta constitucional de Coahuil-tejas*. He subsequently served the state of Tamaulipas in the same capacity at Victoria, where he published its official organ, *Atalaya*, and a news sheet on his own account, entitled *El Telescopio*.

During the life of the Republic of Texas Bangs printed the first newspaper in Galveston and, with the exception of a short stay in Houston, where he printed and wrote for *The Musquito*, he owned, published, and printed an almost continuous succession of newspapers in the "Island City." With annexation he established the *Corpus Christi Gazette*, which was not only the first newspaper in that settlement but the first in English printed west of the Nueces River—in fact the most western newspaper in English on the American continent. With the outbreak of the Mexican War, he was one of the first to establish a newspaper in English and Spanish west of the Rio Grande.

Aside from his prowess as a printer, Samuel Bangs was an American of whom his country should be proud. His enterprising spirit, his courage, his ability to rise above misfortune, his pride in the production of his press, and his determination to succeed —all these make him a figure deserving recognition. When to these is added his contribution to the progress of the press it is surprising that the name of Bangs remained unknown in printing annals for almost a century after his death. Today no authoritative history of the press in Texas or in the neighboring states to

145

the south or west can overlook his name or his work. Someday a monument should honor Samuel Bangs, not only as the first printer in Texas but also as the pioneer of the press in the Southwest.

Epilogue

AMUEL BANGS had indeed deserved better. He had worked hard, and he had been thrifty, but he was too trusting and too generous for his own good. He had received liberal grants from both the Mexican and Texan governments, and he had bought Texas property whenever he could. From the Coahuila and Texas grant three-fourths of the six leagues went to a grasping lawyer who claimed he had secured a gilt-edged title; the remaining league of the Colorado furnished credit for the printing outfit Bangs bought in 1839 from J. W. J. Niles, on which the *Galvestonian*, the *News*, the *Times*, the *Chronicle*, and the *Globe* were subsequently printed. The eight Galveston City lots given him as security for the unpaid balance on the Bastrop County land, he deeded, after the death of Belden, out of sympathy for the widow, to Belden's estate and cancelled the mortgage.[1] The Tamaulipas grant, which had opened to Bangs vistas of a splendid future, was never validated by the Republic of Texas. His 1845 grant from the Republic provided the press for

[1] Samuel Bangs to J. De Cordova, administrator of the estate of John Belden, February 10, 1845; Galveston County, Deed Records, Book E, p. 112.

147

the *Corpus Christi Gazette* and the *Reveille*. All the returns from his Galveston property, acquired through the years, were invested in Point Isabel, which remained for a century little more than a name. The Bangs' furniture and personal effects, together with a complete printing outfit, went to the bottom of the Gulf, and plans for the *Texas Ranger* into the discard.

Only one possible asset, in addition to the Point Isabel property, remained to Caroline and the boys—the land on the Brazos, from which Bangs had not derived one penny, although he had paid the taxes on it when he could. Other people had settled on the land before Ogilvy filed the grant in the newly created Robertson County;[2] and Ogilvy died before legal means had been utilized to clear those settlers from the land.[3] Bangs was too kindhearted to order them off; even had he done so, they might not have left, as they had bought the land in good faith.

The heirs of Bangs were more businesslike. Through G. R. Freeman, a friend in Kentucky, to whom Caroline returned, they employed D. C. Freeman, Jr., an attorney in Austin, Texas, to file suit in 1855 in the United States District Court there against Robert Calvert and J. E. McCampbell, two owners of large tracts of land which fell within the Bangs grant. In time a compromise was effected by which, in 1858 and 1859, Caroline, James Ogilvy, and Samuel K., in return for various sums which amounted to slightly over $6,000, deeded all the land covered by the grant— almost 10,000 acres sloping toward the Brazos River—to the dozen or more settlers living on it.[4] But before the final trans-

[2] Robertson County, Deed Records, Grant of two leagues of land to José Manuel Bangs by the State of Coahuila and Texas, filed March 30, 1839, recorded on April 2, 1839, Book A, pp. 307–320. Written on stamped paper of 1828 to 1835.

The documents in Spanish are the same as those in the Texas Land Office and in the Bastrop County Records.

[3] Ogilvy died after April 30 and "some time before September 28, 1840" ("The Diary of Adolphus Sterne," *SWHQ*, XXXI, 63).

[4] Agreement between Caroline H., J. O., and Samuel K. Bangs and Robert Calvert, January 13, 1858, by D. C. Freeman; Robertson County, Deed Records, Book J, pp. 442–445.

action in 1859 was completed by the payment of the last $3,000, Caroline, too, had gone to her reward.[5] She had been a good wife and a writer of some ability for that day and locality. Her work, under the name of "Cora," is scattered from the early pages of the *Galvestonian* through various Galveston papers of the forties,[6] and was frequently reprinted later.

James lived on in Galveston and worked for many years as a printer on the *Galveston News*, being considered a valued member by the Typographical Association early established there. He married his cousin Josephine French, the daughter of George H. French and Catherine Crosby, who were married in 1842.[7] When the *News* was moved to Houston during the Civil War, James went with it. After he was killed by a fall in 1876,[8] his widow became Mrs. Paul Logre, who, like her mother, Mrs. Cherry—for she, after French's death, had married Wilbur Cherry in 1847—lived on in Galveston in the French, and later the Cherry, home at the northwest corner of Church and 17th Streets until around 1911.[9]

[5] Robertson County, Deed Records, Book M, pp. 388, 458, 576–581, 639; Book N, pp. 209–210.

The references in the obituary to "orphan children" and in the *Telegraph* (November 12, 1845) to "Mrs. Bangs and children" suggest strongly that Caroline and Samuel Bangs had children. If so, they must have died very young as the power of attorney that Caroline H., James O., and Samuel K. gave D. C. Freeman, October 16, 1857, says of James and Samuel "sons and only living descendants" (Book J, p. 440); while the deed that Samuel and James gave to Robert Calvert, June 15, 1859, states that Caroline, since the agreement on January 13, 1858, "has died, and that Samuel and James are *her only heirs*" (Book N, pp. 209–210).

[6] For a story, see the *Galvestonian*, April 1, 1841; for a poem, the *Independent Chronicle*, October 15, 1843. In the article on "Printing in Galveston" in the *Galveston City Directory* for 1859–1860 is a reference to a paper called "the *Times* . . . which commenced in 1845–6; . . . Mrs. Bangs was one of the contributors."

[7] Married January 10, 1842, by John L. Darragh, justice of the peace (Galveston County Marriage Records).

[8] "Death of James O. Bangs on Sept. 19" in Galveston *Daily News*, September 21 and 24, 1876. TxU.

[9] Statement of Miss Alice Cherry, Galveston, Texas, November 27, 1953.

All that remained of the Bangs estate at the time of James' death was the property at Point Isabel, which was so far away that for years it was almost forgotten. Finally, in 1882, Albert C. Howell of Cameron County offered to buy for one hundred dollars the three lots upon which Bangs and his wife had lived, Nos. 1, 11, and 12 of Block 6, as shown on the original map of the old town of Point Isabel. The widow and the son of James signed the deed in Galveston, while Samuel K. signed it on February 21, 1882, in Louisville, Kentucky.[10]

Samuel, the last surviving son, was, like his father, a printer; he also inherited something of his father's philosophical spirit, his sense of humor, and his ability to write easily in either poetry or prose. In 1885 he published a small volume of verse, *Lights and Shadows in the Round of a Typo's Life*,[11] and, from references in it, had apparently issued an earlier one entitled *Ripples on the Stream of Poesy*. In *Lights and Shadows* many of the poems are addressed to his coworkers: to Henry A. Boies (on the title page); to Koogle (p. 17); to Jennie (p. 24); to W. W. Crail, then dead (p. 25); to Henry Charlton, described as "Our Hapless Friend," and to James M. Palmer, both deceased the previous year (pp. 26 and 27); to William F. Foster (p. 28); and to the [Louisville] *Courier-Journal* (p. 39). There is also a comparison of "Past and Present" (p. 29). The general tone ranges from the jocular in "The Dew-Drop Inn," a poem on the Schmitt beer saloon (pp. 8–9), to the elegiac in "Death's Shining Mark," the tribute to Palmer. Humorous touches are frequent, as they had been in the verse of his father.

Edward—whose name is conspicuous in the annals of the Bangs family in Boston[12]—the son of James, became a clerk; he

---

Catherine French married Wilbur Cherry on August 7, 1847 (Galveston County, Marriage Records).

[10] Cameron County, Supplemental Deed Records, Vol. F, pp. 89–90.

[11] [Louisville], Courier Job Printing Co., 1885. 48 pp. Copies in Brown University Library, New Haven, Connecticut, and in the Grosvenor Library in Buffalo, New York.

[12] See Dudley, *History and Genealogy of the Bangs Family*.

was at Bradstreet's in Galveston in 1881–1882, and at the Washington Hotel six years later. He lived on there until 1891,[13] leaving no trace.

Not so with the work of Bangs, of which much, especially of his work in Mexico, has survived. Although his printing of Mina's *Proclamation* at Galveston has not as yet been unearthed, many of his other printings bear witness to his industry and to the type and quality of his work. His earliest printings in Tamaulipas—the *Patriotic Song*, the *Bulletin*, and Mina's variations on the Galveston *Proclamation*—were immediately prohibited by the Inquisition; only a few copies were preserved surreptitiously in Mexico; one set of these has lately been garnered by Yale University. But, since the Spanish governmental system provided that copies of almost everything printed, especially if hostile to the government, be sent to Spain and, in many cases, also to governmental officials in other Spanish colonies, copies of all of these Soto la Marina printings have reposed, almost unnoticed, in Spanish archives, such as the Archive of the Indies in Seville.

Bangs' Monterrey and Saltillo imprints (1820–1823) met a better fate. Not only are there many—crisp and fresh as if printed yesterday—in the Archivo General de la Nación in Mexico City, but, as copies were ordered sent to all the towns of importance in the Eastern Interior Provinces, many reached San Antonio de Bejar, an outpost on the northern frontier of Spain, and were carefully buried there among the heaps of other governmental records. These precious papers were transferred by Bexar County some three-quarters of a century later to the University of Texas for preservation and translation. Many other copies remained among the municipal records of the towns of the Eastern Provinces until their monetary value became known; since then they are to be found in the hands of rare-book dealers in New York and other large centers. Most of the Tamaulipas governmental records, including Bangs' printing of 1827–1828

---

[13] *Galveston City Directory*, 1881–1882; 1888–1889; 1890–1891.

and also those of 1833–1837, were destroyed by fire or negligent handling, but some survive among the discarded materials in the capital at Victoria and among the Prieto and Hernández y Dávalos Papers at the University of Texas.

Specimens of Bangs' printing in Texas have fared worse. The one known second issue of the *Commercial Intelligencer,* formerly in the Rosenberg Library, has disappeared, but fortunately not before the University of Texas and the writer secured photocopies of it. Other issues are now at Yale University. Less than a dozen issues of *The Galvestonian* are known to exist, and only two of the 1842 *Daily News.* Five issues of the *Musquito* are at the University of Texas. One issue of the *Commercial Chronicle* is also there, with an item printed at the *Chronicle* office; the American Antiquarian Society at Worcester, Massachusetts, has another. Of the known issues of the *Corpus Christi Gazette* the largest number in one repository are scattered among the records of the War Department of the United States, in the National Archives in Washington, D.C. In that city, too, is a file of the *American Flag* which includes the issues that Bangs printed.

Further investigations in the Mexican, Cuban, and Spanish archives will certainly bring to light other Bangs imprints.

APPENDIX I

DOCUMENT 1

Proclamation of General Mina[1]

On leaving forever the political group for whose prosperity I have worked from my youthful years, I feel obligated to make clear to my friends and the entire nation the reasons that led to this decision. Never, I know, can I explain to the promoters of the frightful despotism which afflicts my unfortunate country; but I want the oppressed Spaniards, not their oppressors, to know that it is neither vengeance nor any other base passion that has influenced my public and private conduct, but the national interest, the most pure principles, and a deep and irresistible conviction.

It is well known that I was studying at the University of Zaragoza when the dissensions of the royal family of Spain and the base happenings at Bayonne reduced us to becoming the vile prey of a foreign nation or to sacrifice all in the defense of our rights—a choice only between ignominy or death. This tragic alternative pointed the line of duty to every Spaniard in whom the tyranny of the past rulers had not completely weakened their love of country. With many others I was moved by this sacred fire and, faithful to my duty, devoted myself to the common defense by accompanying, as a volunteer, the armies of the right and then of the center. When those armies were unfortunately shattered by the enemy, I fled to my birthplace, in which I was well known; I got together with twelve men, who selected me as their chief, and soon I succeeded in organizing in Navarre respected groups of volunteers, of which the Central Council named me the commanding general. I will pass in silence over the hardships and sacrifices of my companions in arms; let it be enough to say that we fought as good patriots until I had the misfortune to fall a prisoner. The division that I commanded then took my name as an emblem, and chose my uncle, Don Francisco Espoz, to succeed me; the na-

[1] Carlos María Bustamante, *Cuadro histórico de la revolución mexicana*, IV, Letter 17, pp. 5–6.

tional government which approved that decision also permitted my uncle to add to his name that of Mina; and everybody knows how deep the patriotism and how great the glory which distinguished that division under his orders.

When the Spanish nation resolved to enter a struggle so unequal, it can easily be supposed that the object of such risks and privations was not to reestablish the former government in its path of corruption and venality which had reduced us to such poverty. We remembered that we used to have inalienable rights of which our fundamental laws assured us, and of which we had been robbed by force. This recollection alone set everything in motion, and we resolved to conquer or die. The old abuses began to be effectively destroyed; our rights were revived; and we swore solemnly to defend them to the last ditch. This was the principle that moved the Spanish people to accomplish prodigies of valor in the last war.

On reestablishing on our soil the dignity of man and our ancient laws, we believed that Ferdinand VII, who had been our companion and a victim of oppression, would hasten to make amends, through benefits he could confer in his reign, for the misdeeds which the state had suffered under that of his predecessors. We owed him nothing; national generosity alone had called him gratuitously to the throne from which his own weakness and the poor administration of his father had cast him down. We would have pardoned the base acts of which he was guilty in Bayonne and Valencey; we would have forgotten that, more attentive to his own ease than to national honor, he had responded to our sacrifice by trying to entwine himself with the family of our oppressor; we trusted that he would always remember at what price he had been replaced in possession of the scepter, and that, united with those who had freed him, he would heal the deep wounds which, for his sake, the whole nation was suffering.

Spain succeeded at last in reconquering her territory and in securing the freedom of the king she had chosen. Half of the nation had been destroyed by war; the other half was drenched by enemy and by Spanish blood; and when Ferdinand was restored to the bosom of his protectors the ruins that marked his return route would have shown him his indebtedness and his obligations to those who had saved him. Could anyone believe that his famous decree, issued at Valencia the fourth of May, 1814, would be the forerunner of what that ungrateful one was preparing for the whole nation? The Cortes, that ancient aegis of Spanish liberty, to which in our orphaned state the nation owed its dignity and its honor, the Cortes which had just triumphed over its colossal enemy, now witnessed its own dissolution, with its members fleeing in all directions from the persecution of the courtiers [of Ferdinand]. Imprisonment, chains, and presidios were the recompense of those who had sufficient firmness to oppose such scandalous usurpation; the Inquisition, the ancient shield of tyranny—the impious, the infernal Inquisition—was reestablished with all the frenzy of its primitive institution; the Constitution was abolished, and Spain was enslaved anew by him whom she had rescued with rivers of blood and with immense sacrifices.

I, freed at that time from a French prison, rushed to Madrid to see if I could contribute, with other friends of liberty, to the reestablishment of the principles we had sworn to uphold. What was my surprise on seeing the new order of things! The satellites of the tyrant occupied themselves solely in completing the destruction of what our toil had accomplished; they thought only of completing the subjugation of the overseas provinces, and the minister, Don Manuel de Lardizabal, mistaking the sentiments of my heart, offered me the command of a division against Mexico; as if the cause which the Americans defended were different from that which had exalted the glory of the Spanish people; as if my principles likened me to the servile and egoistic [leaders] who ordered, to our disgrace, that America be pillaged and ravished; as if I, who had felt all the weight of the chains that crushed my fellow citizens, would become the hangman of an innocent people.

My wounds, although not entirely healed, pointed in an unmistakable manner to my duty. I retired accordingly to Navarre and in concert with my uncle, Don Francisco Espoz, determined to take control of Pamplona, and offer there an asylum to the Spanish veterans and to the deserving countrymen who had been proscribed, or treated as criminals. During one entire night I was master of that city, but when my uncle was on the way to reinforce me, in order to hold in check, if it should become necessary, a part of the garrison which did not promise cooperation, one of his regiments refused to obey him. Those valiant soldiers who had triumphed so often in defending national independence were now held in check, when it was a question of their own freedom, by shameful preconceptions, deep-rooted prejudices, and by the ignorance we had not been able to dispel. With the undertaking thus frustrated, I, with some of my companions, had to flee to a foreign country. Animated constantly by a love of liberty, I determined to defend that cause wherever my weak efforts might be supported by public opinion and the efforts of the community, wherever they would be most helpful to my oppressed country and most destructive to its tyrants. From the provinces on this side of the ocean the usurper obtained the means to strengthen his arbitrariness; in them, the people were also fighting for their liberty; and from that moment the cause of the Americans became mine.

Spaniards: Do you think me degenerate? Do you conclude that I have abandoned the interest, the prosperity of Spain? Since when did her happiness depend on the degradation of a part of our brethren? Will she be less happy, when the King lacks the means of supporting his absolute rule? be less happy, when there are no monopolists to sustain her despotism? Will she be less agricultural, less industrial, when there are no exclusive concessions to be granted, no employment in the Indies with which to fatten and increase the number of base sycophants? Will she be less given to commerce, if it is less limited to certain and specific persons and passes into the hands of a more numerous and enlightened class?

The more sane and reasonable parts of Spain are thoroughly convinced that it is not only impossible to conquer America again, but impossible and contrary to the best and wisest interests. Aside from the unquestionable justice which the Americans have on their side, what would be the advantages which might be secured in subjugating her again? Who would gain from such iniquity, if it were possible?

Two classes of people are the only and exclusive ones who would take advantage there of the slavery of the Americans—the King and monopolists: the first to strengthen his absolute rule and force us at will; the second, to gain riches with which to maintain despotism and to keep the people in beggary. Here we have the most active agents of Ferdinand and the most cruelly bent enemies of America. The courtesans and the monopolists wish to eternalize the pupilage to which they have brought the nation, in order to erect on the ruins their fortunes and that of their children.

Spain, they say, cannot exist without our Americas. It is clear that by "Spain" these gentlemen understand the small number they, their relatives, and partisans constitute. Because, once America is emanci-

157

pated, there will be no exclusive favors, nor sales of governments, intendancies, and other offices in the Indies for their creatures. Because, once the American ports are opened to foreign nations, Spanish commerce will pass to a more numerous and enlightened class. Because, finally, once America is free, her national industry will revive—an industry now sacrificed to the groveling interests of some few men.

If, from this point of view the emancipation of the Americans is useful and advantageous to the majority of the Spanish people, it is much more so on account of its infallible tendency to establish definitively liberal governments throughout the old monarchy. Without demolishing everywhere that colossus—despotism and monopolies—we shall never be able to recover our dignity. To accomplish this, it is indispensable that all people who speak the Spanish language learn to be free, to know and to exercise their rights. When one single section of America has gained its independence we can flatter ourselves with the fact that liberal principles late or early will extend their blessings to the rest. This is the terrible fact that the agents and partisans of tyranny fear unceasingly. They see, in the height of their desperation, the empire crumbling, and they would be willing, in their impotent fury, to sacrifice it in its entirety.

Under such circumstances, consider, Spaniards, the experience of the past, and in it you will find abundant instructive lessons with which to guide your future conduct. The cause of free men is that of undegenerated Spaniards. One's country is not limited to the place in which he was born, but more properly by that which protects our personal rights. Your oppressors calculate that, in order to reestablish over you and your children their barbarous domination, it is necessary to enslave all. Justly the celebrated Pitt feared similar consequences when he justified, before the British Parliament, the resistance of the Anglo-Americans: "They say that America is obstinate, that America is in open rebellion. I rejoice, sir, that America resists. Three million citizens who, indifferent to the impulse of liberty, voluntarily submit, would be later the most effective means of placing chains on all the rest."

Americans: I have here set forth the principles that led me to join you; if they are right, you will respond satisfactorily to my sincerity. Only for the sake of liberty have I as yet taken up arms; only in its defense will I bear them in the future. Permit me, friends, permit me to take part in your glorious tasks; accept the cooperation of my small efforts in favor of your noble undertaking. . . . Count me among your compatriots. Would that I might merit this title by helping you to win your liberty or by sacrificing my own existence. Then, in recompense, say at least this to your sons: "This happy land was bathed in blood twice by servile Spaniards, abject slaves of a king; but there were also Spaniards, the friends of liberty, who sacrificed their ease and their life for our good."

Galveston, February 22, 1817   *Xavier Mina*

DOCUMENT 2

Bulletin I of the Auxiliary Division of the
Republic of Mexico[1]

The invasion of Spain by the French army in 1808 aroused Don Xavier Mina, among others, to the defense and independence of his nation, an undertaking that was then regarded as hopeless. Mina's military exploits, which date from a tender age and were at first without backing, attracted to him gradually the troops with which he so distinguished himself that he was shortly honored by the Central Council with the command of Navarre, his native country, and by the Council of Aragon with the command of Upper Aragon.

It was young Mina who established the system of guerrilla warfare to which Spain owed, to a large degree, her salvation. After being made a prisoner while carrying out an order of the First Regency, he profited in Vincennes from lessons with General Lahorie and from the excellent library in the castle there. Various turns of fortune followed, among them the defeat of Mina and the unfortunate Porlier, who had been struggling for the regeneration of Spain during the disastrous reign of Ferdinand VII. After seeking asylum in London, where he enjoyed a pension, he was induced by the similarity of the situation in Mexico with that of Spain and by his own steadfast principles to go to the aid of the Mexican patriots who were fighting for

---

[1] The imprint of *Bulletin I* is: "General Headquarters of Soto la Marina," April 28, 1817. [Signed by] The Chief of Staff, Novoa. Original at Yale. Photocopy, LMS.

159

Pioneer Printer

the freedom of their country. Influential persons in England and in North America helped to promote the project. Consequently Mina left England at the middle of May, 1816, and arrived in North America at the end of June.

After making the necessary preparations for the expedition, he left Baltimore September 26 for Port-au-Prince on the island of Santo Domingo, where he disembarked the thirteenth of October, and there organized his forces without delay. When he learned that Commodore Louis Aury was at Galveston with supplies and the intention of cooperating with the insurgents of Mexico, he decided to join that officer. He left Port-au-Prince on October 27 and arrived at the eastern end of St. Louis Island, where the port of Galveston was located, the twenty-second of November. Bad weather and the need to make arrangements for many essential details led Mina to remain there until the sixth of this month. From there, with the land forces concentrated under his command and that of Aury, the expedition set out for the Mexican coast.

It is impossible to describe in detail the disappointments and troubles that were faced during those seven months. Among them were the machinations of the Spanish minister in the United States, Luis de Onís, who even offered his daughter in marriage to Diego Correa, a Canary Islander, as a reward for joining the division for the purpose of assassinating Mina; the pernicious acts of bribed patriots in the United States, at Port-au-Prince, and in Galveston, which resulted in the defection of some officers and men and in the loss of much material; the hurricane of September 18 in Port-au-Prince, which damaged two boats that preceded us and killed an officer and three sailors; the epidemic that took the lives of thirty of our force during the trip from Port-au-Prince to Galveston; the fraudulent tricks of some of those who had joined the division; the dangers, the privations, the bad weather, the discomforts and misfortunes of all kinds, especially during the halt at Galveston. Yet all of these were not sufficient to weaken the valor and determination of these men of varying nationalities who, moved by a moral force, marched to an heroic end under a commander whom they believed would guide them to its attainment.

Having touched at the mouth of the Rio Bravo del Norte [the Rio Grande] to secure fresh water, General Mina issued to his men the following proclamation.

Appendix I

Companions in Arms: You have united under my command for the purpose of working for the liberty and independence of Mexico. For seven years this country has been struggling against its oppressors to attain that noble purpose. Unaided until now, it remains for generous souls to join in the struggle. Thus you, under my command, have undertaken to defend the best cause on earth. We have had to overcome many difficulties; I can bear witness to your loyalty and suffering. Good men will learn to appreciate your courage and soon you will receive your reward— the triumph or the honor which results. You know that when we step on Mexican soil it is not our purpose to conquer, but to help the illustrious defenders of the most sacred of human rights. Let us work then so that their efforts may be crowned with victory, taking an active part in the glorious effort in which they are engaged. I urge upon you to respect the religion, the people, and their property; and I hope you will never forget that valor, the outgrowth of severe discipline, leads to the success of all great enterprises. Rio Bravo del Norte, April 12, 1817. Xavier Mina.

At this point we found a small detachment of Royalists. Thinking we were also Royalists, they told us freely about the poverty and the disorganization of the government that oppressed them and corroborated what we had learned of the actual state of Mexico through correspondence that one of our corsairs intercepted a few days before. Here we lost an esteemed officer and an artilleryman who drowned while attempting to land.

When we reached the bar of the Santander River (which is 23 degrees and 45 minutes of latitude north and 97 degrees and 58 minutes of longitude west, according to the meridian of Greenwich), the General ordered disembarkation, which was effected on the twenty-first in good order and without opposition. Our troops occupied an abandoned hut. In a little while appeared two individuals who, as we learned later, belonged to a Royalist detachment which was stationed there; they withdrew when our boats neared them. Nevertheless they proved friendly and served us as guides. They confirmed the dissension between the viceroy of Mexico and the commandant general of the Interior Provinces and added that the Royalists did not expect us at that point, but at Tampico, where their principal forces were disposed.

Boats from any port can anchor close to the bar, and this can be passed in boats and lighters without difficulty, at least at high tide and in calm weather. The bar itself would be no obstacle if we used pontoons, as there was earlier an opening. The river which empties here forms at the mouth a beautiful bay and is navigable to the town of Soto la Marina, which is fifteen or twenty leagues upstream. For this reason as well as for the proximity to the principal places in the Interior Provinces, this communication is very important and perhaps, in that respect, preferable to others. Therefore the General decided to hold it, by establishing here a military and a naval base.

On the twenty-second the General departed on foot with his troops amid acclamation and rejoicing. The vanguard, under the command of Major Sardá, saw ahead of it, during the march, a squadron of Royalist cavalry under the command of Lieutenant Garza; but it did not venture, in the least, to halt us. The leader had led the inhabitants of Soto la Marina to believe that we were about to burn their homes, lay waste their fields, and ravish their women. As a result, the greater part of the population had abandoned their homes and fled to the woods.

On the twenty-fourth the division arrived at the town. Sardá was received with bell-ringing, and the General was welcomed under a canopy by the priest and some citizens. The rest, seeing that our conduct was the exact opposite of what Lieutenant Garza had led them to believe, slowly joined them. The General made a speech to the people concerning the object of his coming and the justice of the American cause. Monsignor Mier, the vicar of the division, did the same and granted indulgences to those who joined us in good faith in the noble enterprise in which we were engaged. The General instituted such changes in officials as the new order of things demanded, selecting the citizens of best repute and ability to fill the various posts. In a word, the town of Soto la Marina is well satisfied to have us as guests. The landowners have furnished us horses and beef cattle; the young fellows have enlisted with us; and all marvel at our conduct and at our liberal ideas.

Such a favorable outcome, in strong contrast to the many reverses we had earlier suffered, led us to believe that Providence was ready to put an end to the misfortunes that had afflicted this beautiful part of the New World, making it possible that, once emancipated, its riches may reach all other nations, and Mexico may enjoy the opulence which is rightfully hers. But tyranny and darkness have existed here too long to give way easily to liberty and enlightenment. The cooperation of the citizens won over to our cause will help to complete the work in less time than with further aggravation of the evils already suffered. In the end this great accomplishment, through the force of circumstances and the weight of public opinion, is inevitable. The General has decided to publish the proclamation which follows: "To Spaniards and Americans." [Here follows, in condensed form and with the omission of the remarks on the Inquisition and the section addressed to the Spaniards, the proclamation earlier published at Galveston. It is signed by Xavier Mina and dated Soto la Marina, April 25, 1817.]

DOCUMENT 3

A Letter from Samuel Bangs to Dr. Servando de Mier[1]

Saltillo, July 13, 1822

Dr. Servando Mier

My respected and venerated Father:

Since we separated at the time of the Mina Expedition, I have had no reliable news of your whereabouts until now, but this news has given me great pleasure. I am writing this as evidence of my boundless joy and the eternal gratitude I tried to express in return for the kindness you showed me when I was your printer.

I am well and in this city where I have been for three months since I came with the interim Commandant General Don Gaspar López, for you know that Arredondo took possession of the press when we were made prisoners, and that I had the good fortune, through the will of God, to have my life saved, as I was a printer. I have since practiced my profession for the government, but with such miserable wages that I can scarcely buy food. Even now I am paid only eighteen pesos a month, and treated as unjustly as if I were a prisoner, for these gentlemen forget that I also risked my life for the liberty of the North, although it was not won in exactly the way we planned.

In this country I recognize you as a father who has consoled me in adversity and as the outstanding member of the Expedition, for you know what happens to an ignorant foreigner.

Will you have the goodness to let me know if members of the Expedition are being paid or not, so that I may file my petition.

[1] Mier Papers, TxU.

163

If you are contemplating establishing yourself in this country and becoming a director of a press, please give me the preference; and if I can secure a permit to leave the country I will go and bring one from the United States, where I have funds at my disposal.

Please answer me through Don Vicente Mier, your brother and the bearer of this letter, or by mail.

May God guard your precious life many years as a consolation of this foreigner, for so begs your devoted and solicitous servant who kisses your hand,

Samuel Bangs [Rubric]

I must tell you that my name is Manuel so you can put it on the envelope. This was the name they gave me when I was baptized. I am signing "Samuel" so that thus you may recognize me.

DOCUMENT 4

The Application of José Manuel Bangs for Land in Texas[1]

At head: Seal of the Treasury of the State of Coahuila and Texas. [Stamped paper] for the biennium of 1830–1831.

Your Excellency [José María Viesca, Governor]: José Manuel Bangs, a native of the United States of the North, a citizen of this state and a resident of this capital, with all due respect to you, wishes to state:

That on the twenty-sixth of September, 1816, I left Baltimore with the expedition of the illustrious General Xavier Mina, which disembarked at Soto la Marina in May, 1817, employed as a printer. I continued in this capacity throughout this period, and with arms in my hands I defended the fort at La Marina during the attacks which the Spanish General Arredondo made on it until the fifteenth of June of the above-mentioned year of 1817, when I became a prisoner with the garrison which defended the fort.

I was taken to the city of Monterrey and there, as a prisoner, I was forced to work at my trade without any recompense, enduring gnaw-

[1] Certified copy in Texas, General Land Office, Spanish Grants, XXX, fols. 200–201. Photocopy, LMS.

ing hunger and hard work during four long years. In order to barely subsist, I had to engage at night in other work, foreign to my profession, for the tyrannical Commandant did not even give me sufficient food.

In 1821 when the independence of the nation was proclaimed I was freed, and in 1823 I returned to my country. In 1827 I came back with my family and my own press, which I established in the state of Tamaulipas. I sold it to the government of that state in order to move to this capital with another press, which I in turn sold to your government, in whose service I am at present employed.

Since I am now interested in establishing myself permanently in the Department of Texas with my family and devoting myself to agriculture and cattle raising, I respectfully request that you grant me as a colonist six sitios of uncultivated land which that state has on the west side of the Colorado on the road beyond San Antonio, adjoining the land of Colonel Milam. I promise to settle and cultivate the said land in accordance with the Law of Colonization, if granted me in return for my suffering and services on behalf of the country, both of which are attested by the three certificates herewith enclosed and marked respectively as Exhibits Numbers 1, 2, and 3. . . . . City of Leona Vicario [Saltillo], January 20, 1830. [Signed]: José Manuel Bangs.

DOCUMENT 5

The Baptismal Certificate of Samuel Bangs VIII

I, the Rt. Rev. (Msgr.) José María García Siller, movable priest of the Parish of the Sagrario of Saltillo, Coahuila.

C e r t i f y that in the Baptismal Register No. 23 (twenty-three) of the Archive of this parish on Page 151 verso (one hundred fifty and one verso) there is found an Entry which literally says:

In the Margin: "In the Parish Church of the City of Santiago de Leona Vicario on April 5, 1829, the undersigned parish priest Citizen José Ignacio Sánchez solemnly baptized with holy oil and sacred chrism and gave the name of Samuel Salvador to a child of thirteen days, legitimate son of the Citizens Samuel Bang and of María Susana Payne, its paternal grandparents Samuel Bang and Hanah Grice and

165

the maternal John Payne and Maria Lincetta Jones. Godparents were the Citizens Joaquin Barragán and María de la Luz Barragán, to whom I pointed out the obligations contracted and the spiritual parentage. Which I sign, J. Igno. Sánchez (Rubric).
True copy of the original which I certify . . . June 9, 1959.

The Parish Priest
Mons. José María García Siller

APPENDIX II

EXTANT SPECIMENS OF SAMUEL BANGS' PRINTING
A TENTATIVE LISTING[1]

1. WITH THE MINA EXPEDITION

1. *Proclamation* of Mina. Galveston, February 22, 1817. See Appendix I, Document 1. Only the reprint by Bustamante is extant.
2. *Address* of Mina. Rio Bravo del Norte, April 12, 1817. In *Boletín I.*
3. *Canción patriótica.* Soto la Marina, April [22], 1817. TxU.
4. *Proclamation* of Mina. Soto la Marina, April 25, 1817. In *Boletín I.*
5. *Boletín I. (Bulletin of the Auxiliary Division of the Mexican Republic.)* In Appendix I, Document 3. Yale, National Museum of Mexico. Photocopies, TxU and LMS.
6. *Proclamation of Mina to the Spanish and American Soldiers of the King.* Soto la Marina, May 18, 1817. Yale. Photocopies, TxU and LMS.

2. IN THE EASTERN INTERIOR PROVINCES

a. *At Monterrey (1820–1822)*

Blank Forms for Various Purposes, and an Invitation

7. Appointments to military posts. AHE, 1820.
8. Appointments headed by Arredondo's full name and title with coat-of-arms of Spain in lower left-hand corner. AHE, 1820.

---

[1] The purpose of this list of "Extant Specimens" is (1) to give some idea of the types, variety, and volume of a pioneer printer's work, and (2) to point out some of the typographical peculiarities, such as the almost complete absence of accents and the random employment of italics, by which pieces of Bangs' early work, which now have a considerable monetary value, may, in the absence of an imprint, be identified.

Because of the difficulty in locating the now widely scattered specimens of Bangs' printing, this list cannot be definitive.

9. Acknowledgments of receipt of correspondence. AHE, 1820.
10. Classification (of soldiers, employees) as disabled, with orders to Treasury to pay as such.
11. Passports. AHE, 1820.
12. An Invitation—El obispo de Monterrey, el Comandante General de estas provincias, y el Capitán Don José de Castro, Padrino, Abuelo y Padre del Parbulo Don José Joaquín de Castro (que ha sido Dios servido llevarse para si a su Sta. Gloria) suplican a V. el honor de su asistencia al Entierro, y demas oficios que se han de celebrar en la Santa Iglesia Catedral de esta Ciudad a los diez y media de la mañana de hoy 30 del corriente; a cuyo favor [viviran] a V. sumanente reconocidos. AHE, 1820.

Circulars, Decrees, and Pamphlets

13. D. Joaquín de Arredondo . . . Issues a royal *cédula* of Ferdinand VII of Spain (Madrid, November 9, 1819) in which that monarch announces his marriage to María Josefa Amalia of Saxony. Monterrey, April 19, 1820. AGE.
14. D. Joaquín de Arredondo . . . Issues a royal *cédula* on succession to the throne of Spain. Rubric of Arredondo. Monterrey, April 19, 1820. AGE.
15. ———. Issues a bando of the viceroy, Juan Ruiz de Apodaca (May 31, 1820) ordering obedience to the Constitution of 1812 which the king has sworn to support. Rubric of Arredondo. Monterrey, June 13, 1820. AGE.
16. D. Joaquín de Arredondo . . . Issues decree of the Cortes of Cádiz (May 23, 1812) and of Ferdinand VII (March 9 and 17, 1820) regarding elections of alcaldes and *ayuntamientos*. Also orders such elections in the four provinces under his command. Rubric of Arredondo. Monterrey, July 6, 1820. Three separate sheets glued together. AGE.
17. Royal plan (Madrid, March 22, 1820) for putting Constitution into effect. Instrucción for calling of Cortes. 22 sections. No date of Monterrey reprint. 5 pages. Italics *g, m, d, P, A.* Lower case "o" serves as zero. TxU.
18. [No official heading]. Arredondo issues order of the Secretary of State of Spain (March 25, 1820) that all correspondence with the Overseas Ministry be classified and filed separately, according to decree of April 6, 1812. Rubric of Arredondo. In script: "Monterrey, July 21, 1820." 2 leaves. TxU.
19. D. Joaquín de Arredondo . . . Issues a general pardon granted

by the king (December 20, 1819) and issued by the viceroy April 13, 1820. Monterrey, August 1, 1820). AGE.

20. ———. Circular ordering Constitution of 1812 republished on August 15, that all officials take oath to support it, and then visit jails and set prisoners, with few exceptions, free. Rubric of Arredondo. Monterrey, [blank] August, 1820. AGE.

21. "Gaceta extraordinaria del Gobierno de México." Mexico City, August 29, 1820. Announcement that king has sworn (July 9) to support the Constitution. MS copy of Monterrey reprint. TxU.

22. D. Joaquín de Arredondo . . . Issues royal decree (Madrid, April 24, 1820) that teachers and clergy in all schools and universities read and explain the Constitution to students. Rubric of Arredondo. Monterrey, September [blank], 1820. 3 printed pages. TxU.

23. Instructions for holding elections in overseas provinces for deputies to the Cortes of Spain for 1820–1821. Madrid, March [blank], 1820. 19 sections. No date of Monterrey reprint. Italics *d* and *p.* 4 pages. A reprint of pp. 9–12 of a 20-page decree and Supplement (Madrid, March 24, 1820). TxU.

24. Aviso. A report by the secretary, José Eustaquio Fernández, of the meeting of a Junta electoral (October 2, 1820) at which J. B. Valdez and Felipe de la Garza were elected deputies to the Cortes of 1820–1821. Monterrey, October 2, 1820. Half sheet. TxU.

25. Aviso. A report by J. E. Fernández of the election that day of deputies to the Provincial Deputation from each of the four Eastern Interior Provinces. Monterrey, October [in script] 3, 1820. Italic *o* and *d;* "hazendado" [*sic*]. TxU.

26. *Reglamento provisional para la milicia nacional local en la Peninsula e Islas adjacentes.* Madrid, April 24, 1820. In script: "Es copia." Monterrey, 9 de Octubre de 1820. 5 leaves. Italic *g;* "polnico" for *político.* Copied from large broadside issued at Mexico City, September 15, 1820. TxU.

27. D. Joaquín de Arredondo . . . Circular ordering that the swearing of the Constitution be celebrated on October 12 to 14. Monterrey, October 11, 1820. Rubric of Arredondo. TxU.

28. ———. Confirms decree of Ferdinand VII (April 15, 1820) that all laws pertaining to overseas colonies be put into effect. Monterrey, October 17, 1820. Rubric of Arredondo. Italic *R* and *g.* TxU.

29. ———. Issues report from the Ministry of Overseas (Madrid,

July 7 and 10, 1820) that officers of the Cortes have been chosen and oath taken by the king. Rubric of Arredondo. Monterrey, November [6], 1820. TxU.

30. *Habitantes de las Quatro Provincias de Oriente* [Inhabitants of the Four Interior Provinces]. [First address of the Provincial Deputation to those within its jurisdiction.] Unsigned. No rubric. Italic *E*. Monterrey, November 20, 1820. 2 pp. TxU.

31. D. Joaquín de Arredondo . . . Reissues royal order (May 28, 1820) that decrees of September 8, 1813, prohibiting whipping or other forms of corporal punishment be enforced. Monterrey, November 22, 1820. Rubric of Arredondo. TxU.

32. ———. Cordillera. Los Comandantes militares, Jueces territoriales, Dueños y Administradores de Hacienda, de los puntos anotados en la cordillera del margen, darán la mas pronto direccion a [in script]: "1 adjunto Pliego, muy executivo rotulado al Teniente Coronel Dⁿ Antonio Elozua" anotando a continuacion la hora en que [1°] recivan y den curso, por convenir asi al mejor servicio de la Nacion. Sale a las ocho de la noche de esta dia. [Carries other notations of receipt and dispatch en route to Saltillo.]

Full heading of Arredondo with all of *Pelegrin* on second line; *Goberndor* for *Gobernador* and *Coreos* for *Correos*. In script, after *Nacion:* "Monterrey 23 de Nov^e de 1820." Signed "Arredondo" with rubric. AHE. Package labeled "1820."

33. D. Joaquín de Arredondo . . . Royal order (April 22, 1820) that decree of Cortes (November 9, 1812) favoring rights of citizens of overseas provinces, especially Indians, be enforced. Text of decree follows. Rubric of Arredondo. Monterrey, November 25, 1820. Italics *E, A, C,* and *R*. 2 leaves. This decree prohibited personal servitude, enforced labor on roads and public works, and *repartimientos*. TxU.

34. ———. A circular addressed to the newly established *ayuntamientos* whose duties he had earlier outlined to them. As none has complied with the decree of June 23 included in the *Instrucción para el Gobierno Político de las Provincias* he reprints the portion requiring that each such body furnish the political chief quarterly statistical reports, showing births, deaths, marriages, etc. Rubric of Arredondo. Monterrey, December 1, 1820. 4-page folder printed on 2 pages. No heading. TxU.

35. ———. Circular repeating royal decree of May 16, 1820, ordering observance of decree of June 8, 1813, on free establishment of factories and free exercise of all useful industries. Monterrey,

Appendix II

December 5, 1820. Rubric of Arredondo. 7 lines of decree in 6-point; articles 1 and 2 in 8-point leaded. TxU.

36. D. Joaquín de Arredondo . . . Authorizes rewards to the beggars who had aided the Spanish army. Monterrey, December 8, 1820. Library of Vito Alessio Robles.

37. ———. Reprint of decree (April 24, 1820) issued at Monterrey on September [blank], 1820, ordering priests and teachers to read and explain the Constitution of Spain. Also orders editions printed in America sold at cost. 8 sections. Monterrey, January 2, 1821, but over the printed 2 is written in ink 9. Rubric of Arredondo. 1 long leaf. TxU.

38. ———. Royal order (Madrid, July 1, 1820) that decrees of the Cortes, including that of December 4, 1810, and those of January 26, July 14, September 28, November 11, and December 17, 1811, be enforced. Monterrey, January [in script] 16, 1821. Rubric of Arredondo. 1 long leaf. Two sheets fastened together. TxU.

39. ———. Decree (August 17, 1820) granting general pardon to criminals. 11 articles. Reprinted at Monterrey, January [in script] 16, 1821. Rubric of Arredondo. Italic *E*. 1 half sheet. TxU.

40. ———. A reminder that by decree of April 19, 1814, the use of term "magestad" was restricted in application to the king. Monterrey, January [in script] 20, 1821. Rubric of Arredondo. Italic *g, E, R, G*. Note in ink on copy in the Bexar Archives: "Published second time on February 10, 1821." TxU.

41. D. Joaquín de Arredondo . . . Reprint of decree (Madrid, August 24, 1820) ordering the May 11 decree of amnesty to include British prisoners. Monterrey, January 22, 1821. Rubric of Arredondo. Italics *G, R, E, g*. TxU.

42. Provincias Internas de Oriente. Diputación Provincial. An appeal to the "Moradores de estas quatro provincias de Oriente" for contributions with which to arm and equip five hundred soldiers to defend the region against the Indians and an exhortation to each man to do his duty. Signed by Arredondo and José León Lobo, with Rafael Eça y Musquiz as secretary. In script: "Monterrey, February 12, 1821." Italic *l, d*. 4-page folder printed on 3. Page 1 is 8-point; pp. 2–3, 6-point. TxU.

43. D. Joaquín de Arredondo . . . Reprint of a royal decree (June 30, 1820) ordering enforcement of a series of specified decrees, beginning with that of December 1, 1810, and continuing with that of April 11, 1811, May 3 and June 4, 1812, etc. Monterrey,

171

March 13, 1821. Rubric of Arredondo. 1 long leaf, composed of 2 whole sheets and 1 half-sheet fastened together. TxU.

44. Provincias Internas de Oriente. Junta Electoral. Aviso al publico. Announces the election of two deputies to the Cortes and a substitute; also four provincial deputies and two alternates. Monterrey, March 13, 1821. Printed signature of Juan Fr. Gutiérrez. TxU.

45. D. Joaquín de Arredondo . . . Habitantes de las quatro provincias de Esta America Septentrional. Announces the defection of Iturbide. Monterrey, March 13, 1821. Rubric of Arredondo. Italics *S, E, C*, and *c*. TxU.

46. The announcement of Dr. José Eustaquio Fernández that he has been elected one of the deputies to the Cortes from the four interior provinces. Monterrey, March 16, 1821. Library of Vito Alessio Robles.

47. Acknowledgments of receipt of federal correspondence.

Con indice de V. de [blank] de [Marzo ppso] he recibido los oficios que comprende desde el numero [1°] hasta el [14] inclusivo, . . . Monterrey, April 7, 1821. Rubric of Arredondo. Dates and numbers are in script. These bimonthly reports carry the rubric of Arredondo until August 2. TxU.

48. A proclamation "A los habitantes de esta Nueva España" issued by Viceroy Apodaca in Mexico City on April 5, 1821, appealing to all citizens to support the government. Printed signature of "El Conde del Venadito"—the title of Apodaca. Reimpreso en Monterrey, Ymprenta del gobierno. No date of reprint. Note the new form of imprint. TxU.

49. Circular de la consulta hecha a S.M. sobre el plan de autores que deben adoptarse para la instruccion pública en todas las universidades y establecimientos literarios de la Monarquia. Mandada cumplir en Ultramar por el real orden de 9 de Octubre de 1820. Año de 1821. Monterrey, Ymprenta del Gobierno. 18 pp. The most extensive work as yet noted. Has disappeared from the Bexar Archives. TxU.

50. D. Joaquín de Arredondo . . . As result of Iturbide uprising, Arredondo prohibits travel in the four provinces without passport, and announces penalties; restricts printing, and prohibits the circulation of letters or proclamations in regard to the uprising. Monterrey, April 28, 1821. Rubric of Arredondo. Italics, *E, A, C, N, P, l, d.* TxU.

51. ———. Issues circular of Iturbide signed at the Hacienda del Colorado, June 20, 1821, abolishing certain war taxes and im-

positions; reduces the alcabala tax to 6 per cent, and orders enforcement. Rubric of Arredondo. Monterrey, July 27, 1821. First line of heading ends with "Pele." TxU.

52. D. Gaspar Antonio López Teniente / Coronel del Exercito Ymperial Mexicano de las Tres Garantias, Comandante General y Gefe superior-politico interino de las quatro provincias / internas orientales, comandante en gefe del (*sic*) de operación en ellas, & & . . . Issues decree of the Soberana Junta Provisional Gubernativa of October 23, 1821, granting amnesty to military personnel. Monterrey, November 15, 1821. Rubric of López. Italic *E* and *g*. TxU.

53. D. Gaspar Antonio López . . . Issues another decree of October 23, 1821, granting pardon (indulto a los paisanos) to all prisoners, with few exceptions. Monterrey, November 15, 1821. Rubric of López. Italic *E* and *g*. TxU.

54. ————. Issues a decree (approved by the Regency October 22, 1821) limiting freedom of the press on subject of the government. Monterrey, November 18, 1821. In script over 18 is "27." Rubric of López. Heading, 4 lines; closing, 5 lines. Italics. TxU.

55. ————. Issues decree dated October 8, 1821, reducing *alcabala* tax to 6 per cent and freeing some articles entirely (in substance same as signed by Iturbide on June 20 and published at Querétaro on [June] 30th). Monterrey, November 28, 1821. Rubric of López. Italics, *E, l, e, m, t, o*. Large bold-faced capitals. TxU.

56. D. Gaspar Antonio López . . . Issues decree approved by the Regency November [14], 1821, defining the powers and prerogatives of Iturbide and assigning him title of "Generalísimo Almirante." Rubric of López. Monterrey, December, [in script] 18, 1821. TxU.

57. Completed forms, generally bimonthly, showing receipt of correspondence from August, 1821, to December 30, 1821. All these 1821 forms are set in italics. TxU.

58. D. Gaspar Antonio López . . . Issues as a circular the decree of the Soberana Junta Gubernativa (October 26, 1821) dealing with the administration of the tobacco industry and authorizing steps to prevent contraband. Monterrey, January [in script] 12, 1822. Rubric of López. TxU.

59. ————. Issues orders of the captain general of the Eastern and Western Interior Provinces, [Anastacio Bustamante], (Mexico City, December 28, 1821), deploring the great number of desertions, emphasizing the penalties, and outlining means of pre-

vention. Monterrey, January [blank], 1822. Signed "Bustamante." Italics *d, q, p.* TxU.

60. Forms [completed in script] of acknowledgment of correspondence from January 12 to March 26. Rubric of López. TxU.

61. D. Gaspar Antonio López, Comandante General y Gefe Superior Interino . . . Reprints decree of the Soberana Junta (January 3) issued on January 10, 1822, granting permission for free trade in mules by land between the United States and the Eastern Interior Provinces. Monterrey, January 29, 1822. "Segundo de la Independencia de este Imperio." Signed Gaspar López. TxU.

62. D. Gaspar Antonio López . . . Reissues the decree of the Junta (January 12, 1822) suspending issuance of passports to leave the country. Monterrey, January 31, 1822. Rubric of López. Italics *E, p, l, d, q.* TxU.

63. ———. Reprint of decree of the Junta (December 15, 1821) ordering the property confiscated for adherence to the cause of independence returned. Monterrey, February 4, 1822. Rubric of López. Italics *C, n, l, p, q, d, I, B, A.* TxU.

64. ———. Reprints decree of the Junta of December 15, 1821, that the tax on cards remain as of bando published the previous October 9. Monterrey, February 7, 1822. Rubric of López. Italics, *d, l, p, E, I.* TxU.

65. ———. Issues oficio of the Junta (Mexico City, December 28, 1821) inviting all to write on the Constitution to be framed for the Empire. Monterrey, February 8, 1822. Rubric of López. Italics, *d, g, E, I.* TxU.

66. ———. Reprints decree of the Junta on the transportation of money or treasure (December 31, 1821). Monterrey, February 9, 1822, "Segundo de la independencia." Rubric of López. Usual italics. TxU.

67. ———. Reissues decree of the Junta (January 7, 1822) restating the design of the imperial coat of arms, seal, and flag. Monterrey, February 10, 1822. Rubric of López. TxU.

68. *Aclaraciones* of the law of May 23, 1812, concerning city councils with revision of March 28, 1821, by which the number of members in large cities was ordered increased. In script: "Es copia. Monterrey, Febr° 14 de 1822." Juan Antonio Padilla. A Bangs reprint. Italics, *d, l, p, q, c.* TxU.

69. D. Gaspar Antonio López . . . & & Decree approved January 25, 1822, authorizing an increase in the membership of city councils in Querétaro, Guadalajara, and its observance in other cities.

Appendix II

"Es copia. Monterrey, 14 de febrero de 1822." Italics, *D, c, l, p, I.* TxU.

70. ———. Reglamento provisional (November 20, 1821) para el establecimiento de las seis capitanías generales (26 sections) ... approved by the Junta on January 15, 1822, with 7 additional sections outlining the duties of the captain generals of the empire. Monterrey, February 17, 1822. 2 sheets pasted together. TxU.

71. ———. Issues decree approved by the Regency (January 28, 1822) that questions of capital or property utilized by troops during the Revolution be solved according to royal *cédula* of May 31, which urged contestants to try to iron out their own difficulties and only after such failed to apply to the courts. Monterrey, February 19, 1822. Rubric of López. TxU.

72. ———. Issues decree approved by the Regency (December 21, 1821) on contraband in tobacco and orders observance of royal order of December 17, 1813, which is included. Monterrey, February 20, 1822. Rubric of López. TxU.

73. ———. Order of the Soberana Junta that all *ayuntamientos* and juntas provinciales proceed with their work on statistics. Approved by the Regency, January 3, 1822. Issued at Monterrey, March 4, 1822. Full heading of López. TxU.

74. ———. Order of the Junta (approved February 7, 1822) that administration of the navy be combined with that of the army. Issued at Monterrey, March 6, 1822. TxU.

75. ———. Decree (February 24, 1822) setting forth powers of Constituent Congress and oaths to be taken by members and those comprising the Regency. Mexico City, February 26, 1822; Monterrey, March 12, 1822. Italics, *d, l, p, q.* TxU.

76. ———. Regulations of Congress governing reception of the Regency and form of oath to be taken. Mexico City, February 26; Monterrey, March 13, 1822. TxU.

77. ———. On sanctity of persons of deputies. Passed, February 24; issued February 26, 1822. Monterrey, March 13, 1822. TxU.

78. ———. Decree (February 26, 1822) authorizing courts, civil and ecclesiastical, to continue to function. Form of oath at bottom of page. Monterrey, March 14, 1822. Italics, *d, e, l, x.* TxU.

79. ———. Decree prescribing felicitations to Congress to be written and not presented in person. Mexico City, February 26; Monterrey, March 14, 1822. Italics, *d, e, p.* TxU.

80. ———. Issues decree prescribing time and form of thanks for

175

the installation of Congress. Mexico City, February 26; Monterrey, March 14, 1822. TxU.

81. ———. Decree prohibiting the exportation of money in the interest of domestic economy. 8 clauses. Mexico City, February 21; Monterrey, March 17, 1822. TxU.

82. ———. Reissues decree (February 27, 1822) of the Junta on need for more taxes; raises those on foreign liquors. Mexico City, March 5; Monterrey, March 21, 1822. TxU.

83. ———. Decree (February 19, 1822) legitimizing money minted at Zacatecas in 1821. Monterrey, March 22, 1822. TxU.

84. ———. Decree reducing the number of copies of printed works required from printers by the Reglamento de la libertad de imprenta. Mexico City, March 1; Monterrey, March 27, 1822. TxU.

85. ———. Decree of March 1, fixing national holidays—February 24, March 2, September 16 and 27. Monterrey, March 27, 1822. TxU.

86. ———. Decree (March 21, 1822) of the Constituent Congress ordering rewards for services rendered the independence movement since February 24, 1821, by military personnel or *paisanos,* each of whom should report either to military officials or the government in order to be recommended. No imprint. No date. Apparently a copy made by Bangs from an original also in the Bexar Archives. No heading. No closing paragraph. 2 pages. TxU.

87. ———. Same as 86 but apparently a preliminary printing. Italics, *a, d, l, p, q, I.* TxU.

88. ———. Reissues decree of the Soberana Junta (February 21, 1822) repealing various small taxes. The government will take over the Hospital de Naturales and Indians are in the future to be admitted to others as any other citizen. Monterrey, March 29, 1822. TxU.

89. ———. Decree of general pardon to political prisoners and contrabandists. Passed March 15, 1822. Issued at Monterrey, April 3, 1822. Many italics. TxU.

90. ———. Same but applicable to military prisoners. Passed March 15, 1822. Issued at Monterrey, April 7, 1822. TxU.

91. ———. Discount on all salaries decreed (March 11, 1822). Mexico City, March 20; at Monterrey, April 7, 1822. Attached is a "Tarifa de descuentos" and "Notas," dated March 14, 1822. Many italics. TxU.

92. ———. Ciudadanos de las provincias internas de oriente. Urges them to make contributions or voluntary loans to government.

Warns of threat of Spanish invasion; treasury is empty. Signed by López with rubric. Monterrey, April 8, 1822. No imprint. Few italics, *d, p, E*. First line in bold-face type; the second in large capitals. TxU.

93. ———. Decree (March 22, 1822) permitting export of money and departure of individuals; earlier deposits to be returned. Present tariff laws will continue. Passports available to all. Monterrey, April 11, 1822. TxU.

94. El Generalísimo Almirante a los Mexicanos. Begins: "Conciudadanos . . ." Iturbide reports the military victories of Generals Velasquez and Bustamante and praises both. Mexico City, April 4. An *advertencia* addressed "Mexicanos" is signed by Iturbide, April 6, 1822. Issued at Monterrey, April 21, 1822. Date and place are in script. Many italics, including *E*. Two lines (upper light, lower heavy) between "Advertencia" and text. TxU.

95. [No heading of López]. Decree (April 15, 1822) that on next holiday citizens, civic bodies, and Jefe Político will, at high mass, take an oath to support Congress. Troops to be drawn up before flag and take oath. Mexico City, April 18. Reprinted in Monterrey without date. Many italics. At center head, "Num. 19." TxU.

At this point the press and all its furnishings were boxed and shipped mule-back to Saltillo, where López maintained his headquarters.

b. *At Saltillo (1822–1823)*

96. Printed forms of acknowledgment completed in script. The last sent from Monterrey in 1822 is dated May 4; the first from Saltillo is dated June 5. TxU.

97. [López] issues Iturbide's communication of April 24, 1822, remitting message from the secretaries of Congress reporting satisfaction with efforts to maintain order and tranquillity and asking what steps have been taken to clear Mexico of Spanish troops. Saltillo, May 21, 1822. Italics, *d, l, p*. No heading; no concluding paragraph. TxU.

98. D. Gaspar Antonio López . . . Issues decree of May 14, that conspiracy against independence is equivalent to *lesa magestad* and will suffer same penalty. Saltillo, May 26, 1822. TxU.

99. ———. Viva Nuestro Emperador Don Agustin de Iturbide. [Bold Face] Begins: Mexicanos. Me dirijo a vosotros . . . Proclamation of Iturbide (Mexico City, May 18, 1822) asking for

final proof of love. Rubric of López. "Es copia. Saltillo, 27 de mayo de 1822. Segundo de la Independencia. First line of text in 8-point; balance in 6-point. Italics, *p, d, c, q*. TxU.

100. ———. Habitantes de las Quatro Provincias (large, bold-faced type). Announces Iturbide is emperor. Ends: "Viva, viva, viva, nuestro Emperador Agustin Primero." Saltillo, "27 de mayo de 1822. Segundo de la independencia." Signed López with rubric. No closing paragraph. Italics, *D, L, P, Q, S*. TxU.

101. ———. Decree of Congress (May 21, 1822) making Iturbide emperor. Saltillo, May 30, 1822. Signed by López with rubric. Many italics. TxU.

102. ———. S. M. el Emperador . . . [Speech after taking oath of office before Congress.] Begins: "Seame permitido, dignos e ilustres Representantes . . ." At end: "Es copia. Saltillo. 1º de junio de 1822." TxU.

103. ———. Issues Iturbide's order that congratulations be written, not offered in person. Mexico City, May 29, 1822. Saltillo, June 8, 1822. Italics in heading only. TxU.

104. ———. Congress decrees form for name of Iturbide—"Agustin, por la Divina Providencia y por el Congreso de la Nacion, primer Emperador de Mexico." He will sign—"Agustin." Mexico City, May 29, 1822. Saltillo, June 8, 1822. TxU.

105. ———. Orders three-day public prayers; all diversions to cease. Mexico City, May 29, 1822. Saltillo, June 8, 1822. TxU.

106. El emperador al ejercito y al pueblo mexicano. Begins: "Compañeros y conciudadanos." Signed: "Agustin. [May 22, 1822]. Saltillo, June 15, 1822." Printed: Gaspar Lopez [no rubric]. No imprint, but Bangs' type and few italics. At head: "Orden Imperial de 3 de junio de 1822." TxU.

107. D. Gaspar Antonio López . . . El Congreso Constituyente a la nacion mexicana. Begins: "Mexicanos." Justifies its action in selecting Iturbide. Includes as note his proclamation of May 18, beginning: "Mexicanos." Mexico City, May 21, 1822. Saltillo, June 16, 1822. 2 pages. Double line below heading. TxU.

108. ———. All employees are ordered returned to their posts if they held one previously. Mexico City, June 8, 1822. Saltillo, June 22, 1822. TxU.

109. Los Capitulados de Zaragosa [printer's device, two arrows with points extended] desarmados por el coronel don Felipe de la Garza gobernador del Nuevo Santander y obligados a embarcarse por Tampico. Imprenta de la Comandancia General. Saltillo, Año de 1822. Segundo de la Yndependencia del Ymperio.

178

Pamphlet. 9 printed pages. Last document included is dated June 10, 1822. TxU.

110. D. Gaspar Antonio López . . . Iturbide permits notaries to use own judgment about working on the three days of celebration. Mexico, June 12, 1822. Saltillo, June 30, 1822. Under heading of López, Bangs' printer's device—two arrows pointed in opposite directions. TxU.

111. ———. Monarchy is decreed hereditary. Mexico City, June 26, 1822. Saltillo, July 6, 1822. Bangs' arrows. TxU.

112. ———. Regulations for operation of the mint. Mexico City, June 22, 1822. Saltillo, July 6, 1822. Bangs' arrows. TxU.

113. ———. Iturbide issues (June 26) decree of Congress of June 18 concerning establishment of the mint and coinage of money. Saltillo, July 6, 1822. Printed signature of Gaspar López. Rubric with initials. Bangs' arrows. TxU.

114. ———. Laws governing desertion. Mexico City, June 12, 1822. Saltillo, July 8, 1822. Bangs' arrows. TxU.

115. ———. Regulations governing the Consejo del Estado. Mexico City, July 1, 1822. Saltillo, July 13, 1822. TxU.

116. ———. Law governing use of stamped paper. Mexico City, June 26, 1822. Saltillo, July 13, 1822. TxU.

117. El Capitan General y Gefe Superior [18-pt. bold face] Politico Interino de esta provincia a todos sus habitantes. [Large capitals.] [Arrows.] Sings praise of Iturbide. Mexico, July 17, 1822. No date for Saltillo printing. No closing paragraph. 6-point to last 15 lines, which are in 8-point. Begins: "Mexicanos: desaparecieron ya los tiempos de sufrimiento . . ." Italics, *l, s, A*, "intimamedte," "indepedencia [*sic*]." TxU.

118. ———. Congress orders that care be taken that unfit don't get offices. Mexico City, July 10; Saltillo, July 20, 1822. No arrows.

119. ———. Regulations governing temporary imprisonment of Spaniards. Mexico City, July 10; Saltillo, July 20, 1822. 8-pt. type. López with rubric. No arrows. TxU.

120. Don Gaspar Antonio López . . . Reprints decree of Congress imposing taxes on alcoholic beverages [treasury is empty]. Mexico City, August 9, Tacubaya, August 12, 1822, by Iturbide. Saltillo, August 31, 1822. Gaspar López with rubric. Full heading. Printer's arrows. Closing paragraph in italics. Full sheet. TxU.

121. Exposicion del Gobierno a los habitantes del imperio. Begins: "Apenas el gobierno pudo reunir . . . México [8] (o 3) de Sep-

179

tiembre, 1822." Signed: "Herrera." Bangs' arrows. No Saltillo date. In hand of Bangs on verso: "Septiembre de 1822." TxU.

122. D. Gaspar Antonio López . . . El Emperador . . . On treatment and disposition of those below rank of sergeant who deserted Spanish army. Mexico City, August 20, 1822. 6 articles. Has heading, concluding paragraph, italics, arrows. Rubric of López. Saltillo, September 7, 1822. TxU.

123. Don Gaspar Antonio López, & &. [Arrows]. On imposition of taxes on mules, burros, and coaches toward fortifying Veracruz. Tacubaya, August 6, 1822. Saltillo, September 7, 1822. At head in script: "Núm 3." Full heading and closing. TxU.

124. ———. Certified copy of treaty between the Mexican government represented by Anastacio Bustamante and the Lipan Indians represented by Enrique de León, signed at Tacubaya, August 17, 1822. In script: "Es copia de que certifico." 10 articles. Saltillo, September 18 de 1822. No heading, arrows, or closing, but signed by López. TxU.

125. ———. Disposition of Spanish troops. September 9, 1822. Saltillo, September 21, 1822.

126. ———. Decree that the oath and proclamation of Iturbide be celebrated in the provincial capitals. Mexico City, September 5; Saltillo, September 21, 1822. Full heading. Arrows. Closing 5 lines. Italics. TxU.

127. ———. The Constituent Congress refuses to return Secundino Casillas to his former position as governor of Analco. Mexico City, September 13; Saltillo, September 28, 1822. Full form.

128. Congress orders discounts from military pay refunded and discontinued. Mexico City, August 22; Saltillo, September 28, 1822. Full heading, arrows, closing. TxU.

129. Circular of the captain general announcing new limits fixed by Iturbide for the captaincy general to include the Occidental Provinces and those of Guanajuato, Zacatecas, and San Luis Potosí as of September 25, 1822. Signed by Anastacio Bustamante, Mexico City, September 25, 1822. Issued by López with rubric. Half sheet. No imprint. TxU.

130. Gaceta Extraordinaria del Gobierno Imperial de México del Domingo 27 de octubre de 1822. Reimpreso en el Saltillo. Imprenta del Gobierno. [No issuance date.] Nuevo Santander is in a state of complete tranquillity. 4 pages. Signed at Mexico City, October 26, 1822, by Herrera. TxU.

131. [D. Gaspar Antonio López]. El Comandante General y Gefe superior interino a los habitantes de las quatro provincias de

oriente. [Arrows.] Conciudadanos y amigos: Announces that Tamaulipas is at peace and Felipe de la Garza [governor] has come into the Iturbide fold. Saltillo, October 30, 1822. No imprint, but identifiable by rubric of López and Bangs' arrows. TxU.

132. Gaceta Estraordinaria del Gobierno Imperial de México del 1 de noviembre de 1822. Reimpreso en el Saltillo. Imprenta del Gobierno. Bangs' arrows. TxU.

133. D. Gaspar Antonio López . . . Iturbide orders Congress dissolved. Mexico City, October 31, 1822. Saltillo, November 9, 1822. Full form except arrows. TxU.

134. Opinion of the Council of State on steps to be taken toward obtaining the surrender of San Juan de Ulloa. Printed signature of Soto Riva. Mexico City, November 10, 1822. No heading, arrows or closing. No Saltillo date of issuance. Italics *d, p, E* generously sprinkled. TxU.

135. Manifiesto de la Junta Nacional Instituyente. A la Nación. On Iturbide's dissolution of Congress. Mexico City, November 18 [or 13], 1822. Reimpreso en el Saltillo, Imprenta del Gobierno. Año de 1822. 6 point except 12 lines in 8 pt. 1 large sheet. TxU.

136. Iturbide prohibits exportation of money; treasury officials must clear accounts before leaving country. Mexico City, November 8; Saltillo, November 28, 1822. TxU.

137. The Junta Nacional Instituyente prohibits exports to Spain. Spaniards leaving can take only clothes and other necessary articles. Mexico City, November 5; Saltillo, November 2 [3 or 8], 1822. Heading, arrows, italic closing. TxU.

138. Regulations passed by Congress governing handling and sales of tobacco. 16 articles. Mexico City, October 31 [October 29 in *Col. de Ordenes,* II, 87]; Saltillo, November 28, 1822. Full form. 2 sheets pasted together. TxU.

139. Decree of Iturbide outlining regulations to improve administration of the treasury, and to prevent dishonesty of employees. Mexico City, November 8; Saltillo, December 5, 1822. Full form. TxU.

140. Iturbide orders that government correspondence carry dates of writing and of receipt. México, November 27; Saltillo, December 7, 1822. Full form with arrows. TxU.

141. Iturbide rules that *ayuntamientos* follow decree of Spanish Cortes of September 27, 1813. Mexico City, November 3; Saltillo, December 14, 1822. Full form with arrows. TxU.

142. López issues report of José Domínguez on conduct of Antonio

181

López de Santana, dated December 5 at Puebla. At Saltillo, December 15. Heading, arrows, 5-line conclusion. TxU.

143. D. Gaspar Antonio López . . . Conciudadanos y amigos: [in extra large, bold-face type]. Reports the "iniquo y escandaloso atentado" of Santa Anna [Introductory paragraphs to *Documentos* . . . of Lobato.] No heading. Two straight lines above imprint. Saltillo. "15 de diciembre de 1822. Segundo de la independencia. Imprenta de la Comandancia General de Oriente. Jose Manuel Bangs, Impresor." TxU.

144. [Documentos y proclamas de José María Lobato.] Reimpreso en el Saltillo el 21 de Diciembre de 1822. Segundo de la Independencia. Imprenta de la Comandancia General de Oriente. Jose Manuel Bangs, Impresor. Four short introductory paragraphs by López precede the Documentos. 2 pages. TxU.

145. Gaceta Extraordinaria del Gobierno Imperial de Mexico. 19 de Diciembre de 1822. Reimpreso en el Saltillo. Imprenta de la Comandancia Gral. de Oriente. Jose M[anue]l Bangs, Impresor. TxU.

146. Gaceta Extraordinaria del Gobierno Imperial de Mexico, del lunes 23 de diciembre de 1822. Reimpreso en el Saltillo, Imprenta de la Comandancia General de Oriente. Jose Manuel Bangs, Impresor. 5 pp. Pp. 1 and 5 in 8-point; 2–3 in 6-pt.; p. 4 in both 6- and 8-pt. TxU.

147. D. Gaspar Antonio López . . . Militares de las cuatro Provincias de Oriente. [Printer's arrows.] Invites those who have not presented military credentials to do so and receive promised awards. Gaspar López [in print]. No rubric. Impreso en el Saltillo a 28 de diciembre de 1822, Segundo de la Independencia. Imprenta de la Comandancia General de Oriente. Jose Manuel Bangs, Impresor. TxU.

148. D. Gaspar Antonio López, Caballero [bold face] . . . On Santa Anna and the Spaniards at San Juan de Ulloa. Orders of the Secretary of Justice and the Jefe Político, Puebla, December 9, 1822. Signed José Domínguez. Saltillo, December 28, 1822. 11 sections. López heading; arrows, closing. Printed signature of López with rubric. TxU.

149. [Mexico. Ministerio de Guerra y Marina.] Arrows of Bangs. Announces Iturbide's attitude and action toward holding San Juan de Ulloa. Signed Soto Riva. Mexico City, December 21, 1822. No Saltillo imprint. Italics, *d, l, p*. 8 pp. 1–3 in 6-pt.; 4–5, 8-pt. solid; 6–8, 6-pt. leaded. TxU.

150. D. Gaspar Antonio López, caballero de numero de la orden

imperial de Guadalupe, coronel del exercito imperial mexicano de las tres garantias, comandante general y gefe politico interino de las cuatro provincias internas orientales, comandante en gefe del de operaciones en ellas . . . Authorization of the Junta Nacional Instituyente to issue four million pesos in paper money. 14 articles. Mexico City, December 21, 1822. Rubric of López. Saltillo, January 4, 1823. Bangs' arrows. Italics, *E, D, d.* TxU.

151. [In left hand upper corner] Ministerio de Hacienda. Presents Iturbide's solution to the difficulties of the Provincial Deputations in distributing funds to themselves and to the *ayuntamientos.* No imprint. Part in 6 pt. type; last 16 lines in 8 pt. Italics, *d, p, D, l.* TxU.

152. D. Gaspar Antonio López. Reports the reduction of the *alcabala* tax, etc. Saltillo, January 15, 1823. Rubric of López. AGE.

153. ———. Issues decree of Iturbide approving the general colonization law passed by the Junta Nacional Instituyente on January 23. Saltillo, January 20, 1823. TxU.

154. [In left hand upper corner] "Justicia y Negocios Eclesiásticos. Sección Secular." Iturbide orders decree of Cortes of November 22, 1813 (which is printed below) be observed until Constitution is in force. Mexico City, January 21, 1823. Signed: José Domínguez. No Saltillo imprint. Italics, *d, p, E.* "o" has accent. TxU.

155. Comandancia General de Provincias [bold face] Internas de Oriente [I and O italic capitals]. Reprint of imperial order of January 28. Guerrero has disappeared. Iturbide's orders to Armijo and the *oficio* of Armijo are on same sheet. No Saltillo imprint, but carries all the earmarks of Bangs' press. TxU.

156. [In left hand upper corner] "Ministerio de Hacienda." Authorization of Iturbide to mint half million copper pesos. Mexico City, January 29, 1823. No Saltillo imprint. No heading, arrows, or closing. Italics, *d, p, l, D.* "Cicule" for "circule." TxU.

157. D. Gaspar Antonio López. [Heading as on January 4 decree except that "coronel" to "garantias" is dropped and "brigadier de los exercitos nacionales" substituted.] Announces the recognition of Peru, Mexico, January 11, 1823. Saltillo, January 30, 1823. "Tercero de la Independencia." Rubric of López. TxU.

158. ———. Issues communication from Captain General Anastacio Bustamante to the governor of Santander, emphasizing the duty of citizens to serve in the army and authorizing re-

wards to provincial troops. Saltillo, January 30, 1823. Signed by López with rubric. Bangs' arrows and italics, *d, p, l.* TxU.

159. Proclama de S. M. el Emperador al Exercito Trigarante, February 11, 1823. [Arrows] Asks support of his troops. Signed in print "Agustin." Reimpreso en el Saltillo á 22 de Febrero de 1823. Imprenta de la Comandancia General de Oriente, Jose Manuel Bangs, Impresor. TxU.

160. Proclama [arrows] of the province of Querétaro, February 26, 1823. Disclaims any obligation to Iturbide. Saltillo, March 12, 1823. Imprenta de la Comandancia General de Oriente, Jose Manuel Bangs, Impresor. TxU.

161. Acta de juramento de adhesion al Plan de Casa Mata . . . por la Villa de Saltillo. Saltillo, 17 de Marzo de 1823, Segunda de la verdadera libertad. Jose Manuel Bangs, Impresor. On recto: "Nota. Adicciones al Plan de Casa Mata." On verso: "Contestación" of the Junta de Saltillo to that of Monclova. TxU.

162. El Supremo Poder Ejecutivo de la Nacion a sus compatriotas. [Arrows.] La patria se presenta con dignidad segundo vez . . . Signed April 4, 1823, in print on verso by Celestino Negrete, José Mariano Michelena, Miguel Domínguez. Reimpreso en el Saltillo a 20 de Abril de 1823. Tercero de nuestra Independencia y Segundo de la Libertad. Jose Manuel Bangs, Impresor. TxU.

c. *At Monterrey (1823)*

163. Comandancia General de Provincias Internas de Oriente [large capitals in upper left-hand corner]. Felipe de la Garza, *comandante general* and *jefe político*, refuses to cooperate with Antonio López de Santa Anna, who proposes to raise an army to protect Mexican liberty. Monterrey, June 20, 1823. TxU.

164. El Ciudadano Felipe de la Garza [bold face] brigadier del ejército nacional, etc., issues as bando regulations to curb robbery and assassinations. [Arrows.] 6 sections. Signed in print, Felipe de la Garza. No rubric. Monterrey, June 24, 1823. Four closing lines not italic. Some accents, not all correct. TxU.

165. Ministerio de Hacienda. Circular No. 9. Congress decrees (June 27) 3 days' salary per annum as tax to alleviate federal financial difficulties. 20 sections. Mexico City, June 28, 1823. No heading, no Monterrey imprint, no closing. Italics, *d* and *D*. TxU.

166. ———. Circular No. 10. Explains need for decree of June 27 and adds regulations for implementation of it. Signed: Arrillaga. Mexico City, June 28, 1823. No Monterrey imprint. Italic *l.* Closing resembles Bangs'. TxU.

167. Provincias Internas de Oriente. Diputación provincial. President Rodríguez authorizes circularization of instructions, drawn up and approved by a commission of that body, for holding the elections of deputies to the Constituent Congress. Monterrey, July 10, 1823. "3°" "2°" Signed [in print] by José Antonio Rodríguez [rubric]. Italics, *i* and *A*. Enclosed is committee report (2 pp.) and a MS copy of plan advocated. Signed by Julián de Arrese and Agustín Viesca. TxU.

3. In Newly Created Mexican States

a. *At Victoria, Capital of Tamaulipas (1827–1828)*

168. First Legislature. 4th session. Decree No. 40. March 2, 1827. In script of Bangs: "Se publicó el 13 de Abril." TxU.
169. Instrucción General que da el Supremo Gobierno de Tamaulipas a todos los Ayuntamientos para que procedan a formar su ordenanza municipal. Victoria, March 3, 1827. Fourth Session of the Legislature. 6 pages. TxU.
170. Lucas Fernández [Governor of Tamaulipas] a sus habitantes. Proclamation denouncing attempts to declare independence from Mexico and urging citizens of his state to assist in defending their country. Victoria, March 6, 1827. Signed by Fernández and Eleno de Vargas, secretary. TxU.
171. ————. Issues decree on paving streets [of Victoria], keeping animals off, cleaning and sprinkling, excluding foundries, urging obedience to laws, supervision by the *ayuntamiento* of food, weights and measures, etc. Victoria, 1827. Published as bando on March 24. TxU.
172. El Gobernador del Estado de Tamaulipas a los habitantes del mismo estado. Victoria, June 12, 1827. Cuarto de la instalación del Congreso. [In regard to the refusal of Manuel Prieto, secretary of the Comisión Permanente, to attend its meetings.] TxU.
173. Report of the Comisión Permanente to the governor on preparations for elections. Signed José Ignacio Gil. Ordered printed by Lucas Fernández. July 1, 1827. TxU.
174. Gobierno del Estado de Tamaulipas. [Printer's device.] The Government Council to the governor (July 1, 1827) concerning its organization. José Indalecio Fernández appointed Secretary. Victoria, July 1, [1827]. TxU.
175. *Coleccion de Leyes y Decretos de la Primera Legislatura Constitucional del Estado libre de Tamaulipas.* Ciudad Victoria.

1827. Imprenta del Estado. Dirigida por el C. Jose Manuel Bangs. 51 pp. Title, index and erratas, 1 p. each. Yale.

Second Legislature. 1st Session. Decrees.

176. No. 1. August 1, 1827. Declares void elections for vice-governor in Revilla (Ciudad Guerrero) and Palmillas. Rubric of governor. AGT.
177. No. 2. September 6. Repeals laws of January 25 and of October 21, 1825. AGT.
178. No. 7. September 21. On assigning land in San Antonio Tancasnequi. AGT.
179. No. [13]. October 24. To enforce Decree No. 12. Signed Lucas Fernández. AGT.
180. No. 18. November 10. Carries Bangs' printer's device. AGT.
181. No. 20. November 15. AGT.
182. No. 22. December 13, 1827. 3 pages. AGT.
183. No. 25. December 22. Reglamento de la Secretaría del Gobierno del Estado de Tamaulipas. 6 fols. AGT.
184. No. 26. December 28. Sets hour for state government council meetings. AGT.
185. No. 27. December 29, 1827. Sets salaries of jurists. AGT.
186. Report of the Standing Committee to the House of Deputies, August 14, 1827, Victoria, Imprenta del Gobierno del Estado. [Elaborate printer's device.] Dirigida por José Manuel Bangs. 4 pp. P.
187. Report of the Standing Committee to the House of Deputies, August 21, 1827. Victoria, August 23, 1827. Imprenta del Gobierno del Estado. Dirigida por José Manuel Bangs. New printer's device. P.
188. Dictamen sobre prorrogar o no las sesiones ordinarias del Congreso honorable de este estado leido en sesion pública extraordinaria del miércoles, catorce del corriente. Imprenta del Gobierno del Estado de Tamaulipas. Dirigida por el C. José Manuel Bangs. Printer's device above imprint—two straight lines, upper heavy, lower light. P.
189. Parte espositiva que formó la comisión especial para la iniciativa que se dirigió a la Camara de Diputados del Congreso General sobre espulsión de españoles. Ciudad Victoria, Impreso en la Imprenta del Gobierno del Estado de Tamaulipas. Dirigida por el C. José Manuel Bangs. [1827.] P.
190. El gobernador del estado de las Tamaulipas a todos sus habitantes. Calls a special session for December 2 and lists 11 subjects for consideration. Victoria, November 23, 1827. P.

Appendix II

191. Sesión tenido en el salon del Congreso . . . en 22 de Noviembre de 1827, reunido la comisión Permanente y el Consejo del Gobierno sobre convocar al Congreso a sesiones extraordinarias . . . Ciudad Victoria, Impreso en la Imprenta del Gobierno del Estado. Dirigida por el C. José Manuel Bangs. 4 pp. P.

Second Legislature. Second Session. Decrees

192. No. 28. January 14, 1828. AGT.
193. No. 30. January 17, 1828. AGT.
194. No. 31. January 22, 1828. On taxes. AGT.
195. No. 32. January 22, 1828. AGT.
196. No. 33. January 24, 1828. On brands. AGT.
197. No. 34. January 28, 1828. Restrictions on Spaniards. 4 pp. AGT.
198. No. 35. January 30, 1828. AGT.
199. No. 36. February 1, 1828. Grants temporary leave to governor. AGT.
200. No. 37. January 31, 1828. AGT.
201. No. 38. February 7, 1828. On import duties. AGT.
202. No. 39. February 7, 1828. On salary of deputies. AGT.
203. No. 40. February 8, 1828. Fixes salary of *fiscal* of state supreme court. AGT.
204. No. 42. February 8, 1828. Declares adjournment on February 14, 1828. AGT.
205. No. 43. AGT.
206. No. 44. February 12, 1828. Bangs' printer's device. AGT.
207. No. 45. February 12, 1828. Elects a committee on fiscal matters to confer with others in Mexico City. AGT.
208. No. 47. February 12, 1828. Reglamento de la oficina de la Tesorería del Estado de Tamaulipas. AGT.
209. El Presidente de los Estados Unidos Mexicanos a sus conciudadanos. Mexico City, January 2, 1828. Signed in print: "Guadalupe Victoria." Bangs' printer's device. AGT.
210. Dictamen de la comisión de hacienda del Congreso honorable del estado, al presentar el plan de contribuciones e impuestos para subvenir a los gastos del estado en el año de 1828. José Eustaquio Fernández, Diputado Secretario. José Antonio Fernández, Diputado Secretario. Ciudad Victoria, January 4, 1828. 4 pp. P.
211. El gobernador del estado a sus habitantes. Need of taxation and of honesty in paying. Ciudad Victoria, February 4, 1828. Quinto de la instalación del Congreso de este Estado. Signed [in print]: "Lucas Fernández." P.

187

212. Lista en que constan los ciudadanos que hasta la fecha han contestado a la invitación que se les hizo para el préstamo de cincuenta mil pesos . . . [Printer's device]. Ciudad Victoria, February 9, 1828. Quinta de la instalación del Congreso del Estado. P.

213. Lista [Large printer's device]. Under headings of "Ciudadanos" and "Pesos" are the names of donors and amount of donation. Ciudad Victoria, March 26, 1828. Eleno de Vargas, secretario. P.

214. Año de 1828. Ministerio de Hacienda del Estado de Tamaulipas. [Large printer's device.] Corte de caja en la Tesorería. [January 1 to March 31.] 1 folio printed on both sides. Ciudad Victoria, April 1, 1828. José Feliciano Ortíz. P.

b. At Leona Vicario [Saltillo], Capital of Coahuila and Texas (1828–1830)

215. Decree No. 16 of the Constituent Legislature, passed March 24, issued April 4, 1825. Ley de Colonización. Leona Vicario, 1828. Impreso en la Imprenta del Gobierno de Coahuila y Texas. Dirigida por el C. José Manuel Bangs. 4 pp. TxU.

216. Decree No. 54. Arancel de los derechos que deben percibir los escribanos públicos, alcaldes constitucionales, secretario del tribunal de justicia . . . del estado de Coahuila y Texas. 102 articles. Ordered printed, Leona Vicario, May 2, 1828. 12 pp. TxU.

217. Decree No. 58. Reglamento de la milicia nacional local del mismo estado. At head: "Gobierno Superior de Coahuila y Texas." Ordered printed June 23, 1828. No imprint. 10 pp. TxU.

218. Decree No. 62. Regulates fees of commissioner for distribution of land. May 15, 1828. TxU.

219. Reglamento de pasaportes de 1º de mayo de 1828. Reimpreso en la Imprenta del Gobierno del Estado de Coahuila y Texas. Leona Vicario, 1828. Dirigida por el C. J. Manuel Bangs. At head: "Pueda disembarcar el estrangero." Printed in three columns in Spanish, English, and French. 1 sheet, recto and verso. TxU.

220. Decree No. 63. September 23, 1828. Extends Woodbury's contract to explore for coal and iron. TxU.

221. Decree No. 65. September 26, 1828. Orders criminals freed. TxU.

222. Decree No. 66. September 29, 1828. Permits E. M. de Garza to become lawyer without full course. TxU.

223. Decree No. 68. September 30, 1828. Issued October 1, 1828.

Correspondence concerning Decree No. 50 to be handled by governor. TxU.

224. Decree No. 70. Land acquired under federal or state laws not subject to attachment for debts previously contracted. Passed January 13, 1829. Circulated January 22, 1829. Signed by José María Viesca, governor, and Santiago del Valle, secretary. TxU.

225. Decree No. 72. January 29, 1829. Revises Article 63 of the administration of justice. TxU.

226. Decree No. 73. February 4, 1829. Makes La Bahía del Espíritu Santo a *villa* with name of "Goliad." TxU.

227. Decree No. 74. February 4, 1829. Retired military men exempted from certain contributions. TxU.

228. Decree No. 75. February 6, 1829. James Power made citizen of state. TxU.

229. Decree No. 76. February 6, 1829. Clears up definition of *alcalde*. TxU.

230. Decree No. 77. February 12, 1829. Orders selection of ecclesiastics needed for Department of Texas. TxU.

231. Decree No. 78. February 12, 1829. Woodbury contract extended two years. TxU.

232. Decree No. 79. February 26, 1829. Levies a 2 per cent tax on export of money. TxU.

233. Decree No. 80. February 26, 1829. Clarifies Decree No. 28 of November 2, 1827. TxU.

234. Decree No. 81. March 12, 1829. Authorizes a *cofradía* in Saltillo. TxU.

235. Decree No. 82. March 14, 1829. Fixes rent for tax offices in Texas at 200 pesos annually. TxU.

236. Decree No. 83. Prohibits foreigners from engaging in retail trade. TxU.

237. Decree No. 84. March 24 issued March 30, 1829. Personnel and operation of grand juries. TxU.

238. Decree No. 85. March 24. Issued April 2, 1829. Equalizes *alcabala* taxes. TxU.

239. Decree No. 87. April 28. Issued April 30, 1829. To extend session one month (April 29). TxU.

240. Decree No. 88. April 29. Issued April 30, 1829. Circulation of decrees. TxU.

241. Decree No. 89. April 29. Issued April 29, 1829. Committees to visit and inspect *ayuntamientos*. TxU.

242. Decree No. 90. May 8. Issued May 13, 1829. Must contribute 3 days' earnings annually. TxU.

243. Decree No. 92. May 13, 1829. Orders establishment of Lancasterian schools, one in each department. All catechisms of Akermaham [Ackermann] to be used. Ordered printed, May 14, 1829. 20 articles. TxU.

244. Decree No. 93. May 13, 1829. Orders two panoptic prisons constructed. TxU.

245. Decree No. 94. May 13, 1829. Issued May 14, 1829. Orders ports opened at Galveston and San Bernardo. TxU.

246. Decree No. 95. May 13, 1829. Governor to fix limits of state. TxU.

247. Decree No. 96. May 27, 1829. Grants right to bore wells. TxU.

248. Decree No. 97. May 31, 1829. Ordenanzas Municipales para el Gobierno de Parras. AHE.

249. [Decree No. 98.] June 6, 1829. *Ordnanzas [sic] Municipales para el Gobierno y Manejo Interior del Ayuntamiento de la Ciudad de San Antonio de Bejar, 1829.* Ciudad de Leona Vicario. Imprenta del Supremo Gobierno del Estado, a cargo del C. J. Manuel Bangs. 35 pp. preceded and followed by blank leaf. TxU.

250. Decree No. 99. Same for Goliad. 44 pp. TxU.

251. Decree 100. Same for [San Felipe de] Austin. 26 pp. TxU.

252. Decree 101. Passed May 12, 1829. Same for Rosas (later Zaragosa). [Circulated June 9.] AHE.

253. Decree 102. June 9, 1829. Reglamento para el Gobierno Interior de la Secretaría del Despacho del Supremo Gobierno del Estado de Coahuila y Tejas. Ciudad de Leona Vicario. Imprenta del Supremo Gobierno del Estado, a cargo del C. José Manuel Bangs. 16 pp. TxU.

254. Decree No. 103. May 30, 1829. Issued June 7. Limitation on length of service of substitute officials. TxU.

255. Decree No. 105. September 5, 1829. (In *Gazeta*, September 10, 1829.) Regulation affecting male Spaniards who remain in state and other regulations. TxU.

256. Decree No. 106. September 11, 1829. Issued September 18. Forced loans to be governed by federal law of August 17. TxU.

257. Decree No. 107. September 11, 1829. Imposes 2 per cent tax on imported goods. TxU.

258. Decree No. 108. December 31, 1829. Adherence to *pronunciamiento* of Jalapa. TxU.

259. Decree No. 109. Repeals parts of Decree No. 105 of September 5, 1829. TxU.

260. Decree No. 110. January 9, 1830. Extent to which state will cooperate with plan of Jalapa. TxU.
261. Decree No. 111. January 13, 1830. Repeals certain law of the Recopilación. TxU.
262. Decree No. 112. January 15, 1830. Grants citizenship in state to Bangs. TxU.
263. Decree No. 113. January 22, 1830. Clarification of Decree 90 at request of Candela. TxU.
264. Decree No. 114. January 26, 1830. Authorizes *ayuntamiento* for San Miguel de Aguayo. TxU.
265. Decree No. 115. January 26, 1830. Municipal ordinance for San Juan de Allende. TxU.
266. Decree No. 116. January 26, 1830. Municipal ordinance for San Nicolás de Capellanía (now Ramos Arizpe). AHE.
267. Decree No. 117. January 26, 1830. Municipal ordinance for Santa Rita de Morelos. AHE.
268. Decree No. 118. February 19, 1830. Defines qualifications for substitute lawyers. TxU.
269. Decree No. 119. February 19, 1830. Resignations from office to be filled by Congress. TxU.
270. Decree No. 120. February 19, 1830. Clarifies Article 45 of Decree No. 37 on monthly reports. TxU.
271. Decree No. 121. March 6, 1830. Amends Decree No. 17 of July 7, 1825. TxU.
272. Decree No. 122. March 6, 1830. Municipal ordinances for Leona Vicario. AHE.
273. Decree No. 123. March 6, 1830. Municipal ordinances for Santa Rosa (now Musquiz). AHE.
274. Decree No. 124. March 26, 1830. Clarifies Arts. 163 and 166 of Constitution for Monclova. TxU.
275. Decree No. 125. April 3, 1830. Obligations of persons named *asesor general del estado.* TxU.
276. Decree No. 127. April 8, 1830. Revision of criminal law. TxU.
277. Decree No. 128. April 1, 1830. TxU.
278. Decree No. 129. April 13, 1830. Six public schools ordered. TxU.
279. Decree No. 130. April 15, 1830. Authorizes loan of 3,000 pesos to help victims of smallpox. TxU.
280. Decree No. 131. April 18, 1830. Municipal ordinances for San Pedro de Gigedo (now Villa Unión). AHE.
281. Decree No. 132. April 16, 1830. Establishes collection office for *alcabalas* in San Isidro de Palomas. TxU.

191

282. Decree No. 134. April 14, 1830. Municipal ordinances for Guerrero. TxU.
283. Decree No. 137. April 19, 1830. Municipal ordinances for
Abasola. TxU.
284. Decree No. 139. April 23, 1830. Doyle granted permission to
build chapel at [Refugio]. TxU.
285. Decree No. 141. April 22, 1830. Bond for collector of *alcabalas*
at Palomas. TxU.
286. Decree No. 143. April 20, 1830, issued April 30. Court procedure. TxU.
287. Decree No. 144. April 30, 1830. Issued May 1. Orders three
grades of medals to best students, with gold, silver, and plain
edges. Also a sufficient number of copies of "la gramática, or-
tografía castellana, and catecismo de Fleuri." AHE, Vol. 64.
288. Decree No. 146. April 30, 1830. Search-warrant procedure. TxU.
289. [Seal of Coahuiltejas.] El C. José María Viesca Gobernador del
Estado de Coahuila y Tejas . . . [Credential issued to Antonio
Menchaca, second ensign of the second company of national
militia]. Leona Vicario, July 24, 1829. Signed: "Viesca." A form
filled in with name, date, and details in script. TxU.
290. Constitución Política del Estado Libre de Coahuila y Tejas
sancionada por su Congreso Constituyente en 11 de marzo de
1827. Reimpresa por orden del H. Congreso, fecha 27 de Febrero de 1829. Ciudad de Leona Vicario. Imprenta del Gobierno
del Estado, á cargo de J. M. Bangs. AHE; photocopy, TxU.
291. Indice de las órdenes y decretos espedidos por el Honorable
Congreso de este Estado desde el año de 1824 hasta fin de 1828.
Secretaría del supremo gobierno del Estado de Coahuila y
Tejas, 30 de Marzo de 1829. TSA.
292. Alocución que el Congreso del Estado dirije a sus comitentes
con motivo a la data del decreto 90. Signed May 8, 1829 by José
María Cárdenas. Ramón García Rojas, diputado secretario.
Mariano García, diputado secretario. Leona Vicario, 1829. 1
sheet, recto and verso. TxU.
293. Expediente [concerning the abolition of certain state offices
by Decree No. 50, April 17, 1828]. Leona Vicario, 1829. Im-
prenta del Gobierno del Estado de Coahuila y Texas, á cargo del
C. José Manuel Bangs. 92 pp., errata 2 pp. TxU.
294. Cartilla de Tramites para arreglo de los jueces . . . Ciudad de
Leona Vicario. Imprenta del Gobierno del Estado á cargo del
C. J. Manuel Bangs, 1829. [Dated May 31, 1829 in Actas del
Congreso, p. 1078.] TxU.

295. El gobernador del Estado de Coahuila y Tejas a sus conciudadanos . . . Coahuiltejanos—Por noticias oficiales . . . [Warns of
danger of Spanish invasion . . .] Signed: "José Maria Viesca."
August 4, 1829. Ciudad de Leona Vicario, 1829. Impreso en la
oficina del Supremo Gobierno del Estado en Palacio, á cargo
del C. José Manuel Bangs. TxU.

296. La Honorable Diputación Permanente del Estado, á todos sus
habitantes. Conciudadanos: [Appeals for cooperation against
Spanish attack]. Leona Vicario, August 4, 1829. José Manuel
Cárdenas. José María Balmaceda. Ignacio Sendejas, Secretario.
[Same imprint as 295.] TxU.

297. Gazeta Constitucional de Coahuiltejas. Leona Vicario, 1829–
1830. [Same imprint as Item 295.] No. 1, September 3, 1829–No.
41, June 10, 1830. In TxU are Nos. 1–3, September 3, 10, and
17; Extra, September 15; No. 14, December 3, 1829; Nos. 28–29
(March 11 and 18), with Supplement to each; Supplement to
No. 33, April 15, 1830. At Yale are Nos. 32–40 (April 8–27, May
6–27, and June 3). TxU.

298. Gobierno Supremo del Estado Libre de Coahuila y Texas. [No-
tice that Governor Viesca has discarded his former rubric and
now sends samples of the new. Signature of both Viesca and Del
Valle printed, each followed by rubric.] Leona Vicario, September 5, 1829. TxU.

299. Discurso que el día 11 de septiembre de 1829 pronunció el
C. José María Viesca, actual Gobernador del estado de Coahuila
y Tejas, al cerrar sus sesiones estraordinarias el H[1] Congreso del
mismo, y Contestación que en seguida virtió el C. José María
Balmaceda, presidente de dicha H. Asamblea. At end: "Ciudad
de Leona Vicario 1829. Impreso en la oficina del Supremo Gobierno de este Estado, á cargo del C. José Manuel Bangs." TxU.

300. Parte Oficial. Recibido por el estraordinario de hoy a la una de
la mañana. [Leona Vicario, September 18, 1829.] Agreement
for withdrawal to Victoria of defeated Spaniards. Signed at
Campo en el paso de Doña Cecilia, September 11, 1829. Copied
at Victoria, September 14 and reprinted at Leona Vicario, September 18, 1829. Signed [in print] Santiago del Valle [rubric],
secretary. TxU.

301. Mexico. Law, approved by President Guerrero on May 8, 1829,
to liquidate the amount due for the paper money of Texas.
Signed by Lorenzo de Zavala, Mexico City, May 8, 1829. Issued
at Saltillo, October 6, 1829. Signed: "José María Viesca." 4 pp.
folder printed on p. 1. TxU.

302. Mexico. Vicente Guerrero, president, transmits to the Secretary of the Treasury [Zavala] a bill passed by Congress imposing a 5 per cent tax on incomes over $1,000 and more on larger. Dated May 22, 1829. Ordered printed at Leona Vicario, October 6, 1829. Signed: "José María Viesca," who adds instructions for the collection. TxU.

303. Observaciones que la diputación permanente del estado dirije al E. S. Gobernador sobre el decreto general de Septiembre último para que las eleve al superior conocimiento del A. S. Presidente. Leona Vicario, 17 de Octubre de 1829. Signed by Cárdenas, Balmaceda, and Zendejas [as in Item 296]. Impreso en la oficina del Gobierno del Estado dirigida por el C. José Manuel Bangs. Creating an office under the Secretary of the Treasury to supervise administration of money derived through new law. TxU.

304. Mexico. Vicente Guerrero, president, sent to Secretary of the Treasury, Bocanegra, a bill imposing additional taxes. Dated November 6, 1829. Ordered printed in Leona Vicario, December 2, 1829. TxU.

305. Gobierno Supremo del Estado Libre de Coahuila y Tejas. The Governor prints a letter, dated December 5, from his brother Agustín Viesca (who was the Secretary of State and of Foreign Affairs for Mexico from November 3 to December 23, 1829) reporting the Pronuncimiento of Jalapa of December 4. To it he adds his own comments on December 21. 3 printed pages. TxU.

306. El Presidente de la República [Vicente Guerrero] a los Mejicanos. Congress has assembled. Will work for peace. Mexico City, December 11, 1829. Ciudad de Leona Vicario, 1829. Reimpresa en la oficina del Supremo Gobierno de este Estado, á cargo de José Manuel Bangs. On verso: Guerrero's call for a special session of Congress (December 10, 1829) is forwarded from Mexico City by the Secretary of State (Agustín Viesca) to his brother, Governor José María Viesca. He in turn urges citizens to give patriotic support to the federal government of Guerrero—December 22, 1829. TxU.

307. Proclama del Ecsmo. Sr. General don Luis Quintanar. México, December 23, 1829. Signed by Quintanar. Ciudad de Leona Vicario. 1830. Reimpreso en la oficina del Supremo Gobierno de este Estado, á cargo del C. José Manuel Bangs. On verso: "Acta del pronuncimiento de la gran Méjico . . . diciembre 23, 1829." TxU.

308. Acta del pronuncimiento del Ilustre Ayuntamiento y demás

vecindario de esta capital (approving the Plan of Jalapa of December 4, news of which reached Saltillo on December 31 and led to this action). Printed names of 33 signers. Imprint as 307. TxU.

309. Same without names of signers. Issued January 9, 1830? Same imprint as 307 and 308. TxU.

310. [Report to the Congress of the] Comisión de Puntos Constitucionales. [Signed at Leona Vicario, January 8, 1830.] José María Balmaceda, Presidente; Ignacio Sendejas and Vicente Valdéz, secretaries. Impreso en la oficina del Supremo Gobierno de este Estado en Palacio, a cargo del ciudadano José Manuel Bangs. TxU.

311. La catorcena Judith piensa hacer vida privada. Ultima conversacion que tubieron en Catorce Juana y Pasquala, que escribio un curioso que las estubo oyendo. Dialogue in verse. 3 columns. Signed: "El Curioso." Ciudad de Leona Vicario. 1830. Impreso en la imprenta del Supremo Gobierno de este Estado, a cargo del C. José Manuel Bangs. TxU.

312. Gobierno Supremo del Estado Libre de Coahuila y Tejas. Instrucciones a que debe arreglarse el comisionado para el repartimiento de tierras a los [nue] vos colonos . . . segun la Ley de Colonización de 24 de Marzo de 1825. 28 sections. Signed by Governor Viesca and Secretary Santiago del Valle. Saltillo, January 4, 1827. The additional article is dated April 25, 1830. TxU.

313. Instrucción formada para ministrar la vacuna . . . TxU.

314. Gobierno Supremo del Estado libre de Coahuila y Tejas. Governor Viesca publishes an interchange of correspondence between himself and the Secretary of State of Mexico (Lucas Alamán) under dates of April 17 and 24 and May 3 and 10, 1830, in which Alamán asks the cooperation of the state with the federal government in defending Mexico against Spain. The whole is signed by Viesca, Leona Vicario, May 10, 1830, who promises cooperation. 3 pages. On verso is "Instrucciones para colectar y preparar objectos de Historia." TxU.

315. [Same heading.] [Lucas Alamán] to J. M. Viesca, May 7, 1830. Cites his efforts to promote economic progress. Viesca replies July 3, promising cooperation. TxU.

316. Mutilated title: [   ]es Coahuiltejanos
          [   ] a esta vindicación
     su honor atrozmente ultrajado.
          La gratitud
     de uno de sus conciudadanos.

195

Pioneer Printer

Signed: "Leona Vicario, June 18, 1830, by Ignacio Sendejas." A reply to an editorial in No. 41 of the *Gazeta*. "Este comunicado correspondía a la Gazeta del jueves, que se suspendió por órden del Supremo Gobierno." Signed: "Ciudad Leona Vicario, 1830. Impreso en la oficina del Supremo Gobierno, a cargo del C. José Manuel Bangs." TxU.

317. Estado de Coahuila y Tejas. Noticia de los expedientes, oficios y demás asuntos que se han recibidos y despachados por la secretaría de gobierno . . . en todo el mes de junio último. Ciudad de Leona Vicario, Imprenta del Estado á cargo del C. J. M. Bangs. 4 pp. One item included is dated July 1, 1830. TxU.

c. *At Victoria, Tamaulipas (1833–1837)*

Decrees; Official Organ, La Atalaya; *and a Newspaper,* El Telescopio
Decrees (issued with heading "Circular")[1]

318. No. 3. March 1, 1833. Vice-Governor J. N. Molano issues decree of adjournment of 10th session of the Legislature of Tamaulipas on March 2. Signed: "Molano [rubric] and Gabriel Arcos [rubric], official mayor." AGT.
319. No. 4. September 2, 1833. 3 braces as printer's mark. AGT.
320. No. 6. September 4, 1833. 0-0000-0 as printer's device. AGT.
321. No. 7. September 5, 1833. AGT.
322. No. 9, September 6, 1833. 3 braces as printer's device. AGT.
323. No. 10. September 19, 1833. AGT.
324. No. 11. September 10, 1833. AGT.
325. No. 13. September 20, 1833. 0-00-0. AGT.
326. No. 14. September 20, 1833. ——— brace ———. AGT.
327. No. 18. October 5, 1833. Approves Colegio of Tomas Rosell, Fuente de la Libertad. TxU (Prieto Papers).
328. No. 21. October 10, 1833. AGT.
329. No. 22. October 12, 1833. AGT.
330. No. 23. October 12, 1833. 3 braces. AGT.
331. No. 25. October 12, 1833. —00—. AGT.
332. No. 27. November 4, 1833. Mariano Cubi y Soler is made citizen of Tamaulipas. TxU (Prieto Papers).
333. No. 29. November 6, 1833. AGT.

[1] As the substance of these decrees is largely of local interest, only changes in the printer's device are indicated. After *La Atalaya* was established, all decrees were printed in it.

334. No. 32. November 12, 1833. AGT.
335. No. 33. November 13, 1833. 0-0000-0 new printer's device. AGT.
336. No. 35. November 14, 1833. AGT.
337. No. 37. November 15, 1833. AGT.
338. No. 39. November 16, 1833. AGT.
339. No. 40. November 16, 1833. AGT.
340. No. 42. November 17, 1833. Amending earlier colonization law. AGT.
341. No. 44. November 24, 1833. AGT.
342. No. 45. November 24, 1833. AGT.
343. No. 48. May 3, 1834. AGT.
344. No. 50. May 14, 1834. Tampico is renamed Santa Anna de Tampico. TxU (Prieto Papers).
345. A bill, headed "Acuerdo" and dated October 22, 1833, when approved by the Legislature, authorized the government to contract for printing all that emanated from the "supremo poderes del estado," including the treasury and one or two periodicals. The press was either to be bought or rented; the periodicals were to be the responsibility of the *empresario*, the state to furnish the paper, the editor to be approved by the government, which was to get one hundred copies free. The date of issuance seems to have been November 5, 1833. AGT.
346. *Atalaya*. Periódico oficial del gobierno. Victoria (Tamaulipas), 1834–1837. Imprenta de el [*sic*] *Atalaya* dirigida [from No. 11] por Manuel Bangs.
      Vol. I, No. 1 (January 7, 1834) to Vol. III, No. [141] (April 27, 1837). In TxU are Vol. I (1834–1835), Nos. 1, 3, 11, 14, 21 (Alcance), 26, 33, 36, 39, 40, 42–43, 45–49, 55, 57–58, 60; Vol. II (1835), Nos. 1–3, 5–7, 9–12, 14–15, 17–21, 23–29, 31–33, 57–59. In the Matamoros Archives (photostat copies at TxU), Vol. II, Nos. 91–92, 97, 99 (April 23 and 30, June 4 and 18, 1836); Vol. III (1836–1837), Nos. 107–108, 114, 119 (August 13 and 20, October 1, November 12, 1836); Nos. 121–122, 124–128, 130–141 (November, 1836–April, 1837). "Impreso por el C. Manuel Bangs" appears from April 23, 1836, to March 25, 1837.
347. *El Telescopio de Tamaulipas*. Victoria, Tamaulipas. Impreso por el C. José Manuel Bangs. Nos. 1 (c. September 1, 1836) to 32 (March 30, 1837). Publication is suspended with No. 32. At Yale, Vol. I, No. 6 (September 29, 1836). Photocopy, LMS. At TxU in Matamoros Archives (photostat copies), Vol. 25, are Nos. 21 (January 12, 1837) and 23–32 (January 26–March 30, 1837).

4. IN TEXAS OR ON HER BORDER

a. At Galveston

348. *The Commercial Intelligencer.* Weekly. Prospectus dated July 1, 1838.
    Vol. 1. No. 2 (July 27, 1838). TGR. Photocopy, TxU, LMS.
    No. 8 (September 15, 1838). Yale. Photocopy, LMS.
    No. 15 (November 24, 1838). Yale. Photocopy, LMS.
    Editorial column is dated December 1, 1838.
    No. 21 (January 12, 1839). Yale. Photocopy, LMS.
349. *The Galvestonian.* Triweekly.
    Vol. I. No. 2 (March 27, 1839). TxU. Photocopy, LMS.
    No. 15 (May 16, 1839). Illinois. Photocopy, LMS.
    Title changed to *The Daily Galvestonian.*
    Vol. I. [Nos. illegible] (April 3–4, 1840). TxU.
    Nos. 42–43 (March 31 and April 1, 1841). Photocopy, TxU.
    Prospectus in March 31 issue.
    December 6–7, 1841. Lacks front page. TxU.
350. *The Weekly Galvestonian.*
    Vol. I. No. 1 (May 8, 1841). TxU.
351. *Galvestonian.* Address of the Carrier of the *Daily Galvestonian,* January 1, 1842. Galveston, Printed at the Office of the *Galvestonian,* 1842. 2 columns. TGR.
352. *The Daily News.*
    Vol. I. No. 8 (April 19, 1842). Office of the *Galveston News,* Galveston. Facsimile, LMS.
    No. 17 (April 30, 1842). Privately owned.
353. *The Commercial Chronicle.* Weekly. Before August 2, 1842.
    Title changed to *The Independent Chronicle.* Weekly.
    Extra (August 1, 1843). Same as Vol. I, 2d Qta., No. 1. AAW. Photocopy, LMS.
    Vol. I. 2d Qta., No. 8 (October 15, 1841). TxU. Photocopy, LMS.
    Title changed back to *The Commercial Chronicle.* Weekly.
354. Galveston Artillery Company. *The charter and constitution of the Galveston Artillery Company.* Organized September 13, 1840. Printed by S. Bangs, *Galveston Chronicle* Office. [1842]? This constitution was adopted October 26, 1842. TxU.
355. Moore, Edwin Ward, and others. "To the people of Galveston" [by E. W. Moore, in two columns] followed by "To the Public" by James Morgan, defending Moore, in three columns, and

Appendix II

"Proceedings of a Public Dinner" given to Commodore E. W. Moore and Officers, Texas Navy, etc., in three columns. [Galveston, Printed at the Office of the *Independent Chronicle,* 1843.]

Broadsheet, both sides in four columns. At head: *Extra. Independent Chronicle,* Vol. I, 2d Qta., No. 1. By Samuel Bangs, City of Galveston, August 1, 1843. Editor, Publisher, and Proprietor.

At the end is a full account of the public dinner given to Moore and his officers by the citizens of Galveston on July 28. AAW. Photocopy, LMS.

b. *At Houston*

356. *The Musquito.* Triweekly. TxU. Photocopy, LMS.
Friday, February 5, 1841, [No. 58], pp. 230–232.
Sunday, February 7, 1841, [No. 59], pp. 233–234.
Wednesday, February 10, 1841, No. 60, pp. 235–236.
Friday, February 12, 1841, No. 61, pp. 237–240.
Sunday, February 14, 1841, No. [62], pp. 244–246 [*sic*].

c. *At Corpus Christi*

357. *The Corpus Christi Gazette.* Weekly.
Vol. I. No. 7 (February 12, 1846). Wisconsin Historical Society. Photocopies, TxU, LMS.
Extra (March 8, 1846). TxU.
No. 12 (March 19, 1846). Archivo de la Secretaría de la Defensa, Mexico, D.F.
No. 14 (April 2, 1846). AAW. Photocopy, LMS.

d. *At Matamoros*

358. *The Matamoros Reveille.* Weekly. In English and Spanish.
Vol. I. No. 1 (June 24, 1846). The Spanish portion carries title "La Diana de Matamoras." 3 columns in Spanish and one, the last, in English. TxU.
359. *The American Flag.* Tri-weekly. The continuation of *The Republic of the Rio Grande.*
Vol. I. No. 9 (July 6, 1846) to Vol. III, No. 219 (July 29, 1848). LC.
Vol. II. No. 128 (August 28, 1847). TxU. Photocopy, LMS.

BIBLIOGRAPHY

PRIMARY SOURCES

Manuscripts

Alessio Robles, Vito (compiler). "Circulares y proclamas de los comandantes generales de las Provincias Internas de Oriente impresas en Monterrey y Saltillo en 1820–1823 por Samuel Bangs." Typescript prepared by Alessio Robles. LMS.

Arredondo, José Joaquín de. SEE Primary Sources, Manuscripts. México, Provincias Internas de Oriente, Comandante Arredondo.

Bangs, José Manuel. Application for grant of land in Texas (Saltillo, January 24, 1830). Spanish Grants, XXX, fols. 200–215. TLO. Photocopies, LMS.

————. Correspondence with the governor of Nuevo León (1825). File 1824, Legajo 5, No. 5. AGE. Photocopies, LMS.

————. Correspondence with José Servando de Mier (1822). Mi. Photocopy, LMS.

————. Correspondence with Alejandro Uro y Lozano (1821–1835). CBC. Photocopies, LMS.

————. Inventory of the press of the Eastern Interior Provinces (Saltillo, April 12, 1823). AGE. Photocopies, LMS.

————. Inventory and receipt for the press (Monterrey, October 7, 1823). AGE. Photocopies, LMS.

————. Power of attorney to Thomas J. Chambers (Saltillo, May 8, 1831). Spanish Grants, XXX, fol. 201. TLO.

————. "Instancia del impresor Samuel Bangs que pidió su transporte a los Estados Unidos su pais." Legajo 4, Carpeta 5, No. 110. AGE.

Barnett, Thomas (agent of the Leftwich Colony). Letter to Samuel Bangs, from San Felipe de Austin, November 17, 1830. Spanish Grants, XXX, fol. 204. TLO.

Bexar Archives, The. Items from 1817 to 1836 are pertinent. TxU.

Bexar County, Texas, Records of the Probate Court. Inventory of the estate of James Bowie, September, 1837. TSA.

Brush, James A. "The Journal of the Expedition and Military Operations of General Don Fr. X. Mina in Mexico, 1816–1817." Huntington Library, San Marino, California. Typescript, TxU.

Bustamante, Anastacio de. SEE Primary Sources, Printed Materials. México Provincias Internas de Oriente, Jefe superior político (Bustamante).

Cienfuegos, José de. SEE Primary Sources, Manuscripts. Spain, State Department, Legation in the United States.

Coahuila y Texas. Correspondence of the governor and the Constituent Legislature relative to the printing of the Constitution of 1827. ACC.

Coahuila y Texas. Laws and statutes. SEE Primary Sources, Printed Materials. Texas. *Laws and Decrees* . . . ; *The Laws of Texas, 1822–1835.*

Coahuila y Texas, Congreso. "Actas del Congreso del Estado" (1824–1833). 9 vols. Typescript, TxU.

Colección de los decretos y órdenes. SEE Primary Sources, Printed Materials. México, Laws. *Colección de los decretos* . . . ; *Colección de ordenes* . . . ; *Legislación mexicana* . . .

Deed Records, Bastrop County, Texas, Books C (1834), E (1845), and G (1850). Bastrop, Texas.

———, Cameron County, Texas, Books A (1847–1848), B (1849), F (1882). Supplemental. Brownsville, Texas.

———, Galveston County, Texas, Books A (1838–1839), B-2 (1842), E (1845), and F (1848). Galveston, Texas.

———, Harris County, Texas, Books A and C (1838). Houston, Texas.

———, Robertson County, Texas, Books A (1839), J (1858), M (1858), N (1859). Franklin, Texas.

———, Suffolk County, Massachusetts, Book CCXCI (1824). Boston, Massachusetts.

Dyer Collection. [Extract from an undated MS], p. 9. TGR.

Echeandía, Juan J. SEE Primary Sources, Manuscripts. Mexico, Provincias Internas de Oriente, Jefe Político Echeandía.

Erving, George W. SEE Primary Sources, Manuscripts. United States, Department of State.

Expediente sobre pasage con que se auxilió a los Anglo-Americanos que pasaron a Saltillo. [Complaint of the owners who furnished for the Anglo-Americans horses and saddles, which had not been returned six months later. Dated September 5, 1822]. 1820, Legajo 1, Carpeta 6 in bundle of *Bandos y órdenes varios.* AGE.

Galveston County, Land Board. [Recommendation of grant of 1,280 acres of land to Samuel Bangs.] File No. 164, Bexar County, 2nd Class (1845). TLO.

Galveston County, Tenth Judicial District Court. Minutes of 1839–1840, Book A; Minutes of 1840–1843, Book B. Galveston, Texas.

Garza, Felipe de la. SEE Primary Sources, Manuscripts. México, Provincias Internas de Oriente, Comandante De la Garza.

Gorostiza, Manuel Eduardo. Letter to Foreign Office, Mexico, from London, June 22, 1830, with enclosed "Memoria." Expediente Personal de Gorostiza. ASRE.

Great Britain, Public Record Office, London. Papers of the Foreign Office, Mexico, 1820–1850.

Harris County, Eleventh Judicial District Court. Minutes of 1838–1840, Book B-2; Minutes of 1841–1842, Book C. Houston, Texas.

Harris, Eli. Letter to Mirabeau B. Lamar, Providence, Louisiana, January 18, 1841. Lamar Papers, Tx. Printed in *The Papers of Mirabeau Buonaparte Lamar* (C. A. Gulick *et al.*, editors, Austin, Texas, 1921–1928, 6 vols.), III, 483.

Hernández y Dávalos Papers. These represent the unpublished portion, largely 1817–1830, of the documents collected by Juan E. Hernández y Dávalos. TxU.

Lamar Papers, The. Tx.

League, Hosea H. (agent for the Nashville Colony). Letter to Samuel Bangs, August 14, 1830. Spanish Grants, XXX, fol. 203. TLO.

Letter Book of the collector of customs at Matagorda, Texas, 1821–1826. Austin Papers. TxU.

Bibliography

Luacey, Domingo. Letter to Agustín de Iturbide, from Veracruz, March 24, 1822. H-D.

Matamoros Archives (photocopies). The remains of official archives bound into 35 vols. The Arabic volume numbers refer only to the physical volumes in TxU.

McLane, Louis. SEE Primary Sources. Manuscripts. United States, Department of State.

México, Provincias Internas de Oriente, Comandante General José Joaquín Arredondo. Correspondence with viceroys. 4 vols. Historia, XX–XXIII, Operaciones de Guerra, Arredondo, 1813–1820. AGN.

——. Report on the Battle of the Medina, September 18, 1813, Historia XXIII, Arredondo IV, fols. 179–193. Translated in the *Quarterly of the Texas State Historical Association*, XI (January, 1908), 220–236.

——. Report on the capture of the fort at Soto la Marina, June 30, 1817. *Ibid.*, pp. 232–267.

——. Letter declining to spread the news of the reestablishment of the Constitution, May 16, 1820. Historia, XX, Arredondo II, No. 1087 (confidential).

México, Provincias Internas de Oriente, Comandante General Felipe de la Garza. Letter, to the Jefe Político Juan J. Echeandía, from San Carlos, August 11, 1823. AGE.

——. Letter, to the Jefe Político, from San Carlos, September 27, 1823. AGE.

México, Provincias Internas de Oriente, Jefe Político Juan J. Echeandía. Letter, to the comandante general, Felipe de la Garza, from Monterrey, October 6, 1823. AGE.

México, Provincias Internas de Oriente, Jefe Político Superior Anastacio Bustamante. Letter to the acting comandante, Gaspar Antonio López, from Puebla, November 14, 1822. AGE.

México, Secretariat of Foreign Affairs. Correspondence of the Secretary of Foreign Affairs and the Minister of Mexico in London, 1829–1833. ASRE.

Mier Papers. The archive of José Servando de Mier Noriega y Guerra, largely 1820–1823. Includes his MS "Memorias" and "Manifiesto apologético." TxU.

Montemorelos, Mexico. Ayuntamiento. Letter to the governor of Nuevo León, from Montemorelos, May 16, 1826. File 1824, Legajo 5. AGE.

Monterrey, México, Ayuntamiento. Libro[s] de actas del cabildo, 1817–1822; 1822–1827. AM.

Monterrey, Catedral. Libro de bautismos, 1817–1822. The entry for Bangs is dated February 16, 1819, p. 128 v.

The Nacogdoches Archives. Tx.

Nuevo León, Congreso Constituyente. [Decree authorizing the governor to purchase a new press and until its arrival to contract for government printing with Julián Arrese and Co.] Transmitted to governor, September 3, 1824. File 1824, Legajo 5. AGE.

Nuevo León, Governor. Correspondence with José Manuel Bangs. File 1824, Legajo 5. AGE.

Ogilvy, James. "Diary." Tx.

——. Letter to Richard Pakenham, August 20, 1839. SEE Primary Sources, Printed Works. Texas, Republic. *Diplomatic Correspondence* . . ., I, 597–599.

Onís, Luis de. SEE Primary Sources, Manuscripts. Spain, State Department, Legation in the United States.

Prieto Papers. These concern Tamaulipas in particular and the Eastern Interior Provinces of Mexico in general. Collected by Alejandro Prieto. TxU.

Pioneer Printer

Ruiz de Apodaca. SEE Primary Sources, Manuscripts. Spain, State Department, Legation in the United States.

Saltillo, Ayuntamiento. [Reply of the body to the governor of Coahuila and Texas (José M. Viesca) attesting Bangs' good character.] February 18, 1830. Spanish Grants, XXX, fols. 200–201.

Saltillo, [Board of censors. Francisco Salas vs. Samuel Bangs for defamation of character.] 1830. File 75, Document 10. AS.

Saltillo, Catedral. Libro de bautismos, Vol. 23, fol. 151 v., April 5, 1829.

Saltillo, Court records. Enrique Henrickson vs. Samuel Bangs for debt. José Jesús Vidaurre, attorney for plaintiff. Alcalde 2º, 1828. File 73, Document 17. AS.

Sendejas, Ignacio. Power of attorney to Samuel Bangs to handle Texas lands. Bexar County, Records of the Probate Court, Inventory of estate of James Bowie, September, 1837. TSA.

Serna, Mateo de la. SEE Primary Sources, Manuscripts. Spain, State Department, Legation in the United States.

Shaler, William. SEE Primary Sources, Manuscripts. United States Department of State.

Spain, State Department, Legation in the United States. Correspondence of the minister to the United States (Luis de Onís) with the captain general of Cuba (José de Cienfuegos). Historia, Operaciones de Guerra, Notas Diplomáticas, I. AGN.

———. Correspondence with the viceroy of Mexico (Juan Ruiz de Apodaca). Historia, Operaciones de Guerra, Notas Diplomáticas, I. AGN.

———. Correspondence with the secretary of state of Spain, 1816–1819. Legajos 5641, 5645. AHN. Photocopies, LC.

———. Correspondence of the consul general in Philadelphia (Mateo de la Serna) with the secretary of state of Spain. Legajo 5645. AHN. Photocopies, LC.

Suffolk County, Massachusetts. Probate Records, Vol. XCVIII. Boston, Massachusetts.

Texas, General Land Office. Of interest for this study are the Spanish grants (before 1821), the Mexican grants (1822–1836), and the Texas grants to 1850. Austin, Texas.

Trellamull, St. Report of the First Regiment of the Union, Galveston, February 24, 1817. [Accounts for 91 men. No names.] H-D (No. 952).

United States, Bureau of the Census. Cameron County, Texas. U.S. Census, 1850. Microcopy, TxU.

———. Galveston County, Texas. U.S. Census, 1850. Microcopy, TxU.

United States, Department of State. Communications from special agents. William Shaler, II, 1810–1815. With Doc. 82, p. 103, Wm. Shaler to James Monroe, Natchitoches, Louisiana, June 20, 1813, is a copy of the Gaceta de Texas (1 sheet printed both sides). State Department Papers. NA.

———. Louis McLane, letter to United States Secretary of State Van Buren, from London, May 21, 1830. MSS Diplomatic Dispatches from United States ministers to England. State Department Papers. NA.

———. George W. Erving, letters to United States Secretary of State John Q. Adams, March 4 and April 9, 1819, Nos. 98 and 99; Diplomatic Dispatches, Spain, Vol. XVI (1818–1819), State Department Papers. NA. Microcopies, TxU.

Victoria, Tamaulipas, Catedral. Libro núm. 3 de entierros de la parroquia de Sta Maria, 1829–1837.

Bibliography

Wagner, Henry R. "Notes on Early Printing in the Provincias Internas." Typescript, LMS. Photocopy, TxU.

Webb, Isaac W. "Account of Mina's Expedition." Papeles de Estado, Audiencia de México, Legajo 14. AGI. Typescript, TxU.

Williams, Samuel M. Transfer of power of attorney from Samuel Bangs to Isaac Doneho. Bexar County, Texas, Records of the Probate Court, Inventory of estate of James Bowie, September, 1837. TSA.

Printed Materials

Books, Pamphlets, Broadsides, and Decrees

Alaman, Lucas. *Lucas Alamán. El reconocimiento de nuestra independencia por España y la unión de los países hispano-americanos.* Mexico City, 1924. (*Archivo histórico diplomático mexicano,* No. 7.)

Arredondo, José Joaquín. SEE Primary Sources, Printed Materials. México, Provincias Internas de Oriente, Comandante General Arredondo.

Boletín I de la División Ausiliar de la República Mexicana. Soto la Marina, a 26 de abril 1817. 3 pp. Yale. National Museum of México. Photocopies TxU and LMS.

Reproduced in facsimile in *Documentos históricos mexicanos* . . . (México, 1910–1912, 7 vols.), IV. In the "Introducción" (pp. xv–xvi) the editor, Genaro García, attributed the printing to Samuel Bangs. Appendix II, No. 2.

Boston, *City Director[ies],* 1789–1830. Those of 1789, 1796, 1798, 1803, 1805, 1806, 1809, 1816 and 1827 are pertinent. Those of 1789 and 1796 are reprinted in *Miscellaneous Papers (Reports of the Record Commissioners,* No. 10), Boston, 1886.

Boston, Registry Department. *Records relating to the early history of Boston,* Vols. 1–39 (1876–1909). *Boston Town Records.* Vols. 16, 22, 24, 29–31 are pertinent. Vols. 1–22 were issued as *Report of the Record Commissioners;* with Vol. 29, title changed to *Registry Department.*

Boston, *Town Records. Report of the Record Commissioners of the City of Boston,* 1758–1769; 1784–1792 (Boston, 1886 and 1903). Vols XVI and XXXI. BTR.

———. *Report of the Record Commissioners of Boston.* Boston, 1890. Vol. XXII. Contains tax records and census reports. BTR.

———. *Births from 1700 to 1800.* Boston, 1893. Vol. XXIV. BTR.

———. *A Volume of Records relating to the early history of Boston.* Boston, 1900. Vol. XXXIX. BTR.

———. *A Volume of Records relating to the history of Boston containing Boston marriages from 1752 to 1809.* Boston, 1903. BTR. Vol. XXX.

Capitulados de Zaragosa desarmados por el coronel don Felipe de la Garza gobernador del Nuevo Santander y obligados a embarcar por Tampico, Los. Imprenta de la Comandancia General. Saltillo. Año de 1822. Pamphlet. 9 printed pages. BA. Appendix II, No. 109.

catorcena Judith piensa hacer vida privada, La. Ultima conversación que tubieron en Catorce Juana y Pasquala, que escribio un curioso que las estubo oyendo. [Dialogue in verse. 3 columns. Signed "El Curioso."] Ciudad de Leona Vicario. 1830. Impreso en la imprenta del Supremo Gobierno de este Estado, a cargo del C. José Manuel Bangs. TxU. Appendix II, No. 311.

Coahuila y Texas, Congreso. *Ley de Colonización.* Decree No. 16 passed by the *Congreso constituyente,* March 24, 1825. [Issued] Saltillo 4 de abril de 1825.

[At head] Gobierno del Estado de Coahuila y Texas. [At end] Leona Vicario: 1828. Impreso en la Imprenta del Gobierno de Coahuila y Texas. Dirigida por el C. José Manuel Bangs. 4 pp. BA. Appendix II, No. 215.

————. *Arancel de los derechos que deben percibir los escribanos publicos, alcaldes constitucionales, secretario del Tribunal de Justicia . . . del Estado de Coahuila y Texas.* Decree No. 54, passed by the *Congreso constitucional*, May 2, 1828. [At head] Gobierno Supremo del Estado de Coahuila y Texas. [At end] Leona Vicario 2 de mayo de 1828. 12 p. BA. Appendix II, No. 216.

————. *Reglamento de la milicia nacional del mismo estado.* Decree No. 58. Ordered printed June 23, 1828. [At head] Gobierno Superior de Coahuila y Texas. No imprint. 10 pp.

————. *Puede desembacar [sic] el estrangero.* Abbreviated form of the national *Reglamento de Pasapostes de 1º de Mayo de 1828* in three columns in Spanish, English, and French. [At end] Impreso en la Imprenta del Gobierno del Estado de Coahuila y Texas. Leona Vicario, 1828. Dirigida por el C. José Manuel Bangs. 1 sheet, recto and verso. BA. Appendix II, No. 219.

————. Decree No. 98. *Ordnanzas [sic] municipales para el Gobierno y Manejo Interior del Ayuntamiento de la ciudad de San Antonio de Bejar,* 1829. [June 6, 1829.] Ciudad de Leona Vicario. Imprenta del Supremo Gobierno del Estado, á cargo del C. José Manuel Bangs. 35 printed pp. TxU. Appendix II, No. 249.

————. Decree No. 99. *Ordenanzas municipales para el Gobierno y Manejo Interior del Ayuntamiento de la Villa de* [Goliad]. Ciudad de Leona Vicario. Imprenta del Supremo Gobierno del Estado, á cargo del C. J. Manuel Bangs. 44 pp. TxU. Appendix II, No. 250.

————. Decree No. 100. *Ordenanzas municipales para el Gobierno y Manejo Interior del Ayuntamiento de la Villa de San Felipe de Austin.* Ciudad de Leona Vicario. Imprenta del Supremo Gobierno del Estado, á cargo del C. J. Manuel Bangs. 26 pp. Yale. Appendix II, No. 251.

————. Decree No. 112. January 15, 1830. Grant of citizenship in state to José Manuel Bangs. BA. Appendix II, No. 262. Photocopy, LMS.

————. Decree No. 183. April 9, 1832. Gammel's *Laws of Texas,* I, 185.

————. Decree No. 195. April 28, 1832. Gammel's *Laws of Texas,* p. 196.

————. Decree No. 13. March 9, 1833. AHE.

————. Other laws between 1822 and 1836. SEE Primary Sources, Printed Materials. Texas. *Laws and Decrees of the State of Coahuila and Texas.*

French, F. R. Letter to the *Galveston News* concerning the French family, written from Woodward, Oklahoma. *Galveston News,* February 6, 1910.

Gaceta extraordinaria del Gobierno Imperial de Mexico del domingo 27 de octubre de 1822. Reimpreso en el Saltillo. Imprenta del Gobierno. [Report that Nuevo Santander is in a state of complete tranquillity.] TxU. Appendix II, No. 130.

Gaceta extraordinaria del Gobierno Imperial de Mexico del 1 de noviembre de 1822. Reimpreso en el Saltillo. Imprenta del Gobierno. TxU. Appendix II, No. 132.

Gaceta extraordinaria del Gobierno Imperial de Mexico. 19 de Diciembre de 1822. Reimpreso en el Saltillo. Imprenta de la Comandancia Gral. de Oriente. Jose M[anue]l Bangs, Impresor. TxU. Appendix II, No. 145.

Gaceta extraordinaria del Gobierno Imperial de Mexico, del lunes 23 de diciembre de 1822. Reimpreso en el Saltillo, Imprenta de la comandancia general de Oriente. Jose Manuel Bangs, Impresor. 5 pp. TxU. Appendix II, No. 146.

Galveston Artillery Company. *The Charter and Constitution of the Galveston*

Bibliography

Artillery Company. *Organized September 13, 1840.* Printed by S. Bangs, Galveston *Chronicle* Office [1842]. 8 pp. TxU.

Galveston City Directory. Galveston, Texas. The directories of 1859–1860, 1881–1882, 1888–1889, 1890–1891 are pertinent. TGR.

Galvestonian. Address of the Carrier of the *Daily Galvestonian.* January 1, 1842. Galveston, Printed at the Office of the *Galvestonian,* 1842. TGR.

Gammel, H. P. N. SEE Primary Sources, Printed Materials. Texas. *The Laws of Texas, 1822–1897.*

García, Genaro (editor). *Documentos históricos mexicanos . . .* México, 1910–1912. 7 vols. *Boletín I* is reprinted in facsimile in Vol. IV.

Garza, Felipe de la. SEE Primary Sources, Printed Materials. México, Provincias Internas de Oriente, Comandante General De la Garza.

Gonzales, José Eleuterio, *Colección de noticias y documentos para la historia del Estado de Nuevo León.* Monterrey, 1867.

Heitman, Francis Bernard. *Historical Register and Dictionary of the United States Army from . . . 1789 to . . . 1903.* Washington, 1903. 2 vols.

Hernández y Dávalos, Juan E. (compiler). *Colección de documentos para la guerra de Independencia.* México, 1877–1882. 6 vols.

In Vol. VI, Documents 756–1098, is "Causa formada al Dr. Fr. Servando Teresa de Mier y Noriega," a member of the Mier Expedition.

Infante, Joaquín. *Canción patriótica que, al desembarcar el general Mina y sus tropas en la barra de Santander, compuso Joaquín Infante, auditor de la división.* Soto la Marina, 1817. Samuel Bangs, impresor de la División ausiliar de la República Mexicana. Yale.

Iturbide, Agustín de. SEE Primary Sources, Printed Materials. México, Emperador (Iturbide).

Lamar, Mirabeau B. *The Papers of Mirabeau Buonaparte Lamar.* Austin, Texas, 1921–1928. Edited by Charles A. Gulick and others. 6 vols.

Lobato, José María. [*Documentos y proclamas de.*] Reimpreso en el Saltillo el 21 de diciembre de 1822 . . . Imprenta de la comandancia general de Oriente. Jose Manuel Bangs, Impresor. Four short introductory paragraphs by López precede the documents. 2 pp. BA. Appendix II, No. 144.

López, D. Gaspar Antonio. SEE Primary Sources, Printed Materials. México, Provincias Internas de Oriente, Comandante General López.

Lundy, Benjamin. *The Life, Travels and Opinions of Benjamin Lundy, including his Journeys to Texas and Mexico. . . .* Compiled . . . under the direction of his children by Thomas Earle. Philadelphia, 1847.

This includes Lundy's "Diary," covering his travels in Mexico.

[Marín de Porras, Primo Feliciano, bishop of Linares, the Commandant José Joaquín de Arredondo, and his son-in-law Captain José Joaquín de Castro, extend an invitation to the funeral of the small son of the latter, to take place at the Cathedral on May 30, 1820.] In package labeled "1820," AHE. Appendix II, No. 12.

México. *El Supremo Poder Ejecutivo de la Nacion a sus compatriotas.* [Begins] La patria se presenta con dignidad segundo vez . . .]. [Signed in print on verso] Celestino Negrete, Presidente. José Mariano Michelena. Miguel Dominguez. México, 4 de abril de 1823. Reimpreso en el Saltillo a 20 de Abril de 1823. Tercero de nuestra Independencia y Segundo de la Libertad. José Manuel Bangs, Impresor. BA. Appendix II, No. 162.

México, Emperador (Iturbide). *El Generalísimo Almirante a los Mexicanos.* Iturbide reports the military victories of his generals, México, April 4, 1822.

207

An "Advertencia" appended is dated April 6.] [In script] Monterrey, 21 de abril de 1822. BA. Appendix No. 94.

―――. *S. M. el Emperador después de haber jurado* . . . [Begins] "Seame permitido, dignos y ilustres Representantes . . ." [Ends] "Es copia. Saltillo. 1º de junio de 1822." BA. Appendix II, No. 102.

―――. *Proclama de S. M. El Emperador al exercito trigarante.* [Request that his troops support him.] Signed [in print] "Agustín." México, 11 de febrero de 1823. Reimpreso en el Saltillo á 22 de febrero de 1823. Imprenta de la comandancia general de Oriente. Jose Manuel Bangs, Impresor. BA. Appendix II, No. 159.

México, Laws. *Colección de los decretos y órdenes que ha expedido la soberana Junta Provisional Gubernativa y soberanos congresos generales de la nación mexicana.* México, 1829–1840. Segunda edición. 8 vols.

―――. *Colección de órdenes y decretos de la Soberanía Junta Provisional Gubernativa y Soberanos Congresos Generales de la Nación Mexicana.* 2ª edición corregida y aumentada . . . México, 1829–1840.

Vols. 1 and 2 (1829) are pertinent.

―――. *Legislación mexicana o Colección completa de las disposiciones legislativas expedidas desde la independencia de la República.* Edición oficial. México, 1876–1904. Manuel Dublán and José María Lozano, compilers.

Vols. 2 and 3 are pertinent.

México, Ministerio de Hacienda. Circular No. 9. [Congress decrees three days' salary as tax.] Mexico City, June 28, 1823. No Monterrey imprint. BA. Appendix II, No. 165.

―――. Circular No. 10. [Regulations for implementation of Circular No. 9.] [Signed in print] Arrillaga. México, junio 28, 1823. No Monterrey imprint. BA. Appendix II, No. 166.

México, Provincias Internas de Oriente, Comandante General José Joaquín Arredondo. [A royal *cédula* in which Ferdinand VII of Spain announces his marriage to María Josefa Amalia of Saxony.] Madrid, November 9, 1819; Monterrey, April 19, 1820. AGE. Photocopy, LMS. Appendix II, No. 13.

―――. [A proclamation of the viceroy ordering obedience to the Constitution of 1812.] Mexico City, May 31, 1820; Monterrey, June 13, 1820. AGE. Appendix II, No. 15.

―――. [A decree of the Cortes of Cadiz regulating elections of city officials, and order for such elections.] Madrid, May 23, 1812; Monterrey, July 6, 1820. AGE. Appendix II, No. 16.

―――. [A circular ordering that the Constitution of 1812 be republished on August 15 and that all officials take oath to support it.] Madrid, March 22, 1820; Monterrey, August [blank], 1820. AGE. Photocopy, LMS. Appendix II, No. 20.

―――. [An order of the viceroy conceding a general pardon and ordering all Anglo-Americans released.] Madrid, December 20, 1819; Mexico, April 13, 1820; Monterrey, August 1, 1820. AGE. Appendix II, No. 19.

―――. [A royal decree that teachers and clergy in all schools and universities read and explain the Constitution to students.] Madrid, April 24, 1820; Monterrey, September [blank], 1820. 3 printed pages. BA. Appendix II, No. 22.

―――. [A circular ordering that the swearing of the Constitution be celebrated on October 12 to 14.] Monterrey, October 11, 1820. BA. Appendix II, No. 27.

―――. [A proclamation which begins: "Habitantes de las quatro provincias . . ."

Bibliography

In it he announces the defection of Iturbide and pleads for allegiance to Spain.] Monterrey, 13 de marzo de 1821. BA. Appendix II, No. 45.

————. [An order beginning: "Como la tranquilidad que felizmente ha reinado . . ."]. Monterrey, 28 de abril de 1821. BA. Appendix II, No. 50.

————. A los habitantes de Esta Nueva España [all caps]. [Above the heading, in italics] Mexico 5 de Abril de 1821. [An appeal of the viceroy for support of the government]. [Printed signature] El Conde del Venadito. Reimpreso en Monterrey. Ymprenta del Govierno. N.d. BA. Appendix II, No. 48.

————. A reissue of Iturbide's circular dated at the Hacienda del Colorado, June 20, 1821. Monterrey, 27 de julio, de 1821. BA. Appendix II, No. 51.

México, Provincias Internas de Oriente, Comandante general (D. Gaspar Antonio López). D. Gaspar Antonio López Teniente Coronel del Exercito Ymperial Mexicano de las Tres Guarantias, Comandante General y Gefe superior politico interino de las quatro provincias internas orientales . . . [A decree of the Soberana Junta Provisional Gubernativa of October 23, 1821, granting amnesty to military personnel]. Monterrey, November 15, 1821. BA. Appendix II, No. 52.

————. [A decree of the constituent congress that conspiracy against independence is equivalent to lésé majesté and punishable as such]. México, May 14, 1822; Saltillo, May 26, 1822. BA. Appendix II, No. 98.

————. Viva Nuestro Emperador Don Agustín de Iturbide. [all caps]. [Begins] "Mexicanos. Me dirijo a vosotros . . ." [Includes the address of Iturbide asking for final proof of their love for him]. México, 18 de mayo, 1822; Saltillo 27 de mayo de 1822. [Signed by López with rubric]. BA. Appendix II, No. 99.

————. [Proclamation to the] Habitantes de las Quatro Provincias [that Iturbide has been chosen emperor]. [Ends] "Viva, viva, viva, nuestro Emperador Agustín Primero." Saltillo 27 de mayo de 1822. [Signed "López" with rubric.] BA. Appendix II, No. 100.

————. [Law that all former employees be reinstated in their posts]. México, June 8, 1822; Saltillo, June 22, 1822. BA. Appendix II, No. 108.

México, Provincias Internas de Oriente, Comandante general (De la Garza). [Advice to Antonio López de Santana (Santa Anna), who proposes to raise an army to protect México, that he will not cooperate with him]. Monterrey, June 20, 1823. BA. Appendix II, No. 163.

————. Regulations to curb robbery and murder. [signed, in print] Felipe de la Garza. Monterrey, June 24, 1823. BA. Appendix II, No. 164.

México, Provincias Internas de Oriente, Diputación provincial. [President Rodríguez' order for circularization of instructions for holding elections of deputies to the constituent congress]. Monterrey, July 10, 1823. [Signed in print by] José Antonio Rodríguez. BA. Appendix II, No. 167.

México, Secretaría de Guerra y Marina. Colección de documentos históricos mexicanos. México, 1920. 3 vols.

México, Secretaría de Relaciones Exteriores. Lucas Alamán: El reconocimiento de nuestra independencia por España y La unión de los países hispano-americanos. México, 1924. (Archivo histórico diplomático mexicano, No. 7.)

Mina, Francisco Xavier. Exposición de D. Xavier Mina a los Españoles y Americanos. Londres, 2 de mayo de 1816. Hernández, Documentos, VI, 850. A copy bearing this date was among Mier's papers captured at Soto la Marina.

————. Proclama. Galvezton, 22 de febrero de 1817. No original issue known. The earliest reprint is that of Bustamante, Cuadro histórico, IV (México, 1826).

209

————. [Proclama dirigida a sus] *Compañeros de armas.* Rio-Bravo del Norte á 12 de abril de 1817. Included in *Boletín I.*

————. [Proclama] *A los Españoles y Americanos.* Soto la Marina 25 de abril de 1817. An abbreviated form of the Galvezton *Proclama.* In *Boletín I.*

————. *Don Xavier Mina General en Gefe de la División Ausiliar de la República Mexicana.* [Subheadings] Soldados españoles del rey Fernando; Soldados americanos del rey Fernando; Soldados españoles y americanos; Cuartel-general de Soto la Marina á 18 de mayo de 1817. Yale. Photocopies, TxU; LMS.

Moore, Edwin Ward. "To the people of Texas." [An] "Extra" of the *Independent Chronicle,* Vol. I, 2nd Qta., No. 1. By Samuel Bangs, City of Galveston, August 1, 1843. Ed. Pub. and Proprietor. MWA. Photocopy, LMS. Appendix II, No. 355.

Ogilvy, James. "Diary of James Ogilvy." Printed in the *Southwestern Historical Quarterly,* XXX (1926), 139 *et passim,* as the "Diary of Adolphus Sterne."

Rodríguez, José Antonio. SEE Primary Sources, Printed Materials. México, Provincias Internas de Oriente, Diputación provincial.

Sendejas, Ignacio. [A pamphlet with mutilated title, signed by Sendejas (Saltillo, June 18, 1830), which refutes an editorial in the *Gaceta,* No. 41, June 10, 1830]. 3 pp. BA. Photocopy, LMS.

Sheridan, Francis C. *Galveston Island or A Few Months off the Coast of Texas. The Journal of Francis C. Sheridan, 1839–1840.* Edited by Willis W. Pratt. Austin, 1954.

Sterne, Adolphus. "Diary." Printed in *SWHQ,* Vols. XXX and XXXI.

Tamaulipas, Primera Legislatura. Circular No. 40. 2 de marzo de 1827. [Ciudad Victoria, 1827]. [In script of Bangs] "Se publicó el 13 de abril." P. Appendix II, No. 168.

————. *Coleccion de Leyes y Decretos de la Primera Legislatura Constitucional del Estado Libre de Tamaulipas.* Ciudad Victoria. 1827. Imprenta del Gobierno del Estado. Dirigida por el C. Jose Manuel Bangs. 51 pp. Yale. Photocopy, LMS. Appendix II, No. 175.

Tamaulipas, Legislatura. *Informe* [de] *la Comisión Permanente a la Junta de Diputados.* [August] 14, 1827. Victoria, Imprenta del Gobierno del Estado. Dirigida por José Manuel Bangs. 4 pp. P. Appendix II, No. 186.

————. *Informe* [de] *la Comisión Permanente a la Junta de Diputados.* Victoria, 23 de Agosto de 1827. Imprenta del Gobierno del Estado. Dirigida por José Manuel Bangs. P. Appendix II, No. 187.

————. [A bill, headed "Acuerdo" and dated October 22, 1833, giving authority to the government to contract for printing of all necessary work and one or two periodicals. The date of issuance seems to have been November 5, 1833]. AGT. Appendix II, No. 345.

————. Decree No. 44. *Ley de Colonizacion.* November 17, 1833. Ciudad Victoria. Imprenta del Restaurador. 8 pp. AGT.

Texas. *Laws and Decrees of the State of Coahuila and Texas.* Houston, 1839. John P. Kimball, compiler.

————. *The Laws of Texas, 1822–1897.* Austin, 1898–1927. 10 vols. H. P. N. Gammel, compiler. Vol. I contains the laws of the state of Coahuila and Texas, 1822–1836.

Texas, Republic. *Diplomatic Correspondence of the.* George P. Garrison, editor. Washington, D.C., 1908–1911. 3 parts in 3 volumes. Part I is Vol. II of the *Annual Report of the American Historical Association* for the year 1907; Parts

Bibliography

II and III were published as Vol. II (in two parts) of its *Annual Report* . . . *for* . . . *1908*.

————. *Proclamation*. July 29, 1843. Signed by Sam Houston. Original in the Huntington Library, San Merino, California.

U. S. Congress. 30th Congress, 1st Session, House of Representatives, *Executive Document, No. 60*. Washington, D.C., 1848.

Newspapers

American Flag. Matamoros, Mexico, and Brownsville, Texas, 1846–1848. LC.

Atalaya. Victoria, Tamaulipas, 1834–1837. TxU.

Austin City Gazette. Austin, Texas, 1840. Tx.

Baltimore, American, The. Baltimore, 1816–1817. Maryland Historical Society Baltimore.

Commercial Advertiser, The. New Orleans, 1816. City Hall, New Orleans.

Commercial Chronicle. Galveston, 1842–1845. From May, 1843, to January, 1844, title was *Independent Chronicle*. AAW. Photocopy, LMS.

Commercial Intelligencer. Galveston, Texas, 1838–1839. TGR. Yale. Photocopies, TxU; LMS.

Corpus Christi Gazette. Corpus Christi, Texas, 1846. Extra of March 8, TxU; No. 7, Wisconsin State Historical Society, Madison, photocopies, TxU, LMS; No. 12, Archivo de la Secretaría de la Defensa Nacional, México; No. 14, AAW, photocopy, LMS.

Corpus Christi Star, The. Corpus Christi, Texas, 1849. TxU.

Correo Atlántico, El. Mexico City and New Orleans, 1835–1836. Photocopy, TxU.

Daily Galvestonian, The. Galveston, Texas, 1840–1841.

Daily News, The. Galveston, Texas. Originally the *Daily Galvestonian*. Galveston, 1842————. Office of the *Galveston News*, Galveston. Facsimile, LMS.

Daily Picayune, The. New Orleans, 1846–1848. City Hall, New Orleans; TxU.

Gazeta Constitucional de Coahuiltejas. Saltillo, 1829–1830. AHE. TxU. Yale.

Gaceta del Gobierno de México. México, 1817–1821. March 6, 1821; February 20, 1823. TxU.

Gaceta del gobierno imperial de México. México, 1821–1823. TxU.

Gaceta del Gobierno Supremo de México. México, 1823. TxU.

Galvestonian, The. Galveston, Texas, 1839–1842. In March, 1840, this became *The Daily Galvestonian*. On May 8, 1841, *The Weekly Galvestonian and Ladies Saturday Evening Visiter* [*sic*] appeared. TxU; Illinois. Photocopies, TxU, LMS.

Georgetown Herald. Georgetown, Kentucky, 1854. Kansas State Historical Society, Topeka, Kansas.

Independent Chronicle. Galveston, Texas, 1843–1844. SEE *Commercial Chronicle*, Galveston.

La Grange Intelligencer. La Grange, Texas, 1845.

Matamoros Reveille. Matamoros, México, 1846. TxU.

Morning Star, The. Houston, Texas, 1839. Tx.

Musquito, The. Houston, Texas, July, 1840, to March, 1841. TxU. Photocopy, LMS.

Northern Standard, The. Clarksville, Texas, 1842–1848. TxU.

Red-Lander, The. San Augustine, Texas, 1839–1846. Tx. TxU.

Republica de Rio Grande y Amiga de los pueblos. Matamoros, 1846. With No. 9 title changed to *American Flag*. LC.

Pioneer Printer

San Luis Advocate. San Luis Island and Galveston, September, 1840, to 1841. Title changed to *The Texas Times,* 1842. TxU.

Telegraph and Texas Register. Houston, 1838–1848. Tx. TxU.

Telescopio de Tamaulipas, El. Victoria, México, 1836–1837. TxU.

Texas Democrat, The. Austin, Texas, 1846–1847. Tx. TxU.

Texas Times, The. Galveston, 1842–1843. TxU.

Times, The. London, 1825–1833. LC.

Weekly Aurora or General Advertiser, The. Philadelphia, 1816–1817. Pennsylvania Historical Society, Philadelphia.

Weekly Delta, The. New Orleans, 1846–1848. TxU.

Weekly Galvestonian and Ladies Saturday Evening Visiter [sic]. Galveston, Texas, 1841.

Weekly Picayune, The. New Orleans, 1838–1843. TxU.

Weekly Times, The. Houston, Texas, 1840. Tx.

An Interview

Miss Alice Cherry and sister were visited, November 27, 1953, in their home at 911 Avenue E in Galveston. They are descendants of Wibur Cherry and Catherine Crosby French Cherry and have lived in Galveston all their lives. Through them verification of the following facts was obtained:

After the death of George French, his widow married Wilbur Cherry. A daughter of George French and Catherine Crosby, named Josephine, married James Bangs; after his death she became Mrs. Paul Logre and lived in Galveston until around 1911. She had one son, Edward Bangs, who lived in Galveston until 1891.

SECONDARY SOURCES

Manuscripts

Frantz, Joe B. "The Newspapers of the Republic of Texas." Unpublished M.A. thesis, 1940. TxU.

Friend, Llerena B. "The Life of Thomas Jefferson Chambers." Unpublished M.A. thesis, 1928. TxU.

Stuart, Ben C. "A History of Texas Newspapers." Unpublished MS. TGR.

Printed Materials

Alessio Robles, Vito. *Coahuila y Texas desde la consumación de la independencia hasta el tratado de paz de Guadalupe Hidalgo.* México, 1945–1946. 2 vols.

———. *La primera imprenta en Coahuila.* México, 1932.

———. *La primera imprenta en las Provincias Internas de Oriente.* México, 1939.

Appleton's Cyclopaedia of American Biography. Vol. IV, p. 113, has article on Thomas McElrath. New York, 1894.

Bangs, Francis Hyde. *John Kendrick Bangs: Humorist of the Nineties.* New York, 1941.

Bangs, Samuel K. *Lights and Shadows in the Round of a Typo's Life.* Louisville, Kentucky, 1885. 48 pp. Brown University Library, New Haven, Connecticut; Grosvenor Library, Buffalo, New York.

Bibliography

Benson, Nettie Lee. *La diputación provincial y el federalismo mexicano.* México, 1955.

Bolton, H. E. *Guide to Materials for the History of the United States in the Principal Archives of Mexico.* Washington, D.C., 1913. P. 293 locates No. 12 of *Corpus Christi Gazette*, March 19, 1846.

Brigham, Clarence S. "Bibliography of American Newspapers, 1690–1820," *Proceedings of the American Antiquarian Society*, New Series, XXXV (1925), 98.

Bustamante, Carlos María. *Cuadro histórico de la revolución de la América Mexicana* . . . México, 1823–1832. 6 vols. Only Vols. I and IV are pertinent. Includes many firsthand documents. TxU.

Castañeda, Carlos E., and Jack Dabbs (compilers). *A Calendar of the Juan E. Hernández y Dávalos Manuscript Collection. The University of Texas Library.* México, 1954.

Castillo Negrete, Emilio del. *México en el siglo XIX.* México, 1875–1892. 26 vols. In Vol. IX Mina's proclamations are reprinted.

"Cora" (pseudonym of Mrs. Caroline French Bangs [18[?]–1858]). Her stories are in *The Daily* and *The Weekly Galvestonian* and are reprinted in other Galveston papers.

Cossío, David Alberto. *Historia de Nuevo León.* Monterrey, 1924–1933. 6 vols. Vols. IV–V (both printed in 1925) are pertinent.

Dudley, Dean. *The History and Genealogy of the Bangs Family.* Boston, 1896. LC.

Garrett, Julia Kathryn. "The First Newspaper of Texas—*Gaceta de Texas*," *Southwestern Historical Quarterly*, XL (January, 1937), 200–215.

———. *Green Flag over Texas: A Story of the Last Years of Spain in Texas.* New York, 1939.

Handbook of Texas, The. Walter P. Webb and others, editors. Austin, 1952. 2 vols.

Harper, Lathrop C. *Catalogue No. 12 of Books, Pamphlets, Broadsides Printed in Mexico, 1813–1850.* New York, [1961].

Industries of Galveston, The. Galveston, 1887. Pp. 72–73, "The Press of the City."

McMurtrie, Douglas C. "Pioneer Printing in Texas," *Southwestern Historical Quarterly*, XXXV (January, 1932), 173–193.

Moore, Ike. "The Earliest Printing and the First Newspaper in Texas," *Southwestern Historical Quarterly*, XXXIX (October, 1935), 83–99.

National Cyclopaedia of American Biography. New York, 1893. Vol. III, p. 456, article on Thomas McElrath.

Robinson, William Davis. *Memoirs of the Mexican Revolution including a Narrative of the Expedition of General Xavier Mina* . . . Philadelphia, 1820.
  Much of the information concerning the Mina Expedition was obtained from a MS "Journal of the Expedition . . ." of James A. Brush. Listed under Primary Sources, Manuscripts.

Spell, Lota M. "The Anglo-Saxon Press in Mexico, 1846–1848," *American Historical Review*, XXXVIII (October, 1932), 20–31.

———. "Gorostiza and Texas," *Hispanic American Historical Review*, XXXVII (November, 1957), 425–462.

———. "The Mier Archive," *Hispanic American Historical Review*, XII (August, 1932), 359–375.

———. "Samuel Bangs: The First Printer in Texas," *Hispanic American Historical Review*, XI (May, 1931), 248–258. Reprinted in *Southwestern His-*

torical Quarterly, XXXV (April, 1932), 267–278. Translated into Spanish by Francisco Monterde, it appeared in a publication of the Secretariat of Education of Mexico, *El Libro y el Pueblo*, X (May, 1932), 4–9.

Stevens, Abel. *The Life and Times of Nathan Bangs*. New York, 1863.

Streeter, Thomas W. *Bibliography of Texas, 1795–1845*. Cambridge, Massachusetts, 1955–1960. 5 vols. in 3 parts.

Warren, Harris G. *The Sword Was Their Passport*. Baton Rouge, 1943. Account of the Mina Expedition, pp. 146–172.

Webb, Walter P., and others (editors). *The Handbook of Texas*. Austin, 1952. 2 vols.

Whitlock, W. F. *The Story of the Book Concern*. Cincinnati, 1903.

Winkler, Ernest W. "The Texas Republican," *Southwestern Historical Quarterly*, VI (October, 1902), 162; VII (January, 1904), 242–243; XVI (January, 1913), 329–331.

INDEX

215

Index

Index

Corpus Christi Gazette published by, 125–129; *Extra* issued by, 128; and Gideon Lewis, 129, 130, 132; *Rio Grande Herald* planned by, 129; in Matamoros, 129–133; *Matamoros Reveille* published by 130, 131–132; epigraph selected by, 131; *El Liberal* issued from office of, 131; *The Brave Ranger* printed by, 132; closing of office of, by army order, 132; imprisonment of, 132; press of, sold to *American Flag*, 133; as printer on *American Flag*, 133; and unavailability of paper, 133; at Point Isabel, 134–139; plans of, for new printing establishment, 135; press of, lost at sea, 135; and De Villiers, 137; *Texas Ranger* projected by, 138–139; in Kentucky, 142; work on Georgetown *Herald*, by, 142

accomplishments of: unique accomplishments of, 143–145; apprentices trained and established by, 144; sharing of office and press with others by, 144; trade in presses and accessories established by, 144; requisites to success possessed by, 144–145; as pioneer in four Spanish provinces, 145; as government printer in two Mexican states, 145; newspapers in Republic of Texas printed by, 145; most western English-language newspaper in America printed by, 145; place of, in history of press in Texas, 146; survival of imprints of, 151–152; extant specimens of, 167–199

as colonizer: petition for grant of land filed by, 75; six leagues granted to, 75; title of, to land, 77, 78, 83, 90, 94–95, 98, 99, 100, 102–103, 106, 107; trips to Texas by, 77, 78, 94–95; Colorado River land grant of, 78–79, 83, 94, 103; Brazos River land grant of, 79, 94–95, 102–103, 148; employment of Chambers

by, 80, 83; Tamaulipas land grant of, 86, 90, 94–95, 106, 107; and bringing in of colonists, 86; and Benjamin Lundy, 86–89; James Ogilvy as agent for 89–90, 98, 99, 100, 107; and Texas boundary, 90; and *Bangs vs. Houston*, 95, 106; revocation of all powers-of-attorney by, 112

as merchant: study of presses made by, 64; sale of presses and types by, 64–65, 69–71, 72, 80–81, 85, 91, 112; establishment of apprentice system by, 69; business contacts of, 69, 71; business difficulties of, 72; merchandising of, and new law, 80–81; development of business by, 81; Uro y Lozano as Monterrey agent of, 81–85; business methods of, 85; advertising by, in *El Atalaya*, 85; and shipping delays, 91; press and type rented by, 113, 116

as innkeeper: accommodation of transients by, 135; brick hotel erected by, 135; announcement of hotel of, in *American Flag*, 136; loss of trade by, 137–138; transfer of Brick Hotel to wife by, 139; as stage driver, 140

Bangs, Samuel K. (Samuel VIII): birth of, 73; baptismal record of, 73; works on Galveston *Herald*, 110; in Kentucky, 141; work of, on Louisville *Courier*, 142; volumes of poetry by, 150; similarity of, to father, 150

Bangs, Sarah (daughter of Samuel V): shared house with father, 61; married to Daniel Rea, 61

Bangs, Suzanne: marriage of, to Samuel Bangs, 63; in Mexico, 65; character of, 67; mastery of Spanish by, 67; and loss of land, 84–85; Lundy's comments on, 87; death of, 91

Bangs, Thomas G.: employs Samuel Bangs as apprentice, 58

Barragán, Joaquín: as godfather of Samuel VIII, 73

Barragán, María de la Luz: as godmother of Samuel VIII, 73

218

Index

Bastrop, Texas: location of, 78; new capital near, 103

Belden, John: and Bangs' Colorado River grant, 101, 103

Benedict (storekeeper): 115

Benton, Senator Thomas Hart: 120

Bexar Archives: at University of Texas, v; as historical source material, v; abbreviations for location of manuscripts in, xi

Bexar County, records of. SEE Bexar Archives

Bigelow, Horatio: as editor of *Texas Republican*, 6

Boletín, El (Matamoros): press of, used for *The Republic of the Rio Grande*, 130

Bolívar, Simón: 9

Borden (State Land Commissioner): 100

Borden, Thomas P.: as surveyor of Bangs' Colorado River grant, 80

Boston, Massachusetts: contrast of, with Mexico, 58; Bangs family in, 60; as seen by Samuel Bangs, 62

Bowie, James: Bangs leases land from estate of, 78

Brave Ranger, The: printed by Bangs, 132; comments of *Picayune* on, 132; sale of, 132

Brazoria, Texas: capture of, by Santa Anna, 90

Brazos River: Bangs' land grant on, 79, 94–95, 102–103, 148

Bredall (boat captain): 100

Brownsville, Texas: establishment of, 137; and Fort Brown, 137; *American Flag* in, 138

Brush, James A.: on Mina Expedition, 8; diary of, 9, 10, 14 n, 22 n, 27 n–28 n; leaves Soto la Marina with Mina, 27n.

Bulletin I of the Auxiliary Division of the Mexican Republic (issued by Colonel Novoa): printed by Bangs, 25; contents of, 25; results of, 25

Buonaparte, Napoleon: troops of, invade Spain, 18

Burnet, David G.: "The Yucatan Message" by, 120

Butler, Anthony (chargé d'affaires of United States in Mexico): and proposed purchase of Texas, 76; and defeat of Santa Anna, 90

Camargo, Mexico: and Bangs' Tamaulipas land grant, 86

Castro, Captain José de: as son-in-law of Arredondo, 42

Catholic Church: and Mier, 18; and Bangs, 41

Chambers, T. W.: as captain of *Sam Houston*, 105

Chambers, Thomas J.: and Bangs' land grants, 80, 83, 103; fee demanded by, 83; perfidy of, 94

Cherry, Wilbur: as partner of Michael Cronican in *Daily News*, 116

Christian Advocate and Journal: 87

Cincinnati, Ohio: press operated by Bangs in, 95

Civilian and Galveston Gazette: 97, 115, 119

Cleopatra (transport): purchase of, by Mina, 20; capture of, by Spanish ships, 26

Coahuila and Texas, Mexico: as most western of the Eastern Interior Provinces, 36; Miguel Ramos Arizpe in, 54; formation of, 78; Bangs as government printer in, 70–74, 80; political changes in, 81; Bangs' merchandizing in, 85, 89

Coleccion de Leyes y Decretos: printed by Samuel Bangs, 68

Colorado River (Texas): Bangs' land grant on, 78–79, 83, 94, 103

Commercial Advertiser (New Orleans): publishes Herrera decree, 11

Commercial Chronicle (Galveston): Bangs as editor and publisher of, 113; office of, 113; policy of, 113–114; comments on, by other editors, 114; on Mexican invasion of San Antonio, 114; regularity of issues of, 115; *Extras* of, 117; title changes of, 117, 122; under management of B. F. Neal, 125; combined with *Daily Globe*, 125; description of, 125; extant issues of, 152

Commercial Intelligencer (Galveston): as first newspaper in Galveston, 92; as seventh newspaper in Texas, 96;

Index

221

Index

García store (Galveston): wreckage of, 115

Garza, Felipe de la. SEE De la Garza, General Felipe

Gazeta Constitucional de Coahuiltejas: published by Bangs, 73; difficulties with Board of Censors over, 74; discontinuance of, 77

Gazette (Gaceta del Gobierno de México): on Royalist military victories, 40; keeps Bangs in touch with outside world, 51

Gazette de la Louisiane: and *Texas Republican*, 7

Gladwin, "Plain John": as editor of *Galvestonian*, 105; death of, 106

Goliad, Texas: city ordinances of, 73; capture of, by Santa Anna, 90

González, José Eleuterio: as historian of Nuevo León, 3; ideas of, on early presses, 3

González Dávila, Antonio: as government printer, 80

G[onzález?] de Roscio, Juan: and Mina Expedition, 9, 20

Gorostiza, Manuel Eduardo: and colonization, 76; and United States in Texas, 76

Grand Cayman Island: sick of Mina Expedition left at, 14

Grande, Mariano *et al.*: commission from, to Bangs, 78

Greeley, Horace: as publisher of New York *Tribune*, 112; ad of, in the *Daily News*, 112

Green, General Thomas: on Bangs' editorials, 119–120

Grice, Hannah T. SEE Bangs, Hannah T.

Guadalupe Victoria (*pseud.*): as president of Mexico: 66

Gual, Pedro: and Mina Expedition, 10; publishes biography of Mina, 10; publishes *Manifesto* by Mina, 11

Hamlin, G. L.: as co-editor of *Texas Times*, 116

Hammeken, ———: 102

Harris, Eli: as owner of press at Nacogdoches, 6; as publisher of *Texas Republican*, 7

Hawes, William: as guardian of Samuel VII, 61

Hendricksen, Henry: sues Bangs for debt, 72

Hernández y Dávalos, José E.: as publisher of documents, v, 10 n

Herrera, José Manuel: as representative of insurgent Mexican government, 11; appointment of Louis Aury as governor of Texas by, 11; departure of, from New Orleans, 17

Houston, Samuel: as president of Republic of Texas, 94; suit filed against, by Bangs, 95, 99, 106; policy of, 112–113; Bangs' opposition to, 113; refusal of, to retaliate for invasion, 114; proclamation of, 120

Houston, Texas: J. W. J. Niles in, 96

Huntington Library: Brush "Journal" at, 9 n

Independent Chronicle: plans for, 117; *Extra* of, 117–118; location of office of, 118; prospectus of, 118–119; typical issue of, 119–121; comments on, 121–122

Infante, Joaquín: on Mina Expedition, 10, 22; as author of *Patriotic Song*, 22

Inquisition: Mier as prisoner of, 18, 40, 51; Mier on, 19; abolished by Spanish constitution, 51

Intelligencer (Galveston): edited by A. J. Yates, 111

Iturbide, Augustín de: independence of Mexico declared by, 46; proclamations by, 50; decrees of, 50; elevation of, to imperial throne, 50; abdication of, 54

Jack, W. H.: and Bangs' Tamaulipas grant case, 99

Jones, Lincetta: 73

Kidd, G. H.: as manager of Fulton House, 120

Kilby Street (Boston): buildings on, owned by Samuel V, 60, 61; name of Mackeral Lane changed to, 61, 62

Index

Lafitte, Jean: headquarters of, on Galveston Island, 93 n

Lamar, Mirabeau Bounaparte: papers of, 4 n; as candidate for President, 96; administration of, 110

language, Spanish: Bangs' instruction in, 13, 16, 18, 32, 36; instruction of, on Mina Expedition, 16; printers' difficulty with, 16, 32, 39, 46; mastery of, by Suzanne Bangs, 67; mastery of, by James O. Bangs, 67

Leftwich, Robert: colony of, 79

Leona Vicario. SEE Saltillo, Mexico

Leplecher, ————: letter to, from Ogilvy, 100

Lewis, Charles L.: Bangs' dispute with, 98, 99, 103, 105, 108; Bangs' house occupied by, 99, 103; and Bangs vs. Lewis, 105, 108

Lewis, Gideon: as editor of Galveston News, 129; and proposed Rio Grande Herald, 129; and Bangs, 129, 130, 132; and Matamoros Reveille, 130, 131; joins the Texas Rangers, 132

Liberal, El (Matamoros): issued from Bangs' office, 131; Mexican viewpoint of, 132; office of, ordered closed, 132; suspension of, 132; comments on, by Picayune, 132

Little Brazos: SEE Brazos River

"loafers": 97

Lobato, General José María: Documentos y proclamas of, printed by Bangs, 53

Lombardo, James: as resident of Point Isabel, 140; capture of, by Indians, 140

Lometa, Texas: as county seat of Cameron County, 138

London, England: search for Bangs material in, 5; diplomats of, alerted about Texas, 76

Long, General James: expedition of, into Texas, 4, 6; passes through Monterrey, 49

Long Expedition, Second: press of, 4, 6; Bangs' surmised captured with, 4; Eli Harris as printer for, 6; press of, at Nacogdoches, 6; press of, destroyed, 6

Longscope, Captain: and Empresario, 101

López, Gasper Antonio: as temporary commandant of Eastern Interior Provinces, 48; headquarters transferred to Saltillo by, 48; press transferred to Saltillo by, 49–59; Iturbide as emperor announced by, 50–51; succeeded as commandant, 54

López de Santa Anna, Antonio. SEE Santa Anna, General Antonio López de

Lundy, Benjamin: Life of, gives clue to Bangs' origin, 4; and colonization in Tamaulipas, 86, 87; and Bangs, 86–89; diary of, 86–87, 89; grant to, 87, 89, 90; to New Orleans, 89

McElrath, Thomas: as salesman in Methodist Book Concern, 63; as partner of Bangs, 63, 64; as publisher of New York Tribune, 112

Mackeral Lane (Boston). SEE Kilby Street (Boston)

McLaran, John: as printer at Galveston, 16

McLeod, Hugh: in Santa Fé Expedition, 130; as editor of The Republic of the Rio Grande, 131

Madrid, Spain: search for Bangs material in, 5

manners and customs, Mexican: of travel, 33; of treatment of prisoners, 34–36, 40; of freight transportation, 38; of holiday celebrations, 48–49

María Josefa Amalia (Princess of Saxony): marriage of, to Ferdinand VII, 41

Marín de Porras, Primo Feliciano (Bishop of Linares): funeral of godson of, 41–42

Marine Hotel (Galveston): steamer Warsaw as, 104

Marshall, Harriet. SEE Bangs, Harriet

Marshall, John: 49; appropriates Bangs' property, 62

Martenich, Captain: and Mina Expedition, 28

Martínez de Pasamontes, José Fernando: and Mina Expedition, 13 n

Massachusetts: search for Bangs material in, 5

223

Index

Sam Houston (ship): sails between Houston and Galveston, 102, 105
"Samuel Bangs: The First Printer in Texas": as first article on Bangs, 5
San Antonio, Texas: press reported near, 3–4; press purchased for, 69; city ordinances printed in, 73; visited by Bangs, 78–79; postroad from, to Nacogdoches, 103
San Antonio de Bexar. SEE San Antonio, Texas
San Carlos, Mexico: General De la Garza in, 56
Sandovál, José María Práxedis: as government printer, 70 n
Sandusky, ———: 10
San Felipe de Austin, Texas: city ordinances printed for, 73; as headquarters of Stephen F. Austin, 79; on Brazos River, 79; visited by Bangs, 70; capture of, by Santa Anna, 90; Moseley Baker locates family at, 98
San Jacinto River: battle of: 90, 91, 93; Santa Anna captured on, 90; Mexican troops defeated on, 90
San Luis, Texas: 115
San Luis Advocate (San Luis): printing of, 115; Ferdinand Pinkard as editor of, 115; contents of, 115; removed to Galveston, 115; name of, changed to Texas Times, 115
San Luis Island. SEE Galveston Island
San Luis Potosí, Mexico (city): La Balanza de Astrea at, 82
— (state): Bangs' merchandizing in, 85
Santa Anna, General Antonio López de: defection of, 53; as president of Mexico, 81; poem in honor of, 82; experiences of, in Texas, 90; signs treaty with Texas, 90; orders troop withdrawal west of Rio Grande, 90
Santa Fé Expedition: 116
Santa María, Miguel: and Mina Expedition, 10
"Santana." SEE Santa Anna, General Antonio López de
Santander River: new Soto la Marina on, 22; navigation on, 22; called "Saint Anders," 22 n; present name of, 22 n

Sardá, Major José: on Mina Expedition, 16; takes water from Rio Grande, 21; in command at Soto la Marina, 27
Scarborough, E. B.: as editor of American Flag, 138
Sendejas, Ignacio: commission from, to Bangs, 78; transfer of power-of-attorney by, 80
Shaler, William: on Gaceta de Texas, 6
Shelby, A. B. (district judge): and editor of The Musquito, 109; succeeded by Col. Thomas Johnson, 109–110
slavery: in Texas, 77; British opposition to, 77
Smith's Building, Captain: 133
Soto la Marina, Mexico: Mina Expedition at, 20, 24, 26–27, 29, 30; location of, 22; description of, 24; clothing of inhabitants of, 24; food preparation in, 24; fort constructed at, 26; defense of, 26–27, 29; attack on fort at, 27, 29; surrender of, 30; captured men shot at, 30; prisoners at, 30; historical sources about, 30 n; compared with Monterrey, 34; in Spanish province of Nuevo Santander, 36
Spain: Southwest as a part of, 3; Mina Expedition members in, 40; king of, remarried, 41; revolution of 1820 in, 42; king of, accepts Constitution, 42
Spaniards: on Mina Expedition, 13
Spanish language. SEE language, Spanish
Steamboat House (Matamoros): 133
Sterne, Adolphus: as executor of estate of James Ogilvy, 90 n; and "Diary" of Ogilvy, 90 n; "Diary of Adolphus Sterne" by, 90 n
Stewart, Daniel: on Mina Expedition, 8–9; recommended to Iturbide, 9
Stillman, Reverend: performs marriage of Samuel VI, 59
Stuart, Daniel. SEE Stewart, Daniel
Supremo Poder Ejecutivo de la Nacion a sus compatriotas, El: printed by Bangs, 55

Tamaulipas, Mexico: decrees of Legislature of, 68; Bangs' printing in,

228